What Happened to Notre Dame?

Other books of interest from St. Augustine's Press

Charles E. Rice and Theresa Farnan, *Where Did I Come From? Where Am I Going? How Do I Get There? Straight Answers for Young Catholics*

Charles E. Rice, *The Winning Side: Why the Culture of Death Is Dying?*

Thomas Aquinas, *Treatise on Law: The Complete Text*; translation by Alfred J. Freddoso

Francisco Suarez, *On Creation, Conservation, and Concurrence: Metaphysical Disputations 20–22*; translation by Alfred J. Freddoso

Ralph McInerny, *Some Catholic Writers*

Ralph McInerny, *The Defamation of Pius XII*

Ralph McInerny, *Shakespearean Variations*

Ralph McInerny, *Good Knights: Eight Stories*

Ralph McInerny, *The Soul of Wit*

Ralph McInerny, *Let's Read Latin: Introduction to the Language of the Church* (with CD)

Florent Gaboriau, *The Conversion of Edith Stein*; trans. by Ralph McInerny

John of St. Thomas, *Introduction to the Summa Theologiae of Thomas Aquinas*; translation by Ralph McInerny

Thomas Aquinas, *Disputed Questions on Virtue*; translation by Ralph McInerny

Kenneth D. Whitehead, *Mass Misunderstandings: The Mixed Legacy of the Vatican II Liturgical Reforms*

C.S. Lewis and Don Giovanni Calabria, *The Latin Letters of C.S. Lewis*

Servais Pinckaers, O.P., *Morality: The Catholic View*

James V. Schall, S.J., *The Regensburg Lecture*

James V. Schall, S.J., *The Sum Total of Human Happiness*

Josef Pieper, *Tradition: Concept and Claim*

Josef Pieper, *The Concept of Sin*

Josef Pieper, *Happiness and Contemplation*

Peter Kreeft, *The Philosophy of Jesus*

Peter Kreeft, *Jesus-Shock*

Peter Kreeft, *An Ocean Full of Angels*

Edward Feser, *The Last Superstition: A Refutation of the New Atheism*

Richard Peddicord, *The Sacred Monster of Thomism: An Introduction to the Life and Legacy of Reginald Garrigou-Lagrange, O.P.*

Charles Cardinal Journet, *The Mass: The Presence of the Sacrifice of the Cross*

What Happened to Notre Dame?

Charles E. Rice

Introduction by Alfred J. Freddoso

ST. AUGUSTINE'S PRESS
South Bend, Indiana
2009

Manufactured in the United States of America.

1 2 3 4 5 6   15 14 13 12 11 10 09

Library of Congress Cataloging in Publication Data
Rice, Charles E.
What happened to Notre Dame? / Charles E. Rice ;
introduction by Alfred J. Freddoso.
p. cm.
Includes index.
ISBN-13: 978-1-58731-920-4 (paperbound : alk. paper)
ISBN-10: 1-58731-920-9 (paperbound : alk. paper)
1. University of Notre Dame. 2. Catholic universities and colleges –
United States. 3. Catholics – Religious identity. 4. Academic freedom.
5. University autonomy. 6. Obama, Barack. I. Title.
LD4113.R54 2009
378.772'89 – dc22   2009029754

∞ *The paper used in this publication meets the minimum requirements of the American National Standard for Information Sciences - Permanence of Paper for Printed Materials, ANSI Z39.48-1984.*

St. Augustine's Press
www.staugustine.net

To Father Norman Weslin, O.S., Lieutenant Colonel,
U.S. Army (Ret.), paratrooper and priest,
whose legal rights I had the privilege to defend,
and who has put himself on the line,
prayerfully and peacefully,
at Notre Dame and elsewhere
to save the lives of the helpless unborn.

Table of Contents

Acknowledgments

I express appreciation, first of all, to my wife, Mary, mother of ten, grandmother of thirty-nine, much loved and definitely the brains of the outfit. Her encouragement and her perceptive critiques of many drafts were indispensable.

Ellen Rice, who happens to be our daughter as well as a professional editor and technical writer, generously brought her talents to bear in overall management of the project as well as in preparing and editing the manuscript. This project would not have gotten off the ground without her. Her contribution was substantive as well as technical, and essential.

Bruce and Laila Fingerhut, whom we are privileged to count as close friends, *are* St. Augustine's Press. This book project was their idea. I am grateful for their professional competence, integrity and energy which kept the whole thing on track.

Prof. Alfred Freddoso, in volunteering to write the Introduction, raised this project to a much higher level. I am especially appreciative because, over many years, I have regarded him as an exemplar of what Notre Dame ought to be and, we pray, will be again.

Introduction
Alfred J. Freddoso

Why I Was Not Scandalized

WHEN THE White House announced on March 20, 2009, that the University of Notre Dame would be honoring President Barack Obama at its commencement ceremony on May 17, I was neither shocked nor scandalized, despite the fact that in a brief two months since taking office President Obama had, as promised beforehand, taken several significant steps toward promoting the practice of abortion and embryo-destructive stem cell research in the United States and abroad.

The reason I was not shocked was that I had anticipated a few weeks earlier that this very thing might happen. Both sides had much to gain. President Obama could cloak himself in the mantle of Our Lady's university as part of an ongoing campaign to solidify his standing among those many Catholic voters for whom life issues are not very important, or at least not overriding. The university, on the other hand, could reap the great public relations benefits of a presidential visit, once it survived what it undoubtedly expected to be a short-lived protest by the local bishop, John D'Arcy of the Diocese of Fort Wayne-South Bend, and a few hardcore pro-life activists. For an institution like Notre Dame that yearns for the respect of its secular 'peer institutions', the benefits of honoring the President far outweighed what looked like the meager potential costs.

The reason I was not scandalized was that I had, as a member of the philosophy faculty, lived through the last thirty years of those historical trends that Charlie Rice ably identifies in this book: the university's steadily intensifying and often frustrated aspiration to be regarded as a

major player on the American educational scene; the concomitant segregation of faith from reason; the deterioration of the core curriculum
for undergraduates into a series of disjointed 'course distribution
requirements' guided by no comprehensive conception of what an educated Catholic should know; the easy transition from a faculty dominated by 'progressive' Catholics to a faculty more and more dominated by
people ignorant of the intellectual ramifications of the Catholic faith;
the concomitant marginalization of faculty who professed allegiance to,
or even admiration for, the present-day successors of the Apostles; and
a succession of high-level administrators lacking in a philosophical
vision of Catholic higher education and intent on diffusing throughout
the university a pragmatic mentality at once both bureaucratic and corporate. In addition to these trends, there had been a series of 'incidents'
– stretching from the Land O'Lakes Statement and the university's
coziness with the Rockefeller Foundation in the mid-1960s to the tire-
somely recurring debate over the *Vagina Monologues* in the first decade
of the 21st century – which had served to put more and more strain on
the relationship between the university and the Church it claimed to be
serving and even to be 'doing the thinking for', to cite one astonishing-
ly presumptuous catchphrase used by the university to promote itself.
Rice recounts these incidents as well.

All of this, and more, had long ago led me to a personal *modus
vivendi* in my attitude toward the university. Notre Dame is a wonderful place in many ways, and I am deeply grateful to have spent most of
my adult life here. It is a university as universities go these days, and it
is in some obvious sense Catholic. What it is not – and has not been
since I have been here – is a *Catholic university*, i.e., an institution of
higher learning where the Catholic faith pervades and enriches, and is
itself enriched by, the intellectual life on campus. What it is instead is
a national private university that is more open to (or, at worst, more tol-
erant of) Catholic faith and practice than any other national private university I know of. Or, as I like to put it in a less formal idiom, Notre
Dame today is something like a public school in a Catholic neighborhood.

This might sound appalling to some, but it is, I submit, what the
vast majority of present-day administrators, faculty members, students,
and alumni *mean* when they sincerely, though mistakenly, claim that

Notre Dame is a Catholic university. For they assume without much thought that the Catholic character of the university is borne almost entirely by the 'neighborhood', i.e., by the university's sacramental life and associated activities such as retreats, bible study groups, sacramental preparation courses, etc.; by various good works and service projects on and off campus; by a set of faith-inspired rules governing campus life, e.g., single-sex dorms, parietals, restrictions on parties and alcohol consumption, various regulations governing the nature and funding of student organizations, etc.; and by the sheer number of 'outdoor' and 'indoor' manifestations of Catholicism such as the statue of Our Lady atop the Golden Dome, Sacred Heart Basilica, the Grotto, the "Touchdown Jesus" mural, and scores of statues found all over the 'neighborhood'. It is here that virtually all of a student's moral and spiritual formation, if any, will take place. This is where 'faith' resides on campus; this is where the 'heart is educated', to use another of the catchphrases.

The classroom or laboratory, by contrast, is a wholly different venue, despite the presence of crucifixes. This is the 'public school' part of Notre Dame and the locus, by and large, solely of intellectual formation. This is where 'reason' resides on campus and where 'the mind is educated'; and it has little or nothing to do with Catholicism. (It is no accident that the newest science building on campus contains no noteworthy religious symbols in general, and no noteworthy Catholic symbols in particular. That's the way the science faculty wanted it.)

To be sure, there are a number of professors outside the theology department who self-consciously think of themselves as Catholic (or, as the case may be, Christian or Jewish) intellectuals and who can, in combination with one another, provide a student who chooses his or her courses very carefully with something resembling a Catholic education. Moreover, there are more professors of this sort than one would ordinarily expect to find at a national private university in the United States. Nevertheless, they constitute only a small percentage of the total faculty, and their conviction that a Catholic student's intellectual life should be fully integrated with his or her Catholic beliefs and practices is very much a minority view. Most faculty members would, to the contrary, be deeply disturbed by the prospect of having doctrinally orthodox Catholicism intrude itself into the classroom.

Even though this "public school in a Catholic neighborhood" model of Notre Dame conflicts in some crucial ways with at least one of the self-images the university uses to promote itself, it is nonetheless a plausible, even if ultimately unstable, model of Notre Dame that has allowed me personally to set aside bitter disappointment and to focus instead on the remarkable intellectual and apostolic opportunities that the university affords. I will return to this point below.

In any case, given this background, it should be easy to understand why I was not scandalized by the university's decision to honor President Obama. I have come to expect that the teachers and administrators of the public school will periodically decide to tweak the noses of the 'unenlightened' among their Catholic neighbors. That's just the way it often is with public schools in Catholic neighborhoods.

The reaction

Even if I was not scandalized myself, others apparently were. In a moment I will ask why. But first let's recount some of the highlights.

Instead of the brief outcry anticipated by university administrators, the announcement of the honor to be conferred on President Obama evoked a very long and very spirited protest, one that kept making news almost continuously during the eight weeks between March 20 and May 17. This protest had many prongs:

* Bishop D'Arcy, who found out about the invitation to President Obama only hours before the March 20 announcement that the President would in fact be coming to Notre Dame, issued a press release on March 29 rebuking the university for having chosen "prestige over truth." He pointed out that the university's intention to honor President Obama was a violation of a 2004 statement in which the American bishops asked that Catholic institutions "not honor those who act in defiance of our fundamental moral principles." He then made it known that he would not be following his usual custom of attending the commencement ceremony. Just three weeks later, on April 21, D'Arcy would publish a sharply worded letter rejecting the university's self-serving (and, I might add, internally inconsistent) interpretation of the 2004 bishops' statement and lamenting "the terrible breach which has taken place between Notre Dame and the Church."

* On March 28 Cardinal Francis George of Chicago, the President of the National Conference of Catholic Bishops, made the extemporaneous comment, caught on video and soon afterwards broadcast on the internet, that the invitation to President Obama was "an extreme embarrassment to Catholics" and that "Notre Dame didn't understand what it means to be Catholic when they issued this invitation." (He also revealed that before the White House announcement Cardinal Sean O'Malley of Boston "was to have received an honorary doctorate" at Notre Dame's commencement ceremony.) This was followed, over the course of the next seven weeks, by a series of public statements by some 83 individual American bishops taking the university's administration to task, sometimes in extremely harsh terms.

* ND Response, a coalition of eleven student groups brought together by their opposition to the university's decision to honor President Obama, sponsored a protest rally on Palm Sunday (April 5) and a pro-life march on April 17, joined in a previously scheduled Eucharistic Procession on April 26, and organized an alternative program for commencement weekend. Many of the individual students associated with ND Response appeared on national television and radio over the course of the next several weeks explaining the reasons for their protest, and doing it very well. (In a charming moment, Greta Van Susteren of Fox News was taken aback on national television when an ND Response couple, in answer to a question about their post-graduation plans, gleefully revealed that they were getting married in August.)

* On April 8 ten priests of the Congregation of Holy Cross, Notre Dame's founding religious order, published a letter deploring both the university's decision and "especially . . . the fissure that the invitation to President Obama has opened between Notre Dame and its local ordinary and many of his fellow bishops." This letter stood in marked contrast to the absence of any public protest against the university or public support for the bishop from the leaders of the Congregation.

* Alumni groups were formed to protest the university's decision and to urge Notre Dame alumni to withhold contributions from the university. One beneficiary of the publicity surrounding the commencement

controversy was Project Sycamore, a group of alumni and friends of the university that had been created in 2006 in reaction to some of the trends noted above. During the weeks of the protest, this group's e-mail list skyrocketed to over 10,000 subscribers.

* In late March the Cardinal Newman Society, a watchdog organization dedicated in part to exposing violations of Catholic thought and practice by professedly Catholic colleges and universities, started an on-line petition protesting Notre Dame's action. The petition had garnered a remarkable 360,000 signatures by May 17. In addition, bishops and chancery offices in dioceses all over the country received thousands of letters and e-mails in protest. (My brother, who lives just north of West Palm Beach, reported that a notice in his parish bulletin provided contact information for the president of Notre Dame and pleaded with parishioners not to send the diocesan chancery office any more letters or e-mails about Notre Dame.) This suggests that the bishops who publicly scolded the university were at least in part prompted to do so by a groundswell of dismay from below.

* The "Notre Dame scandal" was featured prominently, with plenty of commentary, on popular Catholic blogs and was the subject of many columns critical of the university that appeared on the websites of *The Wall Street Journal*, *National Review*, *First Things* and other conservative-leaning journals.

* There were 'unwelcome' outside protesters as well, themselves scornful of what they felt was too tepid a reaction by Bishop D'Arcy and ND Response. One enterprising fellow, who sneered that ND Response and other campus critics of the Obama invitation were no better than "pro-life pacifists," paid to have an advertising plane drone around the campus airspace for a few hours every day with a trailer depicting a tenth week abortion. While the bishop and ND Response repudiated the rhetoric of these outsider protests, many of us still have vivid images of harmless-looking people, including a priest and a nun, being arrested, it seemed, for doing nothing more than walking down Notre Dame Avenue praying the rosary. Almost all those arrested decided to plead 'not guilty' to the trespassing charges against them, and trial dates were set for August and September.

* Finally, just as the news coverage finally seemed to be petering out, on April 27 Harvard Law Professor and pro-life hero Mary Ann Glendon announced that she was declining the Laetare Medal, which, according to Notre Dame, is "the oldest and most prestigious honor given to American Catholics."

Through all of the turmoil leading up to commencement day, the university and its public relations operation seemed to make one bumbling move after another:

* On two occasions the university privately sent out "talking points" – one set to the faculty and staff of the business school and the other to the members of the Board of Trustees – giving the recipients advice about how to reply to protestors who might contact them personally with complaints about the university's action. On both occasions, these talking points were leaked to journalists and made their way to the internet. (One talking point claimed in effect that Mary Ann Glendon's speech at commencement would balance off President Obama's; it was among the reasons cited by Glendon for declining the Laetare Medal.) In addition, students making fund-raising phone calls to alumni on behalf of the university's development office were given "pro-life talking points" that consisted of a list of pro-life activities at Notre Dame. These were to be invoked to mollify those prospective alumni donors who voiced worries about the university's decision to honor President Obama. However, all the activities listed were initiatives either of the student Right to Life club or of the Notre Dame Center for Ethics and Culture, a unit which is explicitly pro-life, which publicly supported ND Response, and which does not, shall we say, enjoy a particularly warm relationship with the university's central administration. In other words, none of the cited pro-life activities had been initiated by the university as such.

* When the president of the university offered to meet with a group of students from ND Response with no reporters present except his own public relations spokesman (who, as one wag put it, has never met an unpleasant truth he was willing to admit to), the students shrewdly balked, issuing in reply their own set of conditions for the meeting –

including the presence of a journalist of their own choosing. The meeting never took place.

* The president of the university gave a speech to a group of alumni in which he answered Bishop D'Arcy's complaints by pointing out that the university does not normally consult the local bishop about its internal decisions. But he then issued his own interpretation of the 2004 bishops' statement, claiming that, despite what Bishop D'Arcy might think or say, the university had not violated the statement. (As noted above, this interpretation was roundly rejected by D'Arcy.) So one was left to wonder whether the university did or did not care about what the bishops thought. More generally, throughout the affair, the university's dismissive treatment of Bishop D'Arcy, public and pointed as it was, displayed a level of arrogance that was exceptionally high even by academic standards.

* When Glendon declined the Laetare Medal on April 27, the university immediately announced that it would choose another recipient. But this never happened. Instead, a pliant past recipient agreed to give a speech at the commencement ceremony.

* During a regularly scheduled meeting between students and a subcommittee of the Board of Trustees on April 30, one trustee pointed her finger at the student reporting on behalf of ND Response and accused "people like you" of causing the whole controversy.

* Apparently, internal dissent by administrative staff members was not looked upon kindly, either. The following is an excerpt from a story about commencement weekend that appeared on *National Review Online*:

> "Even some university administrators sympathized, with a handful of recognizable figures attending ND Response events over the weekend. Few wanted to discuss the issue publicly, however. 'It has been made clear that dissenting publicly won't be tolerated,' said one administrator who requested anonymity."

During the eight weeks from March 20 to May 17 the university kept insisting that the pro-life agenda was central to its mission, that its pro-life credentials were impeccable, and that honoring President Obama in no way undercut its "unambiguous" pro-life commitment. But the more these claims were reiterated, the less convincing they seemed. To paraphrase Bishop D'Arcy, Notre Dame's action spoke so loudly that it drowned out the university's claim to be unambiguously pro-life. And what the action said is that while abortion and the mentality it cultivates are bad, they are not really all *that* bad – not bad enough, at least, to prevent one of the most reliable political promoters of abortion in the history of American politics from being honored by Our Lady's university. Moreover, as Wilson Miscamble, C.S.C., noted in his speech to 3,000 protestors at the alternative commencement rally on May 17, no one doubts that if the President's beliefs and actions had violated some important tenet of the left-wing political orthodoxy adhered to by most faculty members at the university, he would never have been invited or honored. In short, the consensus among the protestors was that the Obama controversy had cleared the air and allowed the university to be seen for what it is instead of for what it sometimes pretends to be.

Why They Were Scandalized

Anyone who knows the history of the Catholic Church in America realizes that during the first six decades of the 20th century Notre Dame loomed large in the consciousness of the immigrant Catholic communities that had come to populate the eastern seaboard and the Great Lakes region. Notre Dame's success, especially on the football field, was symbolic of the aspirations of hundreds of thousands of Catholic immigrants who were struggling to "make it" in America and to ensure a better future for their many children. If we concentrate merely on material success, then both Notre Dame and its alumni have indeed made it big in the intervening decades. And, in fact, many American Catholics – perhaps a majority, including a majority of Notre Dame alumni – were undoubtedly pleased to hear that the newly inaugurated President of the United States would be visiting Notre Dame to get an honorary degree.

So who were those discontented protesters? This is really no great mystery, despite the ability of some social scientists to muddy even the clearest waters. If you are an American Catholic, then the more central Catholic belief and practice are to your life, the more likely you were to be upset by Notre Dame's decision to honor President Obama. Or, to put it as serious Catholics would themselves put it, the more centered your life is on Jesus Christ and what Vatican II calls your "baptismal call to holiness," the more likely you were to disapprove of the university's decision. You would also be more likely to think of yourself as 'countercultural' in many ways or, to put a more positive slant on it, as part of what Pope John Paul II dubbed the "culture of life," a community of people who first and foremost think of their own lives and the lives of others – both natural lives and supernatural lives – as gifts from God.

But to be upset is not yet to be scandalized. For that, one also has to have gone some way toward accepting at face value Notre Dame's carefully crafted and relentlessly marketed image of itself as the "greatest Catholic university in the world."

So what happened is that "the greatest Catholic university in the world" did something that it considered squarely in line with its claim to be Catholic, and yet a large number of serious Catholics – large enough to keep the story in the news for eight straight weeks – begged to differ, and loudly. The problem was that the university, still stuck in a "pre-JP2" mindset, was wholly out of touch with the new wave of serious Catholics, including a bunch of surprisingly outspoken bishops. Two weeks after graduation I tried to capture this split with brief images in a letter that appeared in the local diocesan newspaper:

> As a faculty member at Notre Dame, I want to apologize to Bishop D'Arcy for the breathtakingly shameful manner in which he has been treated by the administrators of my university. They think the bishop is out of touch. But the fact is that they themselves have lost touch with the faithful Catholics in the pews, the ordinary people who put faith in Jesus Christ at the very center of their lives – the families with lots of kids, including handicapped kids; the people who have spent years helping women with problem pregnancies, both before and after the birth of their children; the

people who take care of one another in emergencies; the younger idealistic 'JP2' Catholics – in short, the very people who have been quietly building an impressive culture of life in our country right under the noses of those who have led Our Lady's university astray. These people do not have to reassure everyone that, despite appearances to the contrary, they are 'unambiguously pro-life'. They just *are* pro-life. And they instinctively recognize a great bishop when they see one."

What one finds in Charlie Rice's book is all the background information needed to understand how this disconnection became a reality. The various factors on the university's side of the split can be accurately summarized by what I call "the four I's," viz., *impatience, infidelity, ingratiation*, and *impenitence*.

As Notre Dame's drive to become a distinguished university was maturing in the late 1950s and into the next three decades, the time was neither right nor ripe for the massive growth that the university would experience. The vision of what this "great Catholic university" would be was too vague, the times were too tempestuous, and the philosophical reflection on the matter was too spotty and too superficial to serve as a guide on rough seas. Yet it was "full steam ahead," nonetheless. This is in part what I mean by *impatience*.

But the really crucial factor was the *infidelity*, which effectively took the form of a gamble – made in the early 1970s in the wake of Vatican II and in the aftermath of the dissenting reaction to Pope Paul VI's encyclical *Humanae Vitae* – that some form of 'liberal' or 'progressive' Catholicism, freed from (or, to put it more neutrally, disengaged from) the philosophical and theological underpinnings of the past, would emerge as the 'serious' Catholicism of the future. Perhaps at the time this did not seem like much of a gamble. After all, a significant percentage of American bishops, along with their closest advisors, seemed perfectly comfortable with progressive agendas. In any case, at Notre Dame the attitude of dissent from and disdain for the Vatican played a significant foundational role in shaping hiring policies, tenure decisions, key administrative appointments, curricular reform, and admissions strategies for the next thirty years.

Impatience and infidelity were then combined with an obsequious desire to imitate those schools that had already attained 'success'. Imitation was really the only possibility left open at this point, given that the 'Thomistic synthesis' that had previously served as the intellectual foundation for the distinctiveness of Catholic higher education had already been jettisoned by the progressives. The result was that, despite some relatively vapid rhetoric to the contrary, neither Notre Dame nor any other large Catholic university was in a position to challenge prevailing models of success in secular higher education with a detailed and self-confidently articulated alternative. So since at least the early 1980s Notre Dame has been struggling mightily to keep up with the Joneses amid what might fairly be called a culture of *ingratiation*. Policies were sometimes adopted for no other reason than that "this is the way they do it at Princeton (or Duke or Stanford or Vanderbilt, etc.)." (For those who need examples, I will cite just two recent ones: the top-down push for quasi-professional 'undergraduate research' in the humanities, and a new rule that prohibits professors from having close relatives enrolled in their courses.) The thought seems to have been that if only we imitate the others, they will accept us as a peer – and the hidden rider was always "despite our Catholicism" (and, one might add, "despite our big-time football program"). To be fair, there were obvious cases in which it was entirely appropriate for a growing Notre Dame to imitate more established and prestigious institutions of higher learning; for instance, by paying close attention to what other similar schools were doing, Notre Dame's endowment management team has become one of the best in the country. But there were just as obvious cases in which such imitation was inappropriate and should have been seen as such. Unfortunately, by this time the intellectual ramifications of the Catholic faith, which might have guided such decisions, had been set aside, the Catholic character of the university having already been relegated to the 'neighborhood'. Despite what the rhetoric of graduation weekend or of festive presidential installations might have suggested, the university was being led by pragmatists who did not have a comprehensive philosophical vision of Catholic higher education, or a correlative plan of action, to guide them. As time went on, the increasing antipathy of the many newly appointed faculty and administrators toward talk of Notre Dame's Catholic character served to reinforce the trends that the original infidelity had initiated. This brings us up to the present day and helps to explain how the more recent vibrant and faithful manifestations of Catholicism have slipped off the university's radar screen.

But there have not been, and likely will not be, any apologies. This is what I mean by *impenitence*. At the beginning of the millennium, everyone on campus was happy to hear Pope John Paul apologize for the most egregious sins of his predecessors in the hierarchy of the Church. But don't expect Notre Dame administrators to issue an apology for past sins, or even to acknowledge those sins. I have often imagined a future president of Notre Dame walking in sack cloth and ashes down the "God quad" that stretches from the front of the domed administration building toward the statue of the Sacred Heart of Jesus and, beyond that, to the statues of Edward Sorin, C.S.C., the founding father of Notre Dame, and of Mary the Mother of God; he would be reciting the most egregious sins of past university administrators, striking his breast and begging for forgiveness. Somehow that could be the beginning of the salvation of the place I love so much.

A pretty picture, to be sure. But short of direct divine intervention, nothing resembling it will ever become a reality – especially now that Notre Dame, like so many big universities, has been infused with the mentality of a frustratingly bureaucratic and, to put it frankly, soul-less corporation. The "four I's" have left little room in the minds of Notre Dame's leaders for Jesus Christ and his faithful followers in the Church. But what these leaders did not count on, and what has now in 2009 helped disperse the fog of ambiguity clouding Notre Dame's relationship to the Church, was the warm sunshine cast by the 26-year pontificate of John Paul II, followed immediately by the papacy of Joseph Ratzinger – along with the profound effect these holy and brilliant men have had and continue to have on the young people whom they have inflamed with love for Jesus Christ and his Church. As one commentator put it with a wry smile, "It almost reminds you of the Gospels."

In the mid-1980s, a short time after John D'Arcy became bishop of Fort Wayne-South Bend, he had the name of the diocesan newspaper changed from *The Harmonizer* to *Today's Catholic*. Knowing the bishop's 'conservative' tendencies ("He's no friend of Notre Dame," I heard more than once in those days), a progressive friend of mine joked that they should have renamed the paper *Yesterday's Catholic* instead.

But, ironically, as I looked around on May 17 at the crowd of mostly young students and young families who were in attendance at the alternative commencement rally on the south quad, I wondered aloud just who "yesterday's Catholics" were in 2009. Whose vision of the Church was leading to a dead end? And whose vision was instead inspiring young people to dedicate their lives to the Kingdom of God in opposition to the surrounding culture? Whose vision was turning out to be sterile and bourgeois? And whose vision was instead turning out to be fruitful?

Since the mid-1990s there has been a continuous presence of what we might call JP2-Catholics within the undergraduate population at Notre Dame. This is still a fairly small minority of students; I would put the number at no greater than 5% of the total undergraduate population at any given time, though this estimate may be a bit on the low side. Still, the overall undergraduate population of the university is 8,500, and so at any given time there are several hundred students on the Notre Dame campus who are on fire with the faith and whose influence extends far beyond their own small circle. My close friend Janet Smith, who was a faculty colleague in the 1980s, turned to me during the alternative commencement rally on May 17 and marveled, "Nothing like this would have been possible in the '80s. We just didn't have as many students of this sort, willing to be witnesses to Christ no matter what others think." These are the young Catholics that the university has lost touch with. These are, in Chesterton's words, the children who are "fanatical about the faith where the fathers had been slack about it."

One might reply that the university can easily survive without such as these. This is true enough in merely human terms. After all, a $6 billion endowment can go a long way in the City of Man. But the Notre Dame mystique has always, until now at least, included a reference to something more noble and more Christ-like than power and wealth and honor and fame. Without that something more, whatever survives might be impressive in many ways, but would it still be Notre Dame?

What Now?

The president of the university received three standing ovations at the annual faculty dinner on the Tuesday following commencement. To be sure, various lower-level administrators were circulating among the tables encouraging faculty members to applaud loudly and often. But most faculty members needed little such encouragement. The university administrators had stood up 'courageously' against their 'oppressors' in the Church, and in the eyes of the vast majority of faculty members they accordingly deserved high praise.

The daily life of the university can undoubtedly go on, at least superficially, as if nothing happened in the spring of 2009 – especially on the premise that football goes well. (During the fall semesters at Notre Dame, campus controversies normally move to the background for as long as the football team has fewer than two losses.)

But there are at least three unstable elements that could lead to further 'incidents' in the relatively short-term future.

The first has to do with the university's relationship with the Church. John D'Arcy is at present the oldest bishop in the country who is still actively governing a diocese. His last public acts on the Notre Dame campus in the spring of 2009 were two impressive appearances at commencement weekend events sponsored by ND Response. Despite his original intention to forego the Sunday rally, "I realized that it was a requirement for the bishop to be present with these beautiful young people and with those whom they had drawn to Notre Dame and to a pro-life rally on the south quad." As long as he remains bishop of Fort Wayne-South Bend, the university is unlikely to reach out to him with anything like a public apology for its actions or its shabby treatment of him in the spring of 2009.

This sad state of affairs in effect gives the new bishop, whenever he happens to come along, a completely free hand in dealing with the university. For 25 years Bishop D'Arcy pursued what might justly be called a conciliatory strategy toward Notre Dame, despite the fact (which he knew) that certain university administrators were continually laughing at him behind his back. On several occasions when I urged him to be a bit more aggressive in his dealings with the university, his reply was always the same: "What you don't know is how much worse the situation could have been if I were not operating as I do." However, given the new post-Obama circumstances, the next bishop will have no particular reason to be at all deferential to the university. Will he perhaps see his role as limited to overseeing the sacramental life on campus (no easy or insignificant task in itself)? Will he perhaps feel disinclined to publicly validate the university every year by showing up as a token churchman at graduation weekend festivities? Will he perhaps even refuse to attend football games regularly as the university's guest? If no reconciliation has occurred before his arrival, will he simply sit back and wait for the university to take a first step toward healing "the breach" that Bishop D'Arcy spoke of?

The answers to these and other similar questions will go a long way toward determining whether Notre Dame will be able to get away with insisting, as it would undoubtedly like to, that the pre-Obama *status quo* with the Church remains in effect, or whether instead the university will at some point be compelled by internal and external pressures to articulate with more precision its own conception of what its relationship to the Church is and should be. This latter, less pleasant, possibility would call for some tough choices on the part of the university.

It is not inconceivable that, if forced to choose one way or the other, the university would decide that its own conception of progress dictates an independence from the Church that goes beyond anything envisioned heretofore. Such a decision would immediately undercut recent attempts to increase the number of Catholic faculty members. More fundamentally, it would raise questions in the minds of faculty members about why the university should want to put an emphasis on hiring Catholics in the first place, or why it should feel compelled to maintain the present mandated level of 85% Catholics in the undergraduate population, or why it should hold on to 'antiquated' rules about student life that put it at a competitive disadvantage relative to its peer institutions, or why it should require undergraduates to take philosophy and theology courses, or even why it should allow the Congregation of Holy Cross to maintain such a high level of influence, out of all proportion to its numbers, in either the 'public school' or 'the neighborhood'.

But suppose that the university chose instead to reinforce its Catholic 'brand' in some robust sense. Then it might well end up taking steps that either antagonize faculty members or conflict with certain institutional goals set by current administrators. Suppose, for instance, that the university decided to back up its claim to be "unambiguously pro-life." One obvious step would be to allow the Women's Care Center, a highly successful local pro-life pregnancy help organization, to open a branch office on campus – a move that, for whatever reason, the university has resisted in the past. Even this relatively innocuous initiative would undoubtedly irritate at least some faculty members. Another initiative, explicitly suggested by ND Response during the Obama controversy, would be to promise that the university will have nothing to do, directly or indirectly, with embryo-destructive stem cell research. But there are at least two ways in which such an initiative might conflict with institutional goals. First, current administrators long for the university to be accepted into the Association of American Universities (AAU), which includes as members all the peer institutions that Notre Dame seeks to emulate. However, the AAU is one of the biggest lobbyists in Washington for embryo-destructive stem cell research. Second, such an explicitly pro-life promise might jeopardize the university's current close relationship with the branch of the Indiana University School of Medicine that is located on the edge of the Notre Dame campus. And, more generally, any new moves that show even the least obeisance to the Church would immediately raise red flags in the eyes of the faculty.

The second element of instability involves the Congregation of Holy Cross. To my mind, the Congregation is the biggest loser in the Obama affair. First of all, the fact that the Congregation's leaders did not respond strongly or straightforwardly to the university's action may very well result in a loss of vocations, which tend to come nowadays from among the JP2 Catholics. Second, I know from personal conversations that many of the Congregation's younger priests, along with a good number of the seminarians, were deeply discouraged by what they saw as the university's betrayal of the Catholic faith in the Obama affair. The Congregation can ill afford to lose any of these young people, but a continuation of the peace-at-any-price mentality that seems to have a grip on the older generation might well discourage them even further and add to tensions within the Congregation itself.

Factors such as these weaken the Congregation and thus play into the hands of the many faculty members and administrators who strongly believe that Notre Dame's ties to the Congregation – beginning with the requirement that the president of the university, along with six of the twelve members of the powerful Board of Fellows, must be priests of the Indiana Province of the Congregation – retard the university's progress toward 'greatness'. It is not inconceivable that at some time in the short-term future there will be an organized movement to abolish such requirements and to push the Congregation into some sort of merely ceremonial relationship to the university.

The third element of instability is just the "public school in a Catholic neighborhood" model itself, independently of the other two elements. Before I get to that, however, I want to emphasize just how attractive a model this is.

First and foremost, it fits the present reality very well.

Second, it makes Notre Dame an attractive school for well-formed Catholic students who are choosing between Notre Dame and other national private universities and who would prefer a general climate that is hospitable to the practice of the faith. (The matter is more complicated if such a student is choosing between Notre Dame and a school like, say, the University of Dallas, which has a core curriculum with a coherent conception of Catholic higher education behind it.)

Third, as things now stand, the neighborhood's Catholic character is still strong enough to have a residual effect on the public school. More specifically, Catholic intellectuals on the faculty have, in most departments, quite a bit of freedom in choosing which courses to offer and which topics to address in the classroom. To use myself as an example, every year I teach at least one course for philosophy majors on St. Thomas's *Summa Theologiae*, something that would be frowned upon, if not forbidden, in many secular philosophy departments. Better yet, I occasionally teach a majors course on G.K. Chesterton, and best of all, last semester I team-taught a course on Joseph Ratzinger. In other words, the public school is still aware that it is located in a Catholic neighborhood, and so it allows deviations from the standard norms of domineering secularism that one tends to find in the academy nowadays. (A few years ago, after having given a lecture on faith and reason in my standard Ancient and Medieval Philosophy course for majors, I was asked by a student whether I would be allowed to teach such a course at Princeton. I wasn't quite sure of the answer.)

This last point is important for understanding an otherwise puzzling phenomenon that occurred during the Obama controversy: Several of the newer Catholic intellectuals on the faculty did not want the students of ND Response to protest against the university's action; I am talking here about devout Catholics and in some cases daily communicants. Why were they of this mind? To put it straightforward-ly, they are very happy at Notre Dame because they feel liberated here, whereas in the past they felt constrained or even oppressed at the more secularized schools where they were teaching. The protestors, they felt, were threatening this wholly acceptable *status quo* and might trigger a negative reaction that would drive the university in the direction of the sort of secularism that they themselves were very happy to have escaped.

I find this an entirely reasonable position – even if not a particular-ly noble one, given what is at stake in the disagreements over begin-ning-of-life issues. I must confess that I myself was tempted to stay out of the fray when the honor for President Obama was first announced. I had long ago given up trying to 'save' Notre Dame, and while the honor for the President was indeed highly objectionable, so were lots of other things the university was doing.

In the end, like Bishop D'Arcy, I came to feel that my place was with "those beautiful young people" of ND Response, many of whom I knew personally as their teacher and academic advisor. What really struck me in talking with them was how they continually and prayerful-ly examined and re-examined *their own* motivations: Is this for Christ or is it for us? Is this justifiable indignation or is it a personal vendet-ta? And so on. "These kids are sort of, well, *holy*," I thought, "Maybe they *can* save Notre Dame." And so I decided to shoot off my mouth one last time. It's been fun.

In any case, the main point I want to make here is that the present situation is inherently unstable. The historical record laid out for us by authors such as George Marsden and James Burtchaell, c.s.c., suggests that what this "public school in a Catholic neighborhood" model describes is just a phase that the university is going through on its way toward eventually losing its soul completely.

I pray that this is not so. So does Charlie Rice. But one purpose of this book, unfortunately, is to show that the movement toward secular-ization at Notre Dame is much further along than most people would have believed before March 20, 2009.

1
Invitation and Reaction

"What the hell happened?"

STEVE MCQUEEN, as Jake Holman, the bad-luck sailor in *The Sand Pebbles*, a tale of a United States Navy gunboat on the Yangtze River in 1926, shouted those final words into the night as he lay, alone and wounded in the mission courtyard, waiting for the advancing Chinese rebels to find and kill him.

Something like Jake Holman's question must have occurred to many friends of the University of Notre Dame when they heard that President Barack Obama would be the principal speaker, and receive an honorary doctor of laws degree, at the 2009 Commencement. The announcement triggered protests from Notre Dame alumni (including subway alumni) and students as well as others. A prominent Cleveland alumnus, echoing Jake Holman, expressed a not uncommon view on Notre Dame's administrators, "Who the hell are these guys?" More than 350,000 persons signed an online petition by The Cardinal Newman Society asking the Notre Dame President, Rev. John I. Jenkins, C.S.C., to rescind the invitation.

Two cardinals, Cardinal Francis George, President of the U.S. Conference of Catholic Bishops, and Cardinal Daniel DiNardo, of Houston, protested the invitation, as did 83 bishops. Cardinal George described Notre Dame as "the flagship Catholic university" and described its honoring of Obama as an "embarrassment."[1]

Archbishop Raymond L. Burke, Prefect of the Supreme Tribunal of the Apostolic Signatura, the Church's highest court, denounced the invitation: "Dialogue and respect for differences are not promoted by the compromise and . . . violation of the natural moral law. The . . . granting of an honorary doctorate at Notre Dame . . . to our President who is aggressively advancing an anti-life and anti-family agenda is a source of the gravest scandal.

Catholic institutions cannot offer any platform to, let alone honor, those who teach and act publicly against the moral law. In a culture which embraces an agenda of death, Catholics and Catholic institutions are necessarily counter-cultural. If we . . . are not willing to accept the burdens and the suffering necessarily involved in calling our culture to reform, then we are not worthy of the name 'Catholic.'"[2]

Bishop John M. D'Arcy of the Fort Wayne-South Bend diocese, in which Notre Dame is located, refused to attend the Commencement. "My decision," he said, "is not an attack on anyone, but is in defense of the truth about human life. I have in mind also the statement of the U.S. Catholic Bishops in 2004: 'The Catholic community and Catholic institutions should not honor those who act in defiance of our fundamental moral principles. They should not be given awards, honors or platforms which would suggest support for their actions.' . . . [T]he measure of any Catholic institution is not only what it stands for, but also what it will not stand for. . . . Let us ask Our Lady to intercede for the university named in her honor, that it may recommit itself to the primacy of truth over prestige."[3] Notre Dame did not care much what Bishop D'Arcy thought. The first thing he knew of the invitation was when he was told by Fr. Jenkins that Obama had accepted it.

Notre Dame officials presented the invitation as a routine gesture to presidents in their first year in office.[4] The record does not support that excuse. President Obama is the ninth president to receive an honorary degree from Notre Dame but only the sixth to address the graduates. President Clinton received neither honor. Nor is there an unbroken custom that, if a president is invited, it must be in his first year. President George H.W. Bush spoke at Commencement in 1992, his fourth year in office, and President Eisenhower spoke in his eighth, in 1960.[5]

We will discuss in Chapters 2 and 3 the reasons advanced by Notre Dame's executives for the invitation. They must have known that the invitation of Obama would dominate and politicize the graduation. They must have known, too, that their conferral of Notre Dame's highest honors on President Obama would imply a general commendation of the man and his policies. In the conflicts over those policies, they committed, in perception but also in fact, the name and prestige of Notre Dame to the side that is hostile to major imperatives of faith and reason affirmed by the Catholic Church. Let's look at some issues.

Abortion

President Obama is the most relentlessly pro-abortion public official in the world. When asked by Rev. Rick Warren of Saddleback Church, during the 2008 campaign, "At what point does a baby get human rights?" Obama replied that "answering that question with specificity is above my pay grade."[6] But with respect to a child who survives an abortion and is alive outside the womb, Obama, in the Illinois Senate, spoke and voted against the Born-Alive Infants Protection Act. That bill provided that "A live child born as a result of an abortion shall be fully recognized as a human person and accorded immediate protection under the law."[7] President Obama supports the Freedom of Choice Act which would establish a "fundamental right" to abortion and would ban practically every federal or state law restricting abortion.[8] On his fourth day in office, Obama overturned the Mexico City Policy that had forbidden organizations receiving federal funds to perform or promote abortions in other countries.[9] He has restored to the UN Population Fund (UNFPA) the funding that President Bush had stopped because of the Fund's support for forced abortions.[10] Obama opposes the Hyde Amendment and similar restrictions that deny public funding for most abortions.[11] As President, his appointments of significant federal officials have predominantly included pro-abortion activists and supporters.[12]

Embryonic Stem Cell Research

President George W. Bush, on August 9, 2001, restricted federal funding for research on embryonic stem cell lines created after that date. President Obama revoked that Bush restriction.[13] The Obama order authorized the Secretary of the Department of Health and Human Services (DHHS) to "support and conduct responsible, scientifically worthy human stem cell research, including human embryonic stem cell research, to the extent permitted by law." Incidentally, Obama's Secretary of DHHS, Kathleen Sebelius, a Catholic, had a strongly pro-abortion record as Governor of Kansas, including persistent vetoes of restrictions on late-term abortions.[14]

Adult stem cells, derived from bone marrow and other sources, have been used successfully in relieving various injuries and medical conditions. Embryonic stem cells have never successfully treated a human patient for anything. Research indicates that "embryonic stem cells injected into patients can cause disabling if not deadly tumors."[15] Federal funding of embryonic stem cell research (ESCR), however, can make it a lucrative, if unfruitful, enterprise.

No moral problems arise in the use, with consent, of adult stem cells. But every embryo is a living human being. To remove the stem cells kills that embryo. It is, in moral terms, a murder. The essential point is that human life begins at conception or fertilization, the joinder of the sperm and the ovum, whether that takes place in the natural way or through artificial means such as in vitro fertilization. As noted below, a type of fertilization can also occur in cloning. After fertilization, the one-cell zygote divides and becomes an embryo, then a fetus at eight weeks, then a newborn and so on through high school, etc. At every stage "the human being is to be respected and treated as a person from the moment of conception."[16]

The Draft Guidelines on Human Stem Cell Research were issued by the National Institutes of Health for DHHS on April 20, 2009. The final Guidelines for Research Using Human Stem Cells went into effect on July 7, 2009. They provide that "[H]uman embryonic stem cells" may be used in research using NIH funds, if the cells were "derived from human embryos ... that were created using in vitro fertilization for reproductive purposes and were no longer needed for this purpose [and] were donated by individuals ['donors'] who sought reproductive treatment and who gave voluntary written consent for the human embryos to be used for research purposes."[17] The Guidelines permit funding of ESCR only on embryos left over from reproductive *in vitro* fertilization techniques in which embryos are created but only some are implanted in the woman's womb to be carried to term. The excuse that such left-over human beings "are going to die anyway" does not justify intentionally killing them any more than it would justify involuntary lethal experiments on condemned criminals.

The Guidelines do not allow federally funded ESCR using embryos specially created for research purposes by in vitro fertilization or cloning.[18] Such "is prohibited," according to the Guidelines, "by the annual appropriations ban on funding of human embryo research . . . otherwise known as the Dickey-Wicker Amendment,"[19] which bars funding for "the creation of a human embryo or embryos for research purposes; or [for] research in which a human embryo or embryos are destroyed, discarded, or knowingly subjected to risk of injury or death greater than that allowed for research on fetuses in utero."[20] Efforts are underway in Congress, however, to terminate the Dickey-Wicker restriction so as to allow federal funding of the creation of embryos, by cloning or *in vitro* fertilization, for use in research.[21]

Cloning

In cloning, the nucleus of a somatic cell, which is any cell of the body other than a sperm or egg cell, is inserted into an egg (ovum) cell from which the egg cell's nucleus has been removed. The egg is then electrically stimulated to react as if it had been fertilized by a sperm cell. The result is a one-cell zygote which divides and develops.[22] For the first eight weeks it is called an embryo. The cloned embryo is genetically identical to the donor of the somatic cell. Depending on the use made of the cloned embryo, cloning can be "reproductive," in which the embryo is implanted in a woman's womb and carried to term, or "therapeutic," in which the embryo is killed by removal of the stem cells for use in research. Both types are condemned by Catholic teaching.[23] "We will ensure," Obama said, "that our government never opens the door to the use of cloning for human reproduction. It is dangerous, profoundly wrong, and has no place in our society, or any society."[24] He opened the door, however, for the worse evil of therapeutic cloning. Once the Dickey-Wicker restriction is removed, we can expect that the Obama Administration will fund the creation of new human beings by cloning for the purpose of killing them and using their stem cells for research.[25] The experiments performed by Nazi doctors on concentration camp prisoners were unimaginative and primitive by comparison. By conferring Notre Dame's highest honors on the national leader who is setting the stage for such an atrocity, Notre Dame's officers acted like "good Germans" who were submissive to their Führer.

In his 2002 book, *God and the World*, Cardinal Joseph Ratzinger, now Benedict XVI, discussed the description in *Genesis* 3 of the posting of angels east of Eden with flaming swords to keep man, after the Fall, from eating of the Tree of Life. After the Fall, man was forbidden to eat of that tree which gave immortality, "since to be immortal in this [fallen] condition would . . . be perdition." People are now, Ratzinger said, "starting to pick from the tree of life and make themselves lords of life and death, to reassemble life.

"[P]recisely what man was supposed to be protected from is now actually happening: he is crossing the final boundary. . . . [M]an makes other men his own artifacts. Man no longer originates in the mystery of love, by . . . conception and birth . . . but is produced industrially, like any other product."

This is serious business. "[W]e can," said Ratzinger, "be certain of this: God will take action to counter an ultimate crime, an ultimate act of self-destruction, on the part of man. He will take action against the attempt to demean mankind by the production of slave-beings. There are indeed final boundaries we cannot cross without turning into the agents of the destruction of creation itself, without going far beyond the original sin and the first Fall and all its negative consequences."[26]

Rationing of Health Care

At the other end of life, the Obama Stimulus Package contains health care provisions that foreshadow a change from current standards under which Medicare pays for treatments that are safe and effective. The Stimulus applies a cost-effectiveness standard that would be likely to entail rationing of health care in some situations.[27] "It doesn't matter what your doctor says," claimed a *Washington Times* editorial. "[T]he Obama administration plans to decide if you will have cancer treatment or heart surgery. Appearing on 'Meet the Press' . . . Lawrence H. Summers, President Obama's chief economic adviser, stated, 'Whether it's tonsillectomies or hysterectomies . . . procedures are done three times as frequently [in some parts of the country than others] and there's no benefit in terms of the health of the population. And by doing the right kind of cost-effectiveness . . . some experts . . . estimate that we could take as much as $700 billion a year out of our health care system.' Let's be clear – Mr. Summers is talking about rationing. . . . Mr. Summers tried to kill the pain by saying it all wouldn't have to be cut right away. That's only comforting if it's not your loved one's transplant that bureaucrats reject. The hypocrisy is enough to make a heart stop. A White House that doesn't think government should intervene between a doctor and a woman deciding whether to have an abortion has no problem telling doctors whether they can perform tonsillectomies or hysterectomies."[28]

As Senator Tom Coburn (R-OK), a physician, put it, "the ultimate result of every government-run healthcare plan around the world is rationing. [M]ost of the expenses come from . . . senior citizens. . . . Most of the cuts will come from . . . payments for those senior citizens. So you . . . will end up with a form of rationing that will have a tremendous impact on care."[29]

Abolition of Conscience Protection

On December 18, 2008, the Bush Administration published new "conscience rules," timed to take effect just before the Obama Administration took office on January 20, 2009. "The . . . regulation cuts off federal funding for any state or local government, hospital, health plan, clinic or other entity that does not accommodate doctors, nurses, pharmacists and other employees who refuse to participate in care they find ethically, morally or religiously objectionable."[30] The regulations were necessary because various statutes[31] "that would otherwise prevent discrimination against hospitals and health care workers were being ignored or overlooked."[32] The Obama Administration has moved to rescind those Bush regulations.[33] The statutes protecting against discrimination are still in effect. But the rescission of the enforcing regulations portends a lack of enforcement, if not an outright repeal, of some or all of those statutes. The regulations made the statutes effective. Why remove the regulations unless the intent is to ignore or even repeal the statutory conscience protections? As Cardinal Francis George put it, the removal of the rule, "that [protects] doctors, nurses and others . . . who have objections in conscience to . . . abortion and other killing procedures . . . would be the first step in moving our country from democracy to despotism."[34] On July 2, 2009, President Obama told representatives of the Catholic press that "I reiterated my support for an effective conscience clause in my speech at Notre Dame."[35] Obama's mention of conscience at Notre Dame was deceptive, as we shall see in Chapter 4.

Many Notre Dame alumni and students are in the health care professions or in pre-medical studies. The University's conferral of Notre Dame's highest honors on the man who is moving to force medical professionals to choose either to leave their profession or participate in the execution of the unborn or other violations of conscience, was an inexcusable betrayal of a fiduciary duty to those alumni and students.

Other Issues

President Obama's record on these life and conscience issues provides abundant reason why he should not have been honored by Notre Dame. Other aspects of his record, including his unprecedented fiscal deficits and such a stunning expansion of executive power and of federal control over private entities and states that it amounts to an extraconstitutional coup, should have alerted Notre Dame's administrators to the recklessness of committing the name and reputation of Notre Dame to Obama in the face of such well-grounded opposition to him and his policies. Unmentioned in the background are the pending lawsuits – not yet finally resolved on the merits – that raise serious questions as to Obama's eligibility for the office.[36] If the challenges are finally upheld and Mr. Obama is held to be ineligible, unprecedented questions of fraud would arise. It was imprudent to honor Obama in the absence of a resolution of those questions.

Despite the erosion of its Catholic character, which we will discuss in later chapters, Notre Dame has endured for many as an icon, a rock, of Catholic integrity. It was more than football and more than the TV ads during football games depicting Notre Dame students and faculty as "Fighting Irish" against global warming and other politically correct foes (but never against abortion). It was tied up with an image, however false, of Notre Dame as sort of a Marine Corps of the Catholic Church. In view of his record, Notre Dame's conferral of its highest honors on Obama gave scandal to alumni, students and the public. It understandably raised Jake Holman's question. We will try to explain what happened. And why.

2

The Justification
Abortion as Just Another Issue

IN HIS introduction of President Obama at Commencement, Fr. Jenkins quoted Pope Benedict XVI, Pope John Paul II, and the Second Vatican Council on the need, in Benedict's words, "to pursue reasoned, responsible and respectful dialogue in the effort to build a more humane and free society." No one could reasonably disagree with that. But that is not what was going on at Commencement. As Bishop D'Arcy said, "[I]t would be one thing to bring the president here for a discussion on healthcare or immigration, and no person of goodwill could rightly oppose this. We have here, however, the granting of an honorary degree of law to someone whose activities both as president and previously, have been altogether supportive of laws against the dignity of the human person yet to be born."[1]

Notre Dame honored Obama not only by conferring on him an honorary degree but also, in the first place, by inviting him to be the Commencement speaker, which itself is a signal honor. At Commencement, Fr. Jenkins said, "we are fully supportive of Church teaching on the sanctity of human life, and we oppose [Obama's] policies on abortion and embryonic stem cell research." But Notre Dame put "the sanctity of human life" aside so as to honor Obama for his stand on intrinsically lesser issues. Notre Dame, in the words of William McGurn, has followed "an approach that for decades has treated abortion as one issue on a political scorecard."[2]

The Excuses Offered

This downgrading of the abortion issue was obvious in the pre-Commencement excuses offered by Notre Dame for the honoring of Obama. "We will honor Mr. Obama," said Fr. Jenkins, "as an inspiring leader who faces many challenges – the economy, two wars, and health care, immigration and education reform – and is addressing them with intelligence, courage and honesty. . . . Of course, this does not mean we support all of his positions. The invitation to President Obama to be our Commencement speaker should not be taken as condoning or endorsing his positions on specific issues regarding the protection of human life, including abortion and embryonic stem cell research. Yet, we see his visit as a basis for further positive engagement."[3]

Fr. Jenkins' reasons were elaborated by Dennis K. Brown, University Spokesman and Assistant Vice President for News and Information, in his responses to critics:

> [P]lease know that the invitation of President Obama to be our Commencement speaker should in no way be taken as condoning or endorsing his positions on specific issues regarding the protection of human life, including abortion and embryonic stem cell research. Our opposition to these matters is and always has been firm and unwavering.
>
> Rather, we are honoring the president for his historic election, for his concern for the poor, for his efforts to improve educational standards, his respect for the role of faith and religious institutions, and for his commitment to ending war. It is of special significance that the Notre Dame family will hear the commencement address from our first African-American president, a person who has spoken eloquently and movingly about race in America. Racial prejudice has been a deep wound in America, and Mr. Obama has been a healer.
>
> The aforementioned issues are dear to the heart of Notre Dame and all Catholics, and the president has elevated these causes and made them his own. We're honoring him for the causes we share, and for the ways in which he's willing to engage us on positions we *don't* share. In doing so, we believe there is an opportunity to build a relationship, create dialogue and find more commonalities. To do otherwise and completely disassociate our University with those who disagree with us – especially the leader of our nation – is to become irrelevant in shaping public debate and public life. We believe Notre Dame brings a distinctive perspective to issues facing our nation, and developing rapport with the

president and his administration will allow us to make ongoing contributions.

I realize this response is unlikely to satisfy you, but I understand your position and am grateful you shared it with us.[4]

The Gravity of Abortion

In "Forming Consciences for Faithful Citizenship," the United States Catholic bishops affirmed in 2008, in accord with Vatican statements, a "consistent ethic of life [which] neither treats all issues as morally equivalent nor reduces Catholic teaching to one or two issues."[5] Abortion, however, is a defining issue, because it is the state-authorized intentional killing of an innocent human being. In *Evangelium Vitae*, Pope John Paul II issued three definitive pronouncements on the intentional killing of the innocent:

> Therefore, by the authority which Christ conferred upon Peter and his Successors, and in communion with the Bishops of the Catholic Church, *I confirm that the direct and voluntary killing of an innocent human being is always gravely immoral.*[6]
>
> *I declare that direct abortion, that is, abortion willed as an end or a means, always constitutes a grave moral disorder.*[7]
>
> *I confirm that euthanasia is a grave violation of the law of God, since it is the deliberate and morally unacceptable killing of a human person.*[8]

The Church has always taught that abortion is a grave evil. "[T]he human being is to be . . . treated as a person from the moment of conception."[9] The law must provide appropriate "penal sanctions for every deliberate violation of the child's rights."[10]

Roe v. Wade

The gravity of legalized abortion can be understood only in light of what the Supreme Court did in *Roe v. Wade*,[11] the 1973 case that overturned the prohibitions and restrictions of abortion in all fifty states. The Fourteenth Amendment to the Constitution, adopted in 1868, protects the right of a "person" to life and to the equal protection of the laws. In *Roe*, the Court stated that if the unborn child is a person, the pro-abortion case "collapses, for the fetus' right to life is then guaranteed by the [Fourteenth] Amendment."[12]

The Court declined to decide whether an unborn child is a living human being, but ruled that he is not a person, since "the word 'person,' as used in the Fourteenth Amendment, does not include the unborn."[13] Whether or not he is a human being, he is not a person. That is the same, in effect, as a ruling that an acknowledged human being is a nonperson. As a nonperson the unborn child has no constitutional rights. The *essential* holding of *Roe*, therefore, is that the unborn child is not a "person" within the meaning of the Fourteenth Amendment.[14]

Once the Court ruled out the rights of the unborn nonperson, the only right remaining was the mother's right of privacy. The Court said that this right is not absolute, but defined it so as to permit, in effect, elective abortion at every stage of pregnancy up to the time of normal delivery. In later cases the Court allowed some marginal restrictions on abortion. But the Court has confirmed the right to abortion as a "liberty interest" protected under the Fourteenth Amendment and has concluded that "the essential holding of *Roe v. Wade* should be retained and once again reaffirmed."[15]

The Depersonalization Principle

The essential principle of legalized abortion, that an innocent human being can be declared to be a nonperson and subjected to death at the discretion of others, is the principle that underlay the Nazi depersonalization and extermination of the Jews and other target groups. "By legally excluding Jews from German life, [the Nuremberg Laws of 1935] helped set the Holocaust in motion."[16]

Notre Dame rightly prides itself on its record as a champion of racial justice. But its failure to stand up for the right of the unborn to live, is especially indefensible in light of the fact that the depersonalization principle of legalized abortion is the principle also of the *Dred Scott* Case, in 1857, in which the Supreme Court held that free descendants of slaves were not citizens and said that slaves were property rather than persons. "[T]he right of property in a slave is distinctly and expressly affirmed in the Constitution. . . . And the Government in express terms is pledged to protect it in all future time, if the slave escapes from his owner."[17] Could you possibly imagine Fr. Jenkins, or any president of Notre Dame, honoring a public official who persistently expresses his approval of the Holocaust or legally enforced racial segregation, because of that official's stand on the economy or health care? That would be unimaginable as well as indefensible.

Can Other Issues Outweigh Abortion?

The unique gravity of legalized abortion, where the state authorizes the intentional killing of innocent human beings, has received definitive treatment by the Magisterium, the teaching authority of the Church, in the context of whether a Catholic voter could morally vote for a pro-abortion candidate. The issue was whether a candidate's position on issues of social justice, immigration, war, etc., could be a "proportionate reason" to justify the material cooperation of voting for that candidate despite his support for legalized abortion. The principles apply to the question of whether Notre Dame would be justified in honoring Obama for his positions on other issues despite his support for legalized abortion and other intrinsic evils.

In 2004, Cardinal Joseph Ratzinger, now Pope Benedict XVI, in a letter to the American bishops, said: "Not all moral issues have the same weight as abortion and euthanasia. For example, if a Catholic were to be at odds with the Holy Father on the application of capital punishment or on the decision to wage war, he would not for that reason be considered unworthy to present himself to receive Holy Communion. While the Church exhorts civil authorities to seek peace, not war, and to exercise discretion and mercy in imposing punishment on criminals, it may still be permissible to take up arms against an aggressor or to have recourse to capital punishment. There may be a legitimate diversity of opinion even among Catholics about waging war and applying the death penalty, but not however with regard to abortion and euthanasia."

In other words, there can be a just war, but there can never be a just abortion. In a postscript, Ratzinger said, "A Catholic would be guilty of formal cooperation in evil, and so unworthy to present himself for Holy Communion, if he were to deliberately vote for a candidate precisely because of the candidate's permissive stand on abortion and/or euthanasia. When a Catholic does not share a candidate's stand in favor of abortion and/or euthanasia, but votes for that candidate for other reasons, it is . . .

remote material cooperation, which can be permitted in the presence of proportionate reasons."[18]

What could be such "proportionate reasons"? Archbishop John J. Myers, of Newark, in response to the 2004 Ratzinger letter, said: "[P]olicies on welfare, national security, the war in Iraq, Social Security or taxes, taken singly or in any combination, do not provide a proportionate reason to vote for a pro-abortion candidate."[19] That makes sense because legalized abortion involves explicit legal authorization of the intentional killing of innocent human beings, with a toll to date of about 50 million surgical abortions since 1973, not including the uncountable victims of the morning-after pill and other abortifacients.

Dennis Brown, speaking for Fr. Jenkins, said Notre Dame honors Obama "for his historic election, for his concern for the poor, for his efforts to improve educational standards, his respect for the role of faith and religious institutions, and for his commitment to ending war," and as a "healer" of racial prejudice.[20] None of those issues, important as they are, involves the legalized execution of the innocent. Notre Dame, for example, honors Obama "for his commitment to ending war." Apart from the inconvenient fact of Obama's escalation of the war in Afghanistan, that excuse fails because of the difference in kind between legalized killing in war and legalized killing in abortion. The toll from legalized abortion in the United States, of course, dwarfs the toll of military and civilian casualties in the current wars in Iraq and Afghanistan.[21] The difference in kind, moreover, exists because in legalized abortion, government explicitly authorizes the intentional killing of innocent human beings. American law does not authorize intentional killing of the innocent in war. The killing of innocents can legitimately occur in war as an unintended "double effect" of justified military action. If United States forces, however, intentionally kill the innocent in war, they are subject to prosecution.[22]

If Obama's "commitment to ending war" cannot justify Notre Dame's honoring of him despite his promotion of abortion, neither can Obama's positions on economic or social issues where innocents are not subjected to death by government authority.

A Culture of Optional Murder

Legalized abortion is a major contributor to a cultural climate in which the intentional infliction of death on the innocent is widely seen as an optional problem-solving technique. Columbine, in 1999, was only the beginning of a string of random shootings. If you have a problem with your fellow students or fellow workers, one option is to blow them away. Under the radar, euthanasia also has become an accepted procedure in some situations. In the *Terri Schiavo* case, Judge George W. Greer of the Pinellas County, Florida, Circuit Court, ordered, at the request of her husband, the starvation and dehydration of a disabled woman who was not dying and was not in significant pain.[23] In his final order, Judge Greer did not merely authorize Michael, her husband, to remove Terri's feeding tube. Rather, Judge Greer, on February 25, 2005, ordered that "the guardian, Michael Schiavo, shall cause the removal of nutrition and hydration from the ward, Theresa Schiavo, at 1:00 p.m. on Friday, March 18, 2005."[24] It was as much a scheduled, state-ordered execution as the executions of convicted criminals in the state prison at Raiford. Even if Terri were able to take nourishment by mouth, as her parents asserted she could, Judge Greer's order would have mandated her execution by starvation and dehydration. In abortion cases, the law authorizes, but does not require, the mother to kill her unborn child. In *Schiavo*, we crossed the line from state-authorized homicide, as in *Roe v. Wade*, to state-ordered homicide.

Nutrition and hydration, administered by tube, may legally be withheld from an incompetent patient if there is evidence that he would have wanted that withholding or, in some states, if a court decides that the withholding would be in his best interest.[25] Where the family and caregivers agree that nutrition and hydration should be withdrawn, it is commonly done without court involvement. The intent to deprive a patient permanently of food and water is essentially an intent to kill. In moral terms it is murder. A benevolent motive does not change that reality. The only reason anyone has heard of the *Schiavo* case is because Michael wanted to kill Terri, and her parents and siblings did not. So the courts got involved. An impasse arising from such disagreement was inevitable in a legal regime which allows family members, who agree, to kill quietly an incompetent relative.[26] Like euthanasia, abortion is moving beyond the reach of the law because chemical and other abortifacients are making it a truly private matter. The Food and Drug Administration has approved over-the-counter sale to persons age 17 and older, of the abortifacient morning-after pill without a prescription.[27]

Notre Dame on the Sidelines

These cultural realities should impel a Catholic university to be counter-cultural, to insist that the law must protect the right to life of all innocent human beings without exception. The "Fighting Irish" should not be on the sidelines in that fight for life. Columnist William McGurn, of the *Wall Street Journal*, a Notre Dame graduate, made the point in an address at Notre Dame:

> And what will history say of our billions in endowment if the richest Catholic university America has ever known cannot find it within herself to mount a public and spirited defense of the most defenseless among us? . . . The discord that this year's commencement has unleashed – between Notre Dame and the bishops, between members of the Notre Dame community, between Notre Dame and thousands of discouraged Catholic faithful – all this derives from an approach that for decades has treated abortion as one issue on a political scorecard. This is not the road to engagement. This is the route to incoherence, and we see its fruit everywhere in our public life. . . . Notre Dame must recognize these realities – and the role she has played in bringing us to this day by treating abortion as a political difference rather than the intrinsic evil it is. . . . Notre Dame remains one of the few institutions capable of providing a witness for life in the fullness of its beauty and intellectual integrity – and America is waiting to hear her voice. . . . In her most public witness, Notre Dame appears afraid to extend to the cause of the unborn the same enthusiasm she shows for so many other good works here. . . . Imagine the witness that Notre Dame might provide on a Fall afternoon, if millions of Americans who had sat down to watch a football game suddenly found themselves face to face with a Notre Dame professor or student standing up to say, "I fight for the unborn."[28]

Perhaps the most pathetic aspect of the politically correct timidity of Notre Dame's officials on abortion is their obliviousness to the harm that Obama, their honoree, is moving to inflict on Notre Dame students and alumni to whom Notre Dame owes a high fiduciary duty. In Chapter 1, we noted Obama's moves to repeal the conscience protections of health care professionals. Fr. Jenkins said Notre Dame would honor Obama for addressing the challenge of "health care . . . with intelligence, courage and honesty."[29] With respect to laws that "legitimize" abortion or euthanasia, Pope John Paul II said "there is *a grave and clear obligation to oppose them by conscientious objection*."[30] Notre Dame's honoree will force his fellow Notre Dame "alumni" to choose: Commit grave evil or leave the health care profession. We will note in Chapter 4 Obama's misleading mention of the conscience issue in his Commencement address.

A few weeks ago, I asked a friend who knows Notre Dame's leaders very well and personally, "How could they not understand the seriousness of abortion?" That person's response was charitable and, unfortunately, credible. In summary it was: "They mean well. But they are ideological, trapped in the 1960s and 1970s. They have no clue that there are ordinary Catholics who, since John Paul II and *Evangelium Vitae*, take the teachings of the Church, especially on abortion, very seriously. They think that when these ordinary Catholics speak out against abortion, it is just a political statement, because that's all they do, themselves, is think in terms of ideology and politics. They can't imagine that anyone does anything else. So that's why they don't pay any attention to people who talk against abortion. They see themselves as elites. They are clueless as to what ordinary Catholics think." That analysis helps to explain what *First Things* editor Joseph Bottum called "the great divergence, in outlook and purpose, between Catholic universities and the Catholic culture of America."[31]

3

The Justification
The Bishops' Non-Mandate

The Bishops' Statement

IN 2004, the United States Conference of Catholic Bishops issued a statement, "Catholics in Political Life." The five points highlighted in the statement described obligations not only of Catholic public officials but of all Catholics and Catholic institutions involved in the political process:

1. We need . . . to **teach** clearly and help other Catholic leaders to teach clearly on our unequivocal commitment to the legal protection of human life from the moment of conception until natural death. . . .
2. We need to do more to **persuade** all people that human life is precious and human dignity must be defended. This requires more effective dialogue and engagement with all public officials, especially Catholic public officials. We welcome conversation initiated by political leaders themselves.
3. Catholics need to **act** in support of these principles and policies in public life. It is the particular vocation of the laity to transform the world. We have to encourage this vocation and do more to bring all believers to this mission. As bishops, we do not endorse or oppose candidates. Rather, we seek to form the consciences of our people so that they can examine the positions of candidates and make choices based on Catholic moral and social teaching.
4. The Catholic community and Catholic institutions should **not honor** those who act in defiance of our fundamental moral principles. They should not be given awards, honors or platforms which would suggest support for their actions.

5. We commit ourselves to **maintain communication** with public officials who make decisions every day that touch issues of human life and dignity.[1]

The Jenkins Version

Point 4, above, applies directly to Notre Dame's honoring of President Obama. Fr. Jenkins gave this clear mandate a remarkably inventive interpretation:

> Because the title of the document is "Catholics in Political Life," we understood this to refer to honoring Catholics whose actions are not in accord with our moral principles. This interpretation was supported by canon lawyers we consulted, who advised us that, by definition, only Catholics who implicitly recognize the authority of Church teaching can act in "defiance" of it. Moreover, fellow university presidents have told me that their bishops have told them that in fact it is only Catholic politicians who are referred to in this document.
>
> In addition, regardless of how one interprets the first sentence, the second is also important. It reads: "They should not be given awards, honors or platforms which would suggest support for their actions." In every statement I have made about the invitation of President Obama and in every statement I will make, I express our disagreement with him on issues surrounding the protection of life, such as abortion and embryonic stem cell research. If we repeatedly and clearly state that we do not support the President on these issues, we cannot be understood to "suggest support."
>
> Finally, the document states that "we need to do more to persuade all people that human life is precious and human dignity must be defended. This requires more effective dialogue and engagement with public officials. . . ." However misguided some might consider our actions, it is in the spirit of providing a basis for dialogue that we invited President Obama.[2]

Bishop D'Arcy Lays It Out

Bishop D'Arcy's response to Fr. Jenkins is conclusive:

1. The meaning of the sentence in the USCCB document relative to Catholic institutions is clear. It places the responsibility on those institutions, and indeed, on the Catholic community itself. . . .

2. When there is a doubt concerning the meaning of a document of the United States Conference of Catholic Bishops, where does one find the authentic interpretation? A fundamental, canonical and theological principle states that it is found in the local bishop, who is the teacher and lawgiver in his diocese. – Canon 330, 375 §§1 & 2; 380; 381 §1; 391 §1; 392, & 394 §1.

3. I informed Father Jenkins that if there was any genuine question or doubt about the meaning of the relevant sentence in the conference's document, any competent canonist with knowledge of the tradition and love for Christ's church had the responsibility to inform Father Jenkins of the fundamental principle that the diocesan bishop alone bears the responsibility to provide an authoritative interpretation.

4. . . . . Father Jenkins . . . consulted presidents of other Catholic universities, and at least indirectly, consulted other bishops, since he asked those presidents to share with him those judgments of their own bishops. However, he chose not to consult his own bishop who, as I have made clear, is the teacher and lawgiver in his own diocese. I reminded Father Jenkins that I was not informed of the invitation until after it was accepted by the president. I mentioned again that it is at the heart of the diocesan bishop's pastoral responsibility to teach as revealed in sacred Scripture and the tradition. . . . I reminded him that it is also central to the university's relationship to the church. . . .

5. Another key point. . . . Father Jenkins declared the invitation to President Obama does not "suggest support" for his actions, because he has expressed and continues to express disagreement with him on issues surrounding the protection of life. I wrote that the outpouring of hundreds of thousands who are shocked by the invitation . . . demonstrates, that this invitation has . . . scandalized many Catholics and other people of goodwill. In my office alone, there have been over 3,300 messages of shock, dismay and outrage, and they are still coming in. It seems that the action in itself speaks so loudly that people have not been able to hear the words of Father Jenkins, and, indeed, the action has suggested approval to many.

     . . . Father Jenkins . . . also says he is "following the document of the bishops" by "laying a basis for engagement with the president on this issue." . . . I, like many others, will await to see what the follow up is on this issue between Notre Dame and President Obama.

6.   [I]t would be one thing to bring the president here for a discussion on healthcare or immigration, and no person of goodwill could rightly oppose this. We have here, however, the granting of an honorary degree of law to someone whose activities both as president and previously, have been altogether supportive of laws against the dignity of the human person yet to be born. . . .

I consider it now settled – that the USCCB document, "Catholics in Public Life," does indeed apply to this matter.

The failure to consult the local bishop who, whatever his unworthiness, is the teacher and lawgiver in this diocese, is a serious mistake. Proper consultation could have prevented an action, which has caused such painful division between Notre Dame and many bishops – and a large number of the faithful.

That division must be addressed through prayer and action, and I pledge to work with Father Jenkins and all at Notre Dame to heal the terrible breach, which has taken place between Notre Dame and the church. It cannot be allowed to continue.

I ask all to pray that this healing will take place in a way that is substantial and true, and not illusory. Notre Dame and Father Jenkins must do their part if this healing is to take place. I will do my part.[3]

Disrespect for the Church

Notre Dame's administration not only rejected the bishops' mandate but also evidenced a contemptuous disregard for the settled procedures by which one obtains an authoritative interpretation of a Church document. Fr. Jenkins chose to rely on the opinions of canonists and university professors rather than consult the bishop of his diocese. Those unidentified canon lawyers advised him that, "by definition, only Catholics who implicitly recognize the authority of Church teaching can act in defiance of it." But the Bishops' statement forbids honoring those who "act in defiance" not "of Church teaching" but "of our fundamental moral principles." The Jenkins statement implies that abortion is wrong only because it violates "Church teaching" and that therefore the teaching of the Church on abortion is applicable only to Catholics. On the contrary, the "ethical precepts" concerning "abortion and euthanasia," are "not a question of 'confessional values' *per se,* because such precepts are rooted in human nature itself and belong to the natural moral law."[4] In an address to European parliamentarians, Pope Benedict XVI stated that in "her interventions in the public arena" the Church draws attention to "principles which are not negotiable [including] protection of life in all its stages. . . . These principles are not truths of faith, even though they receive further light and confirmation from faith; they are inscribed in human nature itself and therefore they are common to all humanity."[5]

It would reduce the bishops' mandate to incoherence to have it apply only to Catholic politicians who "recognize the authority of Church teaching." That would mean that the bishops would approve the bestowal of honors by a Catholic university on an advocate of infanticide or racial apartheid as long as that advocate was not a Catholic or was a Catholic who rejected "the authority of Catholic teaching." Moreover, the invitation to a public official to be the principal speaker at Commencement is an honor equivalent to, if not surpassing, the conferral on him of an honorary degree. It makes no sense, therefore, to object only to the conferral of the degree on Obama. To invite him to speak at Commencement is as indefensible as giving him an honorary degree. A Commencement speaker is offered by a University to its graduates as a role model who stands for principles upon which they can base their choices for their future. A Catholic university ought not to invite a speaker whose record and stated positions will implicitly encourage its students to include among those choices the murder of the innocent whether born or unborn.

The reality is that Notre Dame, while claiming to be a "Catholic" university, has thumbed its nose at the bishops who are, incidentally, the successors of the Apostles. Thus, the statement of Fr. Wilson D. Miscamble, c.s.c., professor of history at Notre Dame, and nine other Holy Cross priests, said: "We express our deep gratitude to Bishop John D'Arcy for his leadership and moral clarity. . . . The University pursues a dangerous course when it allows itself to decide for and by itself what part of being a Catholic institution it will choose to embrace. Although undoubtedly unintended, the University administration's decision portends a distancing of Notre Dame from the Church which is its lifeblood and the source of its identity and real strength. Such a distancing puts at risk the true soul of Notre Dame."[6]

Professor Mary Ann Glendon

Notre Dame's distancing of itself from the Church received special notice from another quarter. Harvard Professor Mary Ann Glendon, former United States Ambassador to the Vatican, had been named in December, 2008, to receive Notre Dame's Laetare Medal at the 2009 Commencement. On April 27, 2009, she wrote to Fr. Jenkins: "[A]s a longtime consultant to the U.S. Conference of Catholic Bishops, I could not help but be dismayed by the news that Notre Dame also planned to award the president an honorary degree. This, as you must know, was in disregard of the U.S. bishops' express request of 2004. . . . That request, which in no way seeks to control or interfere with an institution's freedom to invite and engage in serious debate with whomever it wishes, seems to me so reasonable that I am at a loss to understand why a Catholic university should disrespect it.

> Then I learned that 'talking points' issued by Notre Dame in response to widespread criticism of its decision included two statements implying that my acceptance speech would somehow balance the event:
> * President Obama won't be doing all the talking. Mary Ann Glendon, the former U.S. ambassador to the Vatican, will be speaking as the recipient of the Laetare Medal.
> * We think having the president come to Notre Dame, see the graduates, meet our leaders, and hear a talk from Mary Ann Glendon is a good thing for the president and for the causes we care about.
> A commencement, however, is supposed to be a joyous day for the graduates and their families. It is not the right place, nor is a brief acceptance speech the right vehicle, for engagement with the very serious problems raised by Notre Dame's decision – in disregard of the settled position of the U.S. bishops – to honor a prominent and uncompromising opponent of the Church's position on issues involving fundamental principles of justice.   Finally, with recent news reports that other Catholic schools are similarly choosing to disregard the bishops' guidelines, I am concerned that Notre Dame's example could have an unfortunate ripple effect.
> It is with great sadness, therefore, that I have concluded

that I cannot accept the Laetare Medal or participate in the May 17 graduation ceremony."[7]

Notre Dame invited Judge John T. Noonan, Jr., of the Ninth Circuit United States Court of Appeals, the 1984 recipient of the Laetare Medal, "to deliver an address in the spirit of the award" at the Commencement. Judge Noonan accepted and delivered an address.

The AAUP Applauds

Not surprisingly, the American Association of University Professors said that it "applauds Notre Dame president Rev. John Jenkins for standing firm on the university's decision to invite President Obama and for exemplifying by his actions the words of his predecessor, Rev. Theodore Hesburgh, who stated unequivocally that 'the Catholic university must have true autonomy and academic freedom in the face of authority of whatever kind, lay or clerical, external to the academic community itself.' The opportunity to be confronted with diverse opinions is at the core of academic freedom, which is vital to a free society and a quality education. The AAUP will continue to work to ensure such academic freedom."[8] The words attributed to Fr. Hesburgh are instead from the Land O'Lakes Statement, discussed in Chapter 6. The AAUP's applause for Fr. Jenkins makes sense for the AAUP, because Notre Dame has substituted for the teaching authority of the Church the more peremptory authority of the secular academic establishment. Ask yourself whether you think the Notre Dame of today would defy the AAUP with the ease and arrogance with which it defied the Catholic Church on the honoring of Obama. Not likely.

4
The Obama Commencement

THE PRESIDENT: I also want to congratulate the Class of 2009 for all your accomplishments. And since this is Notre Dame –
AUDIENCE MEMBER: Abortion is murder! Stop killing children!
AUDIENCE: Booo!
THE PRESIDENT: That's all right. And since –
AUDIENCE: We are ND! We are ND!
AUDIENCE: Yes, we can! Yes, we can!
THE PRESIDENT: We're fine, everybody. We're following Brennan's adage that we don't do things easily. (Laughter.) We're not going to shy away from things that are uncomfortable sometimes. (Applause.)[1]

IT IS significant, first, that this interruption and audience response occurred and, second, that the White House included them in the official release as did the media generally in their reports. "When a man sitting in the rafters of the stadium began shouting," said the *New York Times*, "the crowd drowned him out, and he was taken away by security officers. Three other men stood up one at a time within the next few minutes shouting 'abortion is murder' and 'stop killing our children.' The crowd responded by shouting, 'Yes, we can,' Mr. Obama's campaign slogan, and 'We are N.D.,' a Notre Dame chant."[2] It was not clear from the video, which I watched, how many in the audience raised the chants and whether they were students or others. The permanent record of the Commencement, especially in the White House account, however, memorializes an interjection and especially a response that are more appropriate to a Nuremberg Rally than to a Notre Dame Commencement. It reflects no credit on Notre Dame.

This chapter will not attempt a detailed account of the Commencement. Some aspects, however, are especially pertinent to the theme of this book.

Obsequious

Father Jenkins, in his introduction of President Obama, said, "As a Catholic university, we are part of the Church," a strange assertion in light of the "autonomy" Notre Dame has claimed for itself over the past four decades since Land O'Lakes. Father Jenkins praised Obama for coming to Notre Dame "though he knows well that we are fully supportive of Church teaching on the sanctity of human life, and we oppose his policies on abortion and embryonic stem cell research." Fr. Jenkins was so very grateful that Obama was willing to come to the University to speak to [not really with] those people at Notre Dame who support "Church teaching" and oppose "his policies." Fr. Jenkins, however, misspoke. The issues at stake are not about "Church teaching" and "policies." Those issues, including the absolute inviolability of innocent life, are taught by the Church because they are unchanging truths of the natural law, knowable to reason. Those who, like Obama, place innocent life beyond the protection of the law, perpetrate not debatably erroneous "policies" but injustices that ought to preclude the conferral of honors by Notre Dame. The citation for Obama's honorary degree was, of course, laudatory. The publicly available version read: "The University of Notre Dame Confers the degree of Doctor of Laws, *honoris causa*, on the 44th president of the United States, whose historic election opened a new era of hope in a country long divided by its history of slavery and racism. A community organizer who honed his advocacy for the poor, the marginalized and the worker in the streets of Chicago, he now organizes a larger community, bringing to the world stage a renewed American dedication to diplomacy and dialogue with all nations and religions committed to human rights and the global common good. Through his willingness to engage with those who disagree with him and encourage people of faith to bring their beliefs to the public debate, he is inspiring this nation to heal its divisions of religion, culture, race and politics in the audacious hope for a brighter tomorrow. On Barack H. Obama, Washington, District of Columbia." But it was outdone by Fr. Jenkins' introduction:

> We welcome President Obama to Notre Dame, and we honor
> him for the qualities and accomplishments the American
> people admired in him when they elected him. He is a man
> who grew up without a father, whose family was fed for a

time with the help of food stamps – yet who mastered the most rigorous academic challenges, who turned his back on wealth to serve the poor, who sought the Presidency at a young age against long odds, and who – on the threshold of his goal – left the campaign to go to the bedside of his dying grandmother who helped raise him.

He is a leader who has great respect for the role of faith and religious institutions in public life. . . . He is the first African American to be elected President, yet his appeal powerfully transcends race. In a country that has been deeply wounded by racial hatred – he has been a healer.

Fr. Jenkins praised Obama, primarily for his "goals" rather than accomplishments. Interestingly, Arizona State University had President Obama as its commencement speaker but denied him an honorary degree because "his body of work is yet to come."[3] That did not stop Fr. Jenkins, who praised Obama's goals and statements:

He has set ambitious goals across a sweeping agenda – extending health care coverage to millions who don't have it, improving education especially for those who most need it, promoting renewable energy for the sake of our economy, our security, and our climate.

He has declared the goal of a world without nuclear weapons and has begun arms reduction talks with the Russians.

He has pledged to accelerate America's fight against poverty, to reform immigration to make it more humane, and to advance America's merciful work in fighting disease in the poorest places on earth.

As commander-in-chief and as chief executive, he embraces with confidence both the burdens of leadership and the hopes of his country.

Ladies and Gentlemen: The President of the United States.[4]

The Supreme Challenge?

"More than any problem in the arts or sciences – engineering or medicine – easing the hateful divisions among human beings," asserted Fr.

Jenkins earlier in his introduction of Obama, "is the supreme challenge of this age. If we can solve this problem we have a chance to come together and solve all the others." Fr. Jenkins, incidentally, failed to mention one "problem . . . in medicine." His honoree had already set in motion the procedures to deprive some of those graduating students of the right in conscience to refuse to participate in murder in the health care profession to which they aspire. Apart from that, is "easing hateful divisions" the "supreme challenge of this age"? One way to ease such divisions is to establish a social order that is just and respects all persons. But that is not in the cards in light of Obama's insistent denial of the right to life of unborn persons. Another way to ease hateful divisions is for everyone to agree that nothing is worth being divided about. For those who believe in God and an objective moral order in which some things are worth being divided about, their contribution to such a method of "easing" would be to keep quiet and submit. Fr. Jenkins did not distinguish among methods of "easing hateful divisions." What apparently counts is the "easing" itself. That is hardly "the supreme challenge of this age" in light of other problems, the mention of which by Fr. Jenkins would have put a damper on the ecstasy of the moment. Pope John Paul II, in his address to representatives of the world of culture in the Muslim republic of Kazakhstan on September 24, 2001, 13 days after 9/11, cautioned that Islamic republic against adopting "Western cultural models" because they are "marked by the fatal attempt to secure the good of humanity by eliminating God, the Supreme Good."[5] We are, said Cardinal Joseph Ratzinger to the Cardinals before they elected him Pope, in "[a] dictatorship of relativism . . . that recognizes nothing as absolute and which only leaves the 'I' and its whims as the ultimate measure."[6] The body count in the United States from the legalized execution of the unborn by surgical abortion already exceeds the death toll from the Holocaust by a factor of at least eight. An adequate response to these and other large problems ought to include more than a variant of Rodney King, "Why can't we all just get along?"

Dialogue

The repeated Jenkins theme was the need for "dialogue": "As we serve our country, we will be motivated by faith, but we cannot appeal only to faith. We must also engage in a dialogue that appeals to reason that all can accept." Bishop Robert W. Finn of the Diocese of Kansas City-St. Joseph,

Missouri, made the distinction that Fr. Jenkins failed to make. "Dialogue was the big theme of the Notre Dame commencement. Is it possible for the Church to dialogue on abortion?" asked Bishop Finn. "There are many associated elements that have to do with taking care of women in distress, offering alternatives to abortion. We have to work together, discuss and study how best we can provide for the needs of women and families. How can we reduce the number of abortions? These are elements for dialogue. But the rightness or wrongness of abortion – this is an intrinsic evil. The direct taking of an innocent life can never be negotiated."

Dialogue, for Fr. Jenkins, is not limited to the partial issues noted by Bishop Finn. Fr. Jenkins implicitly offered the prospect of a President Obama willing to dialogue and negotiate with Notre Dame on every aspect of abortion including whether it is right or wrong and whether it should be legal. Bishop Finn exposed that prospect as a delusion: "Dialogue is a means to an end. The purpose of dialogue has to be a change of heart. If I listen well and we speak the truth, then the dialogue may have a chance of being productive. But I have to have some authentic principled goal in mind. . . . [T]he President of Notre Dame said that they had invited the President of the United States and decided to honor him for the sake of dialogue. And then the President got up and said that the differences we have on abortion – namely the Catholic Church's staunch opposition to abortion and his staunch support of abortion – were 'irreconcilable.' And at that moment, it would seem to me that the dialogue came to a screeching halt. Father Jenkins' expressed desire for dialogue, whether it was well-founded or justified, at that point got thrown back in his face. The President shut the door on dialogue by saying that there was not going to be any change in his position on abortion and he understood that there was not going to be any change in the Church's position on abortion. To me, that was the lesson of the day. I am glad that Mr. Obama was so clear. And then amazingly, everybody gave him a standing ovation. The perception . . . was that this was a completely acceptable position of his."[7]

Obama: A Triumph but No Opposition

On the one side, the Notre Dame officials behaved like sycophantic courtiers in awe of the great man who deigned to grace Notre Dame with his presence. On the other side, President Obama accepted the adulation. And he did not give an inch. "Those who speak out against stem cell research may be rooted in an admirable conviction about the sacredness of life," he said, "but so are the parents of a child with juvenile diabetes who are convinced that their son's or daughter's hardships can be relieved." Those last words drew applause despite the fakery involved in his use of the term "stem cell research." As noted in Chapter I, the contested issue is *embryonic* stem cell research (ESCR), which has no record of success in curing any human ailment. The worshipful audience probably did not make the distinction between ESCR and the morally unobjectionable use of adult stem cells. And Obama can now claim approval from a Notre Dame audience for his position on "stem cell research." On abortion, he drew applause when he said, "we open up our hearts and our minds . . . that's when we discover at least the possibility of common ground. That's when we begin to say, 'Maybe we won't agree on abortion, but we can still agree that this heart-wrenching decision for any woman is not made casually, it has both moral and spiritual dimensions.' So let us work together to reduce the number of women seeking abortions, let's reduce unintended pregnancies." That drew applause. Obama's technique for reducing "unintended pregnancies," however, is the promotion and funding of contraception, which, as most of the Notre Dame graduates in his audience probably do not know, is, as John Paul II put it, "so profoundly unlawful as never to be, for any reason, justified."[8]

When he spoke at Notre Dame, President Obama had already set in motion the administrative procedures to deny medical personnel, including in the future some of the graduates in his audience, their right of conscientious objection, as health care professionals, to refuse to participate in abortion and other procedures. His treatment of the issue was artful, deceptive and unyielding: "Let's honor the conscience of those who disagree with abortion, and draft a sensible conscience clause, and make sure that all of our health care policies are grounded not only in sound science, but also in clear ethics, as well as respect for the equality of women." In light of Obama's record, there can be absolutely no reasonable doubt that the last phrase reserved the "equality of women" to choose abortion. President Obama met on July 2, 2009, with representatives from the Catholic press, including the *National Catholic Register*, *America*, Avvenire/Vatican Radio, Catholic News Service, *Catholic Digest*, *Commonweal*, *National Catholic Reporter*, and *The Washington Post*. Obama said that, "I'm a believer in conscience clauses. . . . I reiterated my support for an effective conscience clause at Notre Dame."[9] If that is true, why did he rescind the Bush regulations protecting the rights of conscience, as discussed in Chapter 1? If he is "a believer in conscience clauses," it is with a reservation of "respect for the equality of women," which is effectively a reservation of the right to abortion.

Obama as Religious Arbiter

President Obama told the graduates, "Remember, too, that the ultimate irony of faith is that it necessarily admits doubt." That prompted Bishop D'Arcy to reply: "It's against Catholic teaching on faith. I gave a course in the seminary – I taught it for years – on faith. One of the characteristics of faith is it's certain. And [President Obama] says there's no certainty in faith."[10]

The Commencement was a personal and political triumph for President Obama. And a striking exposure of the inadequacy of the President, Fellows and Trustees of Notre Dame. The event was momentous for another reason. Fr. Jenkins's invitation to Obama had triggered a major controversy within the Catholic Church in the United States on several aspects of the teachings of the Church. Over the years, the Supreme Court has developed a sound doctrine that precludes courts, and implicitly government officials in general, from determining "the centrality of particular beliefs or practices to a faith or the validity of a particular litigant's interpretations of those creeds. Repeatedly and in many different contexts we have warned that courts must not presume to determine the place of a particular belief in a religion or the plausibility of a religious claim."[11] Nor may courts or government officials decide whether the beliefs of any religion are true or false.[12] President Obama at Notre Dame crossed that line. George Weigel, the biographer of John Paul II, made the point:

> Passionate debates over doctrine, identity and the boundaries of "communion" have been a staple of the American religious landscape for centuries. . . . Yet never in our history has the president of the United States, in the exercise of his public office, intervened in such disputes in order to secure a political advantage.
>
> Until yesterday, at the University of Notre Dame.

The principal themes of President Obama's Notre Dame commencement address were entirely predictable . . . "common ground"; tolerance and reconciliation amid diversity; Father Hesburgh; respect for those with whose moral judgments we disagree; problem-solving over ideology; Father Hesburgh; saving God's creation from climate change; pulling together; Father Hesburgh; open hearts; open minds; fair-minded words; Father Hesburgh. None of this was surprising, and most of it was said with the president's usual smooth eloquence.

What was surprising, and ought to be disturbing to anyone who cares about religious freedom . . . was the president's decision to insert himself into the ongoing Catholic debate over the boundaries of Catholic identity and the applicability of settled Catholic conviction in the public square. Obama did this by suggesting, not altogether subtly, who the real Catholics in America are. The real Catholics . . . are those like the late Cardinal Joseph Bernardin, who are "congenial and gentle" in persuasion, men and women who are "always trying to bring people together," Catholics who are "always trying to find common ground." The fact that Cardinal Bernardin's . . . geniality and gentility in bringing people together to find the common ground invariably ended with a "consensus" that matched the liberal or progressive position of the moment went unremarked. . . .

Cardinal Bernardin gave a moving and powerful testimony to Christian faith in his gallant response to the cancer that finally killed him. Prior to that . . . however, the late archbishop of Chicago was best known publicly for his advocacy of a "consistent ethic of life," in which the abortion issue was linked to the abolition of capital punishment and nuclear arms control. And whatever Bernardin's intentions in formulating what came to be popularly known as the "seamless garment" approach to public policy, the net effect of the consistent ethic of life was to validate politically the intellectual mischief of Mario Cuomo's notorious 1984 Notre Dame speech and to give two generations of Catholic politicians a virtual pass on the abortion question by allowing them to argue that, hey, I'm batting .667 on the consistent ethic of life.[13]

The Hesburgh Endorsement

The Obama Commencement was a culmination of the autonomy process begun at Land O'Lakes in 1967 (see Chapter 6). Three days before Commencement, Fr. Hesburgh endorsed the invitation to Obama. "The 91-year-old Hesburgh said in an interview with WNDU-TV that universities are supposed to be places where people of differing opinions can talk. 'It's like a common place where people who disagree can get together, instead of throwing bricks at one another, they can discuss the problem and they can see different solutions to difficult problems and those solutions are going to come out of people from universities. They aren't going to come from people running around with signs,' he said."[14] Fr. Hesburgh would surely agree, however, that his statement is subject to the restriction that some moral issues do have absolute answers that are found, not in conversations in universities, but in the natural law and the Commandments which are specifications of that natural law. The authoritative interpreter of those criteria is the Vicar of Christ because Christ is God and the author of that natural law. As we discuss in Chapter 6, Notre Dame refuses to accept the authority of that interpreter.

5
ND Response

A Large Post Office

ON EASTER Monday, April 24, 1916, about 200 Irish rebels, under the command of Pádraic Pearse, captured the General Post Office in Dublin and proclaimed an Irish Republic. After six days they surrendered to the British Army, as did other rebels at other locations.[1] The failed Easter Rebellion was followed by a war against the British which resulted in a limited independent status for 26 of the 32 counties of Ireland and ultimately the establishment of those 26 counties as an independent republic in 1949. Over the years, as Pearse, James Connolly, Sean Mac Diarmada and other executed leaders of the 1916 Rising gained iconic, heroic status, a curious thing happened. The number of Irish men (and women) who claimed to have been "with Pearse in the GPO" was such that, if all the claims were true, that post office would have had to have approached Yankee Stadium in size.

A Gathering for Prayer

We can expect a similar development with respect to the Commencement events at Notre Dame in 2009. There were two Commencements because there are two Notre Dames. The official Commencement, fairly described as The Obama Commencement, had the air of a political rally. The other one, organized by the pro-life (and pro-Notre Dame) student group, ND Response, at Alumni Hall Chapel, the Grotto and the South Quad, had the character of a spiritual retreat. The media, to the extent they noticed it at all, treated it as a protest. But that does not do it justice. It was not a demonstration. On-site demonstrations are counter-productive. It was not a protest. No marches, no chanting, no disruption. It began with Eucharistic Adoration at 9:30, Saturday night, in the Alumni Hall chapel, the largest residence hall chapel on campus; the crowd was wall-to-wall at the opening and at the closing at 10:45 the next morning, with substantial attendance all night. At 11:15 A.M., Fr. Kevin Russeau of Campus Ministry celebrated Mass on the Quad with ten Holy Cross and other priests concelebrating, including Fr. John Corapi and Fr. Frank Pavone, national director of Priests for Life. Following Mass, a rally on the Quad featured short talks by seven speakers.[2] At 2:00 p.m., at which time the Obama Commencement began, Fr. Pavone led a powerful scriptural meditation on the Glorious Mysteries of the Rosary at the Grotto. The total attendance at all the events was fairly estimated by ND Response at about 3,000, compared to 12,000 at the Obama Commencement. Forty graduating seniors, out of a class of 2,600, skipped the Obama Commencement to be with ND Response.

The comparative numbers might lead you to think that the ND Response event was insignificant. Think again. And remember the General Post Office in 1916. For Notre Dame, May 17, 2009, has been rightly described as a "watershed" date. Whichever way it goes, whether Notre Dame begins to return to its Catholic identity or continues on its secularizing course, the wisdom and courage of ND Response will become more obvious. It will be attractive to say, "I was there on the 17th, praying at the Grotto." The ND Response program, which deserves to be called the Notre Dame Commencement, had a power about it that the other, political event could not have. It was essentially an 18-hour prayer of reparation and petition to the Blessed Mother to reclaim her University for her Son. Alumni had come from as far away as California and Texas to be with those students. Others in the thousands, who could not attend, had pledged to support them at that time with the Rosary. The proceedings were peaceful and respectful. The talks were at times appropriately blunt. But there was no hint of hostility or animosity toward anyone who might disagree. Fr. Russeau, in his homily, emphasized the prayerful nature of the student response to the honoring of Obama. He stressed the "instinct for the Eucharist" at Notre Dame. "What has been inspiring for me," he said, "is that our student body had an instinct – an instinct to come to the altar of the Lord to ask for guidance and strength. I can't tell you the number of Rosaries and Masses and prayer meetings that have been intentional responses to what many feel is a concession to the culture of death. Students, family, friends, alumni, and many of you, have spent hours in adoration looking for the proper response. The students that I have come to know here on campus have reminded me that in all things we must respond with love. And to respond with love in hard times, we must ask our Lord for grace."

Bishop D'Arcy

Bishop D'Arcy had opened the Eucharistic Adoration on Saturday night and had not planned to attend on Sunday because of other commitments. But, he later wrote, "I realized that it was a requirement for the bishop to be present with these beautiful young people and with those whom they had drawn to Notre Dame. . . . I was invited to the platform, and said that I would not be so bold as to speak after Bill Miscamble, which was like batting after Babe Ruth. I said that in this time of sadness, I had thought there were no winners. I was wrong. The young people were the heroes. The dignity and the substance and the prayer, which they brought to these events, was extraordinary." The Bishop thanked Mary K. Daly, her brother, John, Michele Sagala and others, for putting the event together. The Bishop then asked Michele to announce the prayer intentions the students had highlighted. The Bishop listed them, "as best as I can remember:

* "The conversion of heart of President Barack Obama;
* "The strengthening of the pro-life movement nationally and internationally;
* "That Catholic universities be strengthened in their Catholic identity;
    "They prayed thousands of rosaries for these intentions.
    "How can you honestly, as a bishop, stay away from a group that has made such presentations and is dedicated to such causes? I told them John D'Arcy was not important, but the Office of Bishop was, and I was honored to be with them."[3]

The Rally

Chris Godfrey, who had first come to Notre Dame in the uniform of a University of Michigan football player and went on to star on the New York Giants Super Bowl XXI champion team, is a member of the class of 1993 at Notre Dame Law School. "I thanked [Our Lady] every morning on my way to class," he said, "for letting me come to her university." Chris, who is the founder of Life Athletes, put the events of that day in focus: "While it was Notre Dame's promise of excellence that attracted many of us to the university in the first place, it is the waning of its commitment that brings us all together today."

The ND Response commitment, in the Notre Dame tradition, was, and is, to life. The history of Notre Dame, said Professor David Solomon, "is inseparable from its commitment to a tradition – intellectual, moral and spiritual – that provides a perspective from which no human being is invisible. In this tradition, everyone counts. In this tradition, Down syndrome infants struggling in the womb are the equals of princes and potentates – even presidents." That Notre Dame commitment to life is not just academic. "Over 25 years ago," said Elizabeth Naquin Borger, "a young professor here at Notre Dame, named Dr. Janet Smith, realized that women facing one of life's major events had no place to go for support and guidance. Like all of you here who care so deeply, she was compelled to take some action. She realized it wasn't enough for her to say she was pro-life. So she gathered together a cross-section of people to provide advice and funding and she founded a crisis pregnancy center just a short distance from this campus." That center was the Women's Care Center. Ms. Borger, its past chairman, said it has become "the largest life-affirming pregnancy center in the United States – with fourteen different centers."

The Notre Dame Commencement, on the Quad and at the Grotto, affirmed both life and the future. Lacy Dodd was three months pregnant at her Notre Dame graduation and Army commissioning in 1999. When she learned she was pregnant, she went to the Grotto. "In my hour of need, on my knees, I asked Mary for courage and strength. And she did not disappoint. My boyfriend was a different story. He was also a Notre Dame senior. When I told him that he was to be a father, he tried to pressure me into having an abortion. Like so many women in similar circumstances, I found out the kind of man the father of my child was at precisely the moment I needed him most. 'All that talk about abortion is just dining-room talk,' he said. 'When it's really you in the situation, it's different. I will drive you to Chicago and pay for a good doctor.'"[4] The Army gave Lacy a delay in her active duty "On All Saints Day in 1999," she said on the Quad, "I was blessed with the gift of a beautiful baby girl. When the doctor placed her in my arms, I knew there was only one name possible for her: Mary. This morning, ten years since my own graduation, I returned to the Grotto to give thanks. This time I was with my nine-year-old daughter. And together we thanked Our Lady for teaching us to be open to God's will . . . to never be afraid of God's will . . . and to recognize that there may be sacrifices and suffering – but God's will also brings great peace and joy. . . . So . . . this is very personal for me. When I learned of Father Jenkins' decision to honor President Obama . . . at . . . graduation, I started thinking about the message this sends. . . . In the article I wrote, I posed a question that I believe is at the heart of this graduation: I asked Father Jenkins this: Who draws support from your decision to honor President Obama? Is it the pregnant Notre Dame woman – who may be sitting in this year's gradua-tion class – who wants desperately to keep her baby? Or those who, like my boyfriend at the time, tell her that the Catholic teaching on the intrin-sic evil of abortion is just 'dining-room talk'?

"I am still waiting for a response but I think we all know what the answer is. . . . At best, Notre Dame's decision to honor the most pro-choice President in our history sends a message of indifference about the sanctity of unborn life. After all, if abortion does not appear to be an important issue to a great Catholic institution such as Notre Dame, many Catholics will conclude that it does not have to be a big deal for them either."

"Well, my daughter and I have a different message!"

Notre Dame: In or Out of the Church?

The main difference between the Obama Commencement and the Notre Dame Commencement involves Notre Dame's relation to the Catholic Church. In his introduction of President Obama, Father Jenkins said, "[a]s a Catholic university, we are part of the Church." The "autono-my" from the Church claimed by Notre Dame at Land O'Lakes puts his claim into the misleading category. Notre Dame is "Catholic" but only in an informal way. As Mary K. Daly, a leader of ND Response, noted, there is "a 'strong subculture within the student body of earnest Catholics: peo-ple who are making sincere efforts to grow in their faith and to discern and live out God's will in their lives.' She described Notre Dame as a place that has 'adoration five days a week on campus, Mass in all the dormitory chapels at least four times a week, and priests in every dorm.' Thus, Daly said, 'If you are serious about your Catholic faith and want to grow in your personal relationship with Christ, this is an excellent place to do so,' though, she acknowledged, you have to be willing to 'challenge yourself.'"

At Notre Dame, as Christina Holmstrom, a 2008 graduate and Campus Ministry intern, said, "faith 'finds its source and summit in the Eucharist and active participation in the Church and is lived out in a life of service to others.'"[5]

The problem is that Notre Dame cannot have it both ways. It cannot be Catholic without accepting the role of the Church as defined by the Church. As we will see in the next chapter, it won't work. It brings to mind Onnie Jay Holy, in Flannery O'Connor's *Wise Blood*, who founded the "Holy Church of Christ Without Christ."[6]

Father Miscamble

An eloquent reminder of Notre Dame's responsibility to the Catholic Church was the talk by Fr. Wilson D. Miscamble, C.S.C. We include the full text as Appendix A in this book. Please read it or, even better, see it on video.[7] Fr. Miscamble spoke not as a Notre Dame professor, but "primarily as a Holy Cross priest." He recounted Notre Dame's early survival despite adversity. Its founders "built Notre Dame into a distinctive place that nurtured its students' religious and moral development, as well as their intellectual lives. Notre Dame challenged them to serve God and neighbor. And . . . it proudly proclaimed its Catholic identity and its loyal membership in a Church that was and is unafraid to speak of moral truths and foundational principles. . . . Notre Dame came to hold a special place in the hearts of Catholics all across America. Now friends, jump ahead to today. The formal leadership of the University still proclaims its fidelity to this vision. . . . Of late . . . [i]nstead of fostering the moral development of its students Notre Dame's leaders have planted the damaging seeds of moral confusion. . . . The honor extended to Barack Obama says very loudly that support for practically unlimited access to abortion – and approval for the destruction of embryonic life to harvest stem cells – are not major problems for those charged with leading Notre Dame. . . . Friends, just ask yourselves whether anyone – regardless of their other accomplishments – would be honored here at ND if they held racist or anti-Semitic sentiments. They would not – and rightly so! . . . [T]he administration has distanced the University from the Church that is its lifeblood – the ultimate source of its identity. . . . Yet when we look back on these days, I have a sense that what will stand out is how a group of dedicated prolife students, wonderful alumni, and ordinary Catholics who cherish this place refused to acquiesce in the Administration's willingness to wink at its most fundamental values in exchange for the public relations coup that attends a presidential visit. . . . – Let us move forward together and let us never turn back. – Let us take our instruction from the Lord, in the words that the great champion of life, John Paul II, used at the outset of his papacy: BE NOT AFRAID. – Let us labor in this vineyard, so that Notre Dame might regain its true soul . . . be faithful in its mission as a Catholic University . . . and truly become the 'powerful means for good' that Father Sorin dreamed about."

The question is whether Notre Dame's present administrators, or Fr. Miscamble and the Holy Cross priests who joined in their respectful protest against the honoring of Obama, represent the future of Notre Dame.

The Gates of Hell

Fr. John Raphael, ssj (ND '89), principal of St. Augustine High School in New Orleans, made a point on the Quad that captures the spirit of that "Notre Dame Commencement." Fr. Raphael quoted the words of Christ to St. Peter: *"Thou art Peter, and upon this rock I will build my Church, and the gates of hell shall not prevail against it (Mt 16:19)."* Then Fr. Raphael said:

> The passage also tells us something about our gathering today. . . . [U]pon hearing these words we frequently conjure up the wrong image, that of the Church surrounded . . . by a strong and impregnable wall. But note, this passage refers not to the Church's gates, but to the gates of hell!!! It is not the Church that is hunkered down in defensive posture, afraid of the enemy at the gates, it is hell! The forces of darkness and the prince of this world will ultimately collapse, not the Church! The Church is leading the charge, raising the siege! The gates of hell shall not prevail. . . . Until that ultimate victory has been won, each generation is called to play its part, and that is why we are here today.

The Church is on the offense, not the defense. The Church *is* the winning side. We pray that Notre Dame, through the grace obtained by Mary for her University, will survive in full commitment to the mission of the Church. And then you can tell your grandchildren: "Of course, I was there at the Grotto on May 17th." Along with the many tens of thousands.

Land O'Lakes

At the Obama Commencement, Notre Dame obsequiously conferred its highest honors on a politician, occupying the office of President, who favors, among other things, the legalized exposure of all unborn children to execution. As Fr. Miscamble, Fr. Raphael and others stressed, however, the dispositive issue posed by the Obama invitation is Notre Dame's institutional relation to the Catholic Church. That issue cannot be understood except in the context of the "autonomy and academic freedom" in the face of "external" authority "of whatever kind, lay or clerical," claimed by Notre Dame and other Catholic universities in the Land O'Lakes Statement of 1967. In Chapters 6 through 11 we will consider that Statement and some applications of it by Notre Dame.

6
Land O'Lakes

The Statement

"LAND O'LAKES." When you hear that name, what pops into your mind? Butter? Maybe, with the "Indian maiden" logo with trees and a lake in the background. Or maybe: A northern Wisconsin town with a population of 912. Both are right. But "Land O'Lakes" means a lot more for Notre Dame:

> In July 1967 a small group of Roman Catholics – 26 men, almost all priests and educators – gathered at Chicago's O'Hare Airport and boarded a chartered plane bound for a conference center in Land O'Lakes, Wisconsin, which was owned by Notre Dame University. Their goal . . . was on the surface simple: to discuss ways Catholic universities might join in the renewal of the Church sparked by Vatican II. But . . . the Wisconsin group began a revolution they could not have foretold. As the Church would be permanently changed by Vatican II, North America's Catholic universities would be forever changed by the meeting and resultant statement that became known simply as "Land O'Lakes."[1]

The meeting was held under the auspices of the North American region of the International Federation of Catholic Universities, whose president, Fr. Theodore M. Hesburgh, C.S.C, was then President of Notre Dame.

Notre Dame's honoring of President Obama was a predictable result of the change of course that Catholic universities made at Land O'Lakes. The Land O'Lakes Statement declared:

> The Catholic university today must be a university in the full modern sense of the word, with a strong commitment to and

concern for academic excellence. To perform its teaching and research functions effectively, the Catholic university must have a true autonomy and academic freedom in the face of authority of whatever kind, lay or clerical, external to the academic community itself. To say this is simply to assert that institutional autonomy and academic freedom are essential conditions of life and growth, and indeed of survival, for Catholic universities as for all universities.[2]

The Statement, as Fr. George Rutler noted, "neglects to explain what 'the full modern sense of the word' is and why a university 'must' conform to it."[3] Nevertheless, most Catholic universities, around that time, severed their juridical connection with the Church and transferred control to lay-dominated boards of trustees. "Putting it very bluntly," said Rev. Leo McLaughlin, S.J., president of Fordham University, earlier in 1967, "one reason that the changes are being made in the structure of the boards of trustees is money. . . . These colleges simply cannot continue to exist without state aid. In the not too distant future . . . the choice offered to Catholic institutions is going to be quite clear: changes will have to be made within the structure of the Catholic institutions which will make them eligible for federal and state aid or many of them will have to close their doors."[4] The concern that structural changes were needed to qualify the institutions for government aid was genuine but turned out to be exaggerated:

> The presidents were fearful that litigation under way might disqualify their colleges and universities from receiving federal or state funds for building construction, student aid, and noncategorical grants. Two major lawsuits touched them closely, for they involved states where Jesuit colleges were at risk: the *Maryland* case and the *Connecticut* case.[5]
> In its final outcome (in 1976) the litigation would vindicate the capacity of most religiously affiliated colleges and universities to receive public funds because they were not so "pervasively sectarian" that such appropriations would constitute the establishment of religion forbidden by the First Amendment. But in 1966 that outcome was far from clear. The Jesuit presidents were intensely aware that if ultimate control by outside religious authorities were to block their access to needed funding, the schools to which

they had dedicated their ministries were liable to be destroyed. The stakes had been raised from excellence to survival.[6]

A Prelude to Land O'Lakes

Notre Dame's interest in expanded sources of funding was evidently a motivating factor in its sponsorship of a series of annual meetings on population policy, held at Notre Dame from 1963 to 1967 and sponsored by the Ford Foundation and the Rockefeller Foundation. Those meetings and related developments were analyzed by Professor Donald T. Critchlow, of St. Louis University, in a study described by Notre Dame Professor Emeritus J. Philip Gleason as "a superb account of the evolution of federal policy on population issues, family planning, and abortion. Based on prodigious research in little used sources, it illuminates the interaction of philanthropic foundations and popular pressure groups in shaping policy."[7] Professor Critchlow's account provides useful background to the issues raised by Land O'Lakes:

> Organized by George Shuster, special assistant to Father
> . . . Hesburgh . . . these annual meetings called "Conference
> on Population Problems" brought concerned liberal
> Catholics in the church and the academy together with rep-
> resentatives from the foundation community, PPFA [Planned
> Parenthood Federation of America] activists, and public offi-
> cials. Shuster had come to Notre Dame in 1960 at the urging
> of Hesburgh to help transform the university into a premier
> institution of higher learning. Hesburgh believed that the
> key to this lay in receiving public and private funding for
> further research. . . . When Cass Canfield of PPFA men-
> tioned to population activist Fr. John A. O'Brien at Notre
> Dame that he would like to hold a national conference,
> Shuster . . . proposed that the conference be hosted by Notre
> Dame. Canfield readily accepted. Here was the long-sought
> opportunity that the population movement had dreamed of –
> cultivating liberal opinion in the Catholic Church.
>   . . . .[B]oth sides knew what they wanted: a liberal
> forum to create an oppositional voice within the Catholic
> Church on the issue of family planning. . . . [O]fficials from
> PPFA and the Population Council worked closely with Notre

Dame officials in setting the conference agenda and select-
ing the guest list for the conference. Attending the first
meeting were twenty-four participants, including James
Norris of Catholic Relief Services, Richard Fagley of the
Commission of the Churches on International Affairs, Alan
Guttmacher of Planned Parenthood, Frank Notestein of the
Population Council, Leland DeVinney of the Rockefeller
Foundation, and Oscar Harkavy of the Ford Foundation. . . .
A mutual interest in liberalizing the church's position on
family planning brought together progressive Catholics and
population activists at Notre Dame in what a PPFA official
later described as "historic." . . . The birth control movement
had long viewed the Catholic Church's opposition to artificial contraception with aversion, which sometimes found
expression in public statements and private correspondence
that revealed deep anti-Catholic prejudice. Cognizant of this
unproductive sentiment, and astutely aware of the importance of changing the Catholic Church's position on birth
control, John D. Rockefeller 3rd and others within the foundation community saw the Notre Dame meetings as an
opportunity to form an alliance with Catholic intellectuals
and academics who could help change opinion within the
hierarchy. In turn, Father Theodore Hesburgh, while sincere
in his desire to explore the population and family planning
issue, realized that association with the established foundation community could only benefit his university by impart-
ing a certain respectability that comes from associating with
eastern philanthropic foundations.

Hesburgh had to walk a cautious path in pursuing this
relationship, though. From the outset of these meetings in
1963, participants understood that they were coming together in order to formulate an acceptable liberal position for the
church on family planning. Only liberal Catholic academics
were invited to these conferences, which were designed to
introduce them to experts in population. As a consequence,
a quasi secrecy prevailed in the meetings from the beginning.
. . . [T]hirty-seven scholars attending the Notre Dame conference in 1965 . . . signed a . . . statement . . . to the Vatican
commission on birth control urging the pope to reverse the
church's opposition to artificial contraception. . . .

Hesburgh's willingness to engage in intellectual exchange with the population community, and his political skill in handling controversy, won him friends in the foundation community. In 1965 the Ford Foundation awarded Notre Dame a $100,000 grant to host further population conferences. That same year the Rockefeller Foundation awarded a major grant to a Notre Dame social service project in Chile, and AID awarded the university over $550,000 to study family and fertility changes in Latin America. As Hesburgh told Robert West of the Rockefeller Foundation, "I also understand that there is a general belief that Notre Dame is in a good position to exert a liberalizing influence on certain sectors of intellectual life in Latin America."

During these same years, Hesburgh developed a close personal friendship with Rockefeller. In 1966 Hesburgh was appointed to the executive committee of the Rockefeller Foundation with an understanding that he would abstain on voting on issues involving contraception, sterilization, and abortion. Nonetheless, Hesburgh understood that the Rockefeller Foundation was actively funding family planning projects. . . . Hesburgh's extensive travels led to a genuine concern with the poor peoples of the world and the problem of overpopulation. . . . Hesburgh arranged a highly confidential meeting between Rockefeller and Pope Paul VI to discuss the world population issue.[8]

The Fellows Control

Notre Dame made changes in its governing structure, which were approved by the relevant Church authorities, before the Land O'Lakes conference:

Operating under its founding charter from the State of Indiana adopted on January 15, 1844, the University of Notre Dame for many decades had been governed by a self-perpetuating Board of Trustees comprised of six Holy Cross priests.

On March 28, 1967, the above Board of Trustees approved the statutes of the University . . . providing for six laymen to join with the six . . . priests in a body which replaced the then existing Board of Trustees and is known as "The Fellows of the University of Notre Dame du Lac." . . .

On April 8, 1967, at a meeting of the Fellows, the
Statutes were ratified and new Bylaws were approved, which
delegate the general power of governance of the University
to a Board of Trustees.[9]

The Fellows, however, have the leading role: "The Fellows of the
University are a 'self-perpetuating body,' consisting of six members whom
[*sic*] at all times must be 'members of the Priests Society of the
Congregation of Holy Cross, Indiana Province, and six of whom shall be
lay persons.' The Fellows are the 'successors and associates in office' of the
original founders of the University and shall perform the following duties
of office:

* Determine powers to be delegated to the Board of Trustees;
* Elect the Trustees of the University in accordance with the
  Bylaws;
* Adopt and amend the Bylaws of the University;
* Approve the sale and transfer of substantial parts of the
  University's physical property;
* Ensure that the University maintains its essential character as a
  Catholic institution of higher learning;
* Ensure that the University's operations make full use of the skills
  and dedication of the members of the Priests of Holy Cross,
  Indiana Province, Inc.;
* Ensure that the University "continues its long-standing policy of
  admitting students of any race, color, national and ethnic origin."[10]

President Fr. Edward A. Malloy, in 1992, described the role of the
Fellows as "protective" of the University: "From 1842 to 1967 [Notre
Dame] was owned by the Congregation of Holy Cross. In 1967, governance . . . was transferred to a predominantly lay Board of Trustees [and]
the Statutes of the University created a body . . . known as The Fellows.
They have . . . all power and authority granted by [the charter of the
University]. . . . [T]he establishment of The Fellows was intended to be a
protective mechanism for the University."[11] The Holy Cross priests, who
are six of the twelve Fellows, if united, can prevent any University action
of which they disapprove. The Fellows also have the duty to maintain the

"essential character of the University as a Catholic institution." At present the Fellows are:

Rev. E. William Beauchamp, C.S.C.
William M. Goodyear
Enrique Hernandez, Jr.
Rev. Peter A. Jarret, C.S.C.
Rev. John I. Jenkins, C.S.C.
The Most Rev. Daniel R. Jenky, C.S.C., D.D.
Hon. Diana Lewis
Patrick F. McCartan
Terrence J. McGlinn
Richard C. Notebaert
Rev. Timothy R. Scully, C.S.C.
Rev. David T. Tyson, C.S.C.[12]

Purpose and Effect of the Changes

The changes in governance at Notre Dame were in the spirit of the later Land O'Lakes Statement. Those changes were well intended, as was the Land O'Lakes Statement itself. "From the start, Land O'Lakes was controversial, but the argument was not primarily about ideas. Controversy instead grew heated because the statement provided a rationale for bold institutional reform. Hesburgh and Paul Reinert, S.J., of St. Louis University – indeed an entire generation of academic leaders and the religious communities to which they belonged – came to believe that their colleges and universities could best serve God and God's people by seeking excellence in teaching and research under new, independent governance structures in which religious leaders shared responsibility with laypeople. As Hesburgh would comment in an interview years later, while others were debating about Catholic identity, he and his colleagues at Notre Dame were arranging to give away the university."[13] The author of that article does not provide a source for the statement he attributed to Fr. Hesburgh in the last quoted sentence. In any event, Notre Dame did not give away the university in the way you would transfer a house to a new owner. Rather, Notre Dame continued under its original charter but changed the identity and composition of its governing body which, in practical terms, is now the Fellows. The Holy Cross priests reduced themselves from 100 percent to 50 percent of that governing body. The Congregation of Holy Cross does not own or govern Notre Dame. Nor does the Catholic Church. The retention of Holy Cross priests, however, as 50 percent of the governing body ensures their continuing complicity in the consequences of Land O'Lakes "autonomy."

The changes were prompted by a perception that autonomy from the Church was necessary to protect the academic and even spiritual integrity of Notre Dame. The record does not support that perception as we shall see in later chapters of this book. Incidentally, *Ex Corde Ecclesiae* (ECE), the 1990 Apostolic Constitution on Catholic Universities, does not require the Catholic university to have a juridical connection with the Church. *Ex Corde* provides that "A Catholic University possesses the autonomy necessary to develop its distinctive identity and pursue its proper mission."[14] The Application by the United States bishops of *Ex Corde* to the United States affirms that "Catholic universities enjoy institutional autonomy: as academic institutions their governance is and remains internal to that institution."[15] The "autonomy" claimed by the universities at Land O'Lakes is not explicitly contrary to *Ex Corde* or its *Application* to the United States. The problems with Land O'Lakes "autonomy" arise from its lack of context and its potential to be used as a license for actions contrary to the nature of a Catholic university. Father Richard John Neuhaus and the editors of *First Things* commented in 1991 on an article by Notre Dame Professor George Marsden in that issue analyzing the secularization of American universities founded as Protestant institutions.[16] Fr. Neuhaus said: "The essential formula of Land O'Lakes is to be found in the 'mission statement' of hundreds of colleges and universities that still maintain a plausible seriousness about being religious institutions. Not for long will they maintain it, for the formula is a perfect invitation to follow in the footsteps of those who have gone the way so incisively traced by George Marsden."[17]

Over the past four decades, as discussed in Chapters 7 through 11, Notre Dame's implementation of Land O'Lakes autonomy has been inconsistent in various ways with *Ex Corde*'s mandate that one of the "essential characteristics" of a Catholic university is "fidelity to the Christian message as it comes to us through the Church."[18] Or, as the *Application* of *ECE* puts it, the "Catholic identity" of the university includes a "[c]ommitment to be faithful to the teachings of the Catholic Church [and a] [c]ommitment to Catholic ideals, principles and attitudes in carrying out research, teaching and all other university activities."[19]

"Every Catholic University, without ceasing to be a University," says *ECE*, has an "essential relationship to the Church [such that] the *institutional* fidelity of the University to the Christian message includes a recognition of and adherence to the teaching authority of the Church in matters of faith and morals."[20] It is difficult to imagine a more flagrant disrespect for that teaching authority than Notre Dame's bestowal of its highest honors, in defiance of the mandate of the nation's bishops, on a person with the record and stated purposes of President Obama.

The Protestant Precedents

Notre Dame's separation of itself from the authority of the Magisterium to determine the nature of a Catholic university makes it predictable that Notre Dame will follow the pattern by which the Protestant universities went, as Professor George Marsden subtitled his book, "From Protestant Establishment to Established Nonbelief."[21] A similar analysis of that secularizing process was offered by Fr. James T. Burtchaell, C.S.C., in *The Dying of the Light.*[22] Fr. Burtchaell analyzes the process by which colleges and universities founded in the United States by Congregationalists, Presbyterians, Methodists, Baptists, Lutherans, Evangelicals and Catholics gradually lost their religious identity. The Catholic institutions Burtchaell examines are Boston College, the College of New Rochelle and Saint Mary's College in California. His comments on the events leading up to the Land O'Lakes statement, and the impact of that statement, are perceptive. He notes that the Land O'Lakes claim of autonomy from authority "external to the academic community" meant that: "The sovereign 'academic community' would be, not the individual Catholic university, but the educational establishment. The conferees, who had meticulously emancipated their institutions from the church, though somewhat less from the state (whose rights to incorporate and regulate were left unchallenged), were unreservedly prepared to confide their universities to the canons, dogmas, and authority internal to academia. In 1967 they harbored no misgivings about how confining that obedience could prove to be."[23]

Earlier, Fr. Burtchaell had written a two-part article in *First Things.*[24] Using Vanderbilt as the model, he describes the secularization of the Protestant universities in the period, 1870–1910, and then examines, without naming any institutions, the comparable secularization of Catholic universities. Burtchaell notes that, at Vanderbilt and elsewhere, "the estrangement from sponsoring church occurred at a time when the funding the church may have provided was clearly inadequate for the new academic ambitions of the university, and when new, secular sources were offering an infusion of funds."[25]

Burtchaell concludes that, *"The only plausible way for a college or university to be significantly Christian is for it to function as a congregation in active communion within a church."* He suggests that "secularization is rapidly bleaching the Catholic character out of that church's universities and colleges, with all the elements we saw typified in the Vanderbilt story." Once autonomy is declared, the secularization process is gradual and regrettably familiar: "[A]s a century earlier [with the Protestant universities] the Catholic institutions enjoyed an immediate honeymoon period wherein autonomy actually enhanced the institution as both a faith community and a house of liberal learning. But then the slow and inexorable gravity pull of the secularism dominant in the force-field of the academy begins to retard and then counteract the inertial momentum that has hitherto set the course of the Catholic college or university, until, after a period when the forms and symbols of Christian identity are gradually evacuated of their conviction, the institution finally emerges as a wraith of the Christian community it once was."[26]

False Autonomy

Notre Dame's honoring of President Obama gained the applause of the American Association of University Professors. AAUP General Secretary Gary Rhoades said he "applauds Notre Dame president Rev. John Jenkins . . . for exemplifying", in effect, the autonomy asserted in the Land O'Lakes Statement.[27] The Land O'Lakes claim of autonomy from "external" authority however, is fantasy. Catholic universities are subject to dozens of external authorities, including government agencies, accrediting bodies, the NCAA, academic groups like the AAUP, etc. In some respects, outside agencies control even hiring decisions. For example, try hiring an illegal alien for the faculty. Or a law school could face an interesting accreditation review if it appointed a disbarred lawyer to its faculty. The universities accept mandates and supervision from secular authorities but, pursuant to Land O'Lakes, they reject a limited oversight by the Church.[28]

The problem with Land O'Lakes autonomy is truth in labeling. For four decades Notre Dame has promoted itself as a Catholic university, according to its own private definition of that term rather than that of the Church which alone has authority to define it. The mind-set is Protestant. Protestants, however, have the consistency not to claim to be Catholic. ND 2010, the strategic plan, says the University "must take into account with . . . sensitivity and respect the formal teaching role of the Magisterium in the life of the Church." But Notre Dame does not accept Church teaching as binding on the University. The Magisterium is practically irrelevant. Thus, in their April 2, 2008, "statement on the rationale for hiring faculty who will enhance our Catholic mission," Fr. Jenkins and the Provost, Dr. Thomas G. Burish, went on for six pages about keeping Notre Dame "truly Catholic" without once mentioning the Catholic Church. That is like explaining the game of baseball without mentioning the ball.[29]

The Officers, Fellows and Trustees do not own Notre Dame. They are, and their predecessors were, temporary fiduciaries obliged to preserve the identity of Notre Dame as a Catholic university in accord with the definition of that term by the Catholic Church. In the context of that obligation, Land O'Lakes' assertion of autonomy from the Church was a mistake with predictably negative and potentially terminal consequences.

The Broader Context of Land O'Lakes

The Land O'Lakes Statement may appear to raise a narrowly Catholic issue of the allocation of authority between two Catholic entities, the Church and the university. Broader issues are involved. The Statement not only rejects a claim of jurisdiction by the Church. It also rejects any authority external to the university. That latter rejection is illusory since the university is subject to many "external" authorities. More basic, however, is the Statement's misperception of the Church's Magisterium. As we will discuss in later chapters, the Magisterium is not an external entity issuing peremptory orders. It is rather an indispensable aid to the formation of conscience, a gift provided by the God who is love and who is also the author of the moral law. All human beings, and not just Catholics, need an authoritative interpreter of that moral law. The alternative is the "dictatorship of relativism" in which, because there is no acknowledged, objective moral norm, life is reduced to a conflict of interests. The result, as John Paul II made clear, is the rule of the strongest, and, in political terms, totalitarianism. Notre Dame and other "Catholic" universities have lost coherence by claiming to be Catholic while rejecting the Magisterium of the Church. Great good can come from that experience, however, if it prompts a re-evaluation of the constructive nature of the Magisterium and of the need that we all have for such an acknowledged interpreter of the moral law.

Autonomy at Notre Dame
"A Small Purdue with a Golden Dome"?

Today Notre Dame is no longer a Catholic university. We
have intently aped our worsers, and have finally achieved the
status of a non-denominational university. Just like Harvard,
and Yale – and De Paul . . . I . . . think that the faculty at a
Catholic school should be predominantly Catholic. . . . One
may argue – it makes no difference, "Math is Math." But it
does make a difference, for there may be abstract subjects,
but there are no abstract teachers. . . . But parents – among
them my own – were and are willing to sacrifice because
they thought Notre Dame was different, was better. It is no
longer different. It is a small Purdue with a Golden Dome.
And so few give a damn. . . . At one time we were the envy
of those who for various reasons were not allowed the order
and the beauty and the effectiveness of academic and moral
discipline. Now we have joined the throng and we apologize
for being Catholic and try to hide our Faith in small-case letters, so that we can be "accepted" by those who wish they
could follow us. – Prof. Edward J. Cronin, Address, *Notre
Dame Forum,* March 17, 1970

PROFESSOR EDWARD J. Cronin, a 1938 graduate, taught literature at
Notre Dame from 1949 to 1998. "His focus on teaching rather than published research recalled an earlier age for academia" and "[h]is teaching
was so valued that it wasn't unusual to hear a student remark, 'I've got to
get my Cronin course before I graduate.'"[1]

Ed Cronin knew Notre Dame and he knew that the deterioration he
described in 1970 had set in well before the Land O'Lakes assertion of

autonomy in 1967. Land O'Lakes, however, had a decisive impact because it formalized an alienation from the Church that is draining the University of its Catholic character.

Positive Elements at Notre Dame

Professor Ed Cronin, however, would have been the last to discount the positive factors that make Notre Dame "a special place," including especially the students. For example, ND Response, the on-campus protest against the honoring of Obama, was organized by students. It was positive and effective.[2] Campus Ministry, the Institute for Church Life, the Center for Social Concerns and other entities conduct many ministries and service projects for students during the school year and summers. The Alliance for Catholic Education places Notre Dame students and grads in the teaching profession in Catholic schools throughout the nation. Student clubs include effective pro-life groups. The practice of Eucharistic Adoration is growing at the initiative of students and Campus Ministry. The students benefit especially from the ministry and friendship of the Holy Cross priests including, notably, the younger ones. Since 1931, a unique Notre Dame institution, the Bengal Bouts, conducts an annual boxing tournament that has contributed major sums every year to the Holy Cross missions in Bangladesh. More than 200 student boxers competed in 2009. They are impressively motivated by the desire to help the poor in the missions and they participate in a summer service project in Bangladesh.[3]

Spending Spiritual Capital

These are but a few of the positive elements that still make Notre Dame a sound choice for a prospective student who could find a way to pay for it, who would be careful in his selection of courses, who would not drink or do drugs, and, most important, who would be committed to fighting to live a sound moral and spiritual life. Catholic students in particular have abundant sacramental and other spiritual resources available at Notre Dame. Of course, such a student could survive well at a state school like Purdue or the University of Illinois and would surely do well at any of the unapologetically Catholic colleges and universities. Notre Dame, however, is still special and the fight to determine its future is far from over. Many alumni, including especially in Project Sycamore, are effectively working to restore Notre Dame to its mission.[4] Any criticisms in this book of University policies are not intended to minimize those positive elements of life at Notre Dame. However, the occasion for writing this book – Notre Dame's honoring of Obama – is a wake-up call.

In a 1999 address at Notre Dame, Professor Alasdair MacIntyre pointed to "two rival conceptions of a Catholic university, one in which the university recognizes itself as Catholic, not only because of its religious practices, but because of the philosophical and theological dimensions of its teaching and its enquiries, and the other in which a Catholic university is a standard secular university to which Catholic religious practices together with a set of individual Catholic academic concerns have been superadded."[5] Notre Dame is moving rapidly toward the latter conception. Some indications of that movement are described in Chapters 8 through 11. In drawing its public relations benefit from the Catholic presence on campus, Notre Dame is spending the spiritual capital built up by previous generations. The false autonomy of Land O'Lakes, however, has cut Notre Dame off in major respects from the Church, the source of that spiritual capital. Professor Ed Cronin saw that problem as early as 1970. And he saw where it would lead.

8
Autonomy at Notre Dame
The "Research University"

Megalomania

"MEGALOMANIA. THAT'S what ails Notre Dame." A now-deceased Holy Cross priest told me that, referring to Notre Dame's abandonment of its historic mission in pursuit of "big school" prestige. The mission of Notre Dame had been the provision of affordable education in the Catholic tradition to undergrads, with research and graduate programs, especially in the sciences, playing an important but complementary role.

"Megalomania," according to the Oxford American Dictionary, is "an obsessive desire to do things on a grand scale." That could describe Notre Dame's great leap forward: its definition of itself as a "National Catholic Research University." The signs proclaiming that change appeared on Notre Dame Avenue in 1991. A professor at a state university, not a Notre Dame grad, saw the signs and told me, "That's humiliating. If they were one, they wouldn't have to say it." Notre Dame's proclamation of itself as a "Research University," however, dates back to 1978.

In the late 1970s, Notre Dame followed the "big schools" as they went heavily into the research business. One objective was secular prestige. "The reputations of universities," said the President, Father Edward Malloy, in 1992, "are driven by the research and graduate programs, not by the undergraduate schools."[1] Another objective was simpler: Money.

Student Loans

The Guaranteed Student Loan Act of 1965 had strict income limits and by the mid-1970s relatively few students had taken advantage of it. "Then, in 1978, President Jimmy Carter signed the Middle Income Student

Assistance Act into law. It removed the previous income restrictions so that a Kennedy kid could qualify for a guaranteed loan almost as easily as a Katzenjammer kid. The new policy made some people nervous. Fortune magazine warned, 'Anything that makes it easier to pay tuition bills will also make it easier to raise tuition charges.' Fortune was right. Before 1978, tuition increases tended to run a percentage point or so behind inflation. By the 1980's, the increases were running at twice the inflation rate."[2]

"One result of the federal government's student financial aid programs is higher tuition costs at our nation's colleges and universities."[3] As the federally supported loans expanded, the universities raised tuition, then lobbied Congress for more loan funding, then raised tuition again. And so on.

One purpose of the research enterprise for Notre Dame was to make the University a player on the national academic and political scene. "As the leading Catholic institution in the country," said Fr. Malloy at the Board of Trustees meeting at the Ritz-Carlton Hotel in Manalapan, Florida, "we think we should have greater input into national policy decisions and into ethical preparations for decisions. We think we're capable of operating in the same world as the Ivys, Stanford, Vanderbilt, Duke, Southern Cal and Northwestern."[4]

The Price of Research Greatness

Notre Dame and its students have paid a fourfold price for the pursuit of Research Greatness:

1. **Cost.** The federal loan programs were a Big Rock Candy Mountain for the universities. They financed their building and research enterprises on the backs of borrowing students. Notre Dame was far from the worst offender but it was in on the action. In 1978–79, when Notre Dame proclaimed itself a "Research University," undergrad tuition, room and board at Notre Dame totaled $5,180. In 2009–10, it is $48,850. If it had kept pace with the Consumer Price Index, it would now be $17,353. Notre Dame's financial aid office does excellent work in reducing the debt burden of students, but the student or parent loan remains a major form of "financial aid." The loan burden distorts the career and family options of students, especially if they contemplate grad study.[5] The trend is toward a Notre Dame where the only non-wealthy students will be those whose test scores won heavy

discounts, scholarship athletes, ROTC students, minority scholarship students, faculty and staff children and those non-wealthy students, diminishing in number, who choose Notre Dame even at the price of a crippling loan burden.

2. **The Campus.** The "building binge" has transformed the formerly pastoral Notre Dame into a crowded urban-style research campus. And it continues. Athletic fields and open spaces have disappeared under concrete. It used to be the general custom to name buildings after saints or persons in Notre Dame history. Now the question is which donor will have the most buildings named after him or her. And which lucky donor will get to put his or her name on the inevitable parking garage? A senior professor in another college at Notre Dame explained to me a few years ago his theory as to why the research university has to keep adding buildings: "Before, each professor usually taught three courses. Now they teach one so they can do research. And to help with that research and to teach courses the professors are no longer teaching, each professor will have one, or more likely two, grad student assistants. But those assistants need office space, as do the additional adjunct or regular professors who have to be hired to teach the courses the professors are no longer teaching. And we need more staff." His theory has the ring of truth. You might ask: How does that process help the undergrad students who pay the bills? Good question.

3. **Dimunition of the undergrad experience.** Research, especially in the sciences, can be supportive of teaching and, with student participants, can be itself an excellent teaching and learning experience. One result, however, of a general research priority is a diminished emphasis on undergrad teaching. The rhetoric insists on the importance of teaching. But undergrads and untenured faculty know better. David O'Connor, a tenured philosophy and classics professor at Notre Dame, says that "research in fact counts for much more in the tenure process. 'You really don't have to have any impact on the undergraduates [to get promoted],' he says, 'You just need [to have written] a book.' One major reason for this emphasis is that the university stands to gain more financially from research than from quality teaching."[6]

4. **In Fiscal Year 2007, Notre Dame received** $53,974,000 from the federal government for research; Notre Dame's total research expenditures were $77,467,000. "Notre Dame 2010: Fulfilling the Promise," the provisional strategic plan for the University, emphasized funding for research. "[W]e must take the next step," it said, "to move forward as a center of outstanding research and scholarship." In the "allocation of resources," we "must focus on those academic areas that give us the greatest opportunity for growth and funding in our research endeavors." Translation: Get the bucks. ND 2010 hopes to "increase externally sponsored research expenditures to . . . $100 million a year, . . . double the current levels."

ND 2010 says that hiring and promotion should be limited to "only those faculty for whom superior teaching is a high priority." Don't bet on it. That same section lists, among the "Fundamental and Defining Premises," "a heightened sense of urgency for the centrality of research and scholarly publication," including "competition for federal, state and private dollars to support the research enterprise." This "centrality of research" applies to "every academic unit." ND 2010 stresses the importance of hiring new faculty, reducing teaching loads, improving research sabbatical support and increasing support for graduate student programs.[7]

Research in the humanities, explained Professor Ralph McInerny, bears "only the most remote relation to what goes on in classrooms. Research is what professors do on their own, it enhances their own reputation, it is addressed to a dozen or so others interested in the same things. The results might trickle down into classroom teaching, but this becomes increasingly doubtful. . . . Increasingly, the tendency is for a university to seek prestige though the research of its professors, to raise and allocate funds chiefly for research, to put a premium on research. A junior colleague today would be foolish to think that his future depends upon his excellence as a teacher. Promotion and tenure are said to depend on several factors, teaching, publications, collegiality. No one believes this, because it isn't true. A churlish colleague who is a lousy teacher but whose publications cause a stir is safe. A young professor who devotes himself to students, publishes sparingly, carries a fair share of the work of the department, will be on the job market soon. Of course no one is penalized for teaching well, provided he publishes. All this is of course old hat so far as universities go; universities being defined as institutions which offer graduate as well as undergraduate degrees. The sad thing is that colleges are being affected as well. It is as if the only sure appraisal of those with whom we work comes from elsewhere, from referees of submitted papers and articles. These anonymous voices will always override those of students and colleagues. Thus it pays the teacher to ignore the living, breathing students before him and to write things western civilization would not be poorer without."[8]

A Catholic college or university ought to have a better approach.

5. **Impact on Catholic identity.** In 1992, David Lutz, then a Notre Dame Ph.D. candidate and now professor of philosophy at the Catholic University of Eastern Africa in Nairobi, identified the "real danger" to Notre Dame's Catholic identity as those "who believe that Notre Dame can strive for ever-higher standards of academic excellence – and use the same criteria . . . by which . . . secular universities . . . are judged to be excellent – without forfeiting the Catholic character of the University."[9] "Elite universities," Dr. Lutz later wrote, "are ranked by the quantity and quality of the research they produce. One . . . problem with emphasizing research is that teaching may be de-emphasized, but a far more important, though less-noted, danger is that emphasizing research causes Catholicism to be de-emphasized. This is true, not because there is any problem with doing excellent Catholic research, but because it is more difficult to publish such research in prestigious journals and with elite university presses than to publish the kind of scholarship respected by secular universities."[10]

6. **Since Notre Dame, in 1978**, defined itself as a "research university," the percentage of Notre Dame faculty who are Catholic has declined. Notre Dame's redefinition of itself as a "research university" appears to have contributed to that decline. An underlying question, which we will take up in the next chapter, is the status of Catholic faith as a professional qualification for appointment to the faculty of a Catholic university.

9

Autonomy at Notre Dame
A Catholic Faculty?

IN THE three decades since Notre Dame defined itself as a "research university," the percentage of Catholic faculty has declined. In the 1970s more than 80 percent of the Notre Dame faculty identified themselves as "Catholic." In 1986 it was 66 percent. Now it is 53 percent, including all self-identified Catholics regardless of practice or strength of belief. Those retiring include proportionately more Catholics, creating a prospect for further decline of the proportion of Catholics. The Notre Dame Administration is taking steps, with some initial success, to identify and recruit outstanding Catholic faculty.

"A Predominant Number"

Ex Corde Ecclesiae "provides that "[i]n order not to endanger the Catholic identity of the University . . . the number of non-Catholic teachers should not be allowed to constitute a majority within the Institution, which is and must remain Catholic."[1] The *Application* of *Ex Corde* to the United States requires that "the university should strive to recruit and appoint Catholics as professors so that, to the extent possible, those committed to the witness of the faith will constitute a majority of the faculty."[2] The Notre Dame Mission Statement requires "a predominant number" and goes into more detail:

> The intellectual interchange essential to a university requires, and is enriched by, the presence and voices of diverse scholars and students. The Catholic identity of the University depends upon, and is nurtured by, the continuing

presence of a predominant number of Catholic intellectuals. This ideal has been consistently maintained by the University leadership throughout its history. What the University asks of all its scholars and students, however, is not a particular creedal affiliation, but a respect for the objectives of Notre Dame and a willingness to enter into the conversation that gives it life and character. Therefore, the University insists upon academic freedom that makes open discussion and inquiry possible.

Students and the entire Notre Dame community benefit greatly from the presence of faculty who are not Catholic. And the Catholic/non-Catholic distinction is an oversimplification. A faculty member's support for the mission of the University is not simply reducible to whether he or she checks the "Catholic" box.[3] That reality, however, does not diminish the reasonableness of having on the faculty a predominant number of Catholics "committed to the witness of the faith."[4] "[T]here may be abstract subjects," as Professor Ed Cronin noted, "but there are no abstract teachers."[5]

Faith as a Professional Qualification

The point of this chapter is narrow. It is that the Catholic faith of a Notre Dame faculty applicant ought to be regarded not as an esoteric, non-rational preference but as a professional qualification.

Fr. James T. Burtchaell, C.S.C., drew from his study of the secularization of religiously founded universities the conclusion that "*In every one of its component elements – governors, administrators, faculty, and students – the academy must have a predominance of committed and articulate communicants of its mother church.* This must be regarded, not as an alien consideration, but as a professional qualification. . . . Various academic qualifications can be and are traded off against one another, but when any one of them is systematically subordinated to the others, it will shortly disappear from the institution. Communal faith is in one sense, however, unique among professional credentials: apparently the only qualification which, if lost, is institutionally unrecoverable, is commitment in a church to Christ."[6] Notre Dame ought not to subordinate Catholic faith as a professional qualification for the academic life of the University.

Faith and Reason

There is no reason why a Catholic university could not be a "research university" while maintaining its Catholic identity in every respect including the composition of its faculty. Notre Dame, unfortunately, pursues research recognition according to secular standards which tend to regard faith as non-rational and therefore irrelevant to academic quality. The false dichotomy between faith and academic quality distorts reason as well as faith. Pope John Paul II affirmed the "profound and indissoluble unity between the knowledge of reason and the knowledge of faith. . . . [R]eason and faith cannot be separated without diminishing the capacity of men and women to know themselves, the world and God in an appropriate way."[7] The function of reason is "to find meaning, to discover explanations which might allow everyone to come to a certain understanding of the contents of faith. . . . Faith asks that its object be understood with the help of reason; and at the summit of its searching reason acknowledges that it cannot do without what faith presents."[8] It was especially St. Thomas Aquinas who gave "pride of place to the harmony which exists between faith and reason. Both the light of reason and the light of faith come from God, he argued; hence there can be no contradiction between them."[9] In later chapters we will note the legal as well as cultural consequences that have resulted from the separation of faith and reason and especially from the treatment of all assertions about God as non-rational. Our point here is that the Catholic university cannot coherently buy into that basic error. Commitment to the Catholic faith is not a non-rational preference irrelevant to suitability for the academic life of a Catholic university.

Indeed, John Paul II describes the "knowledge which is peculiar to faith" as "surpassing the knowledge proper to human reason."[10] "Faith," said Pope Benedict XVI, "is an encounter with the living God – an encounter opening up new horizons extending beyond the sphere of reason. But it is also a purifying force for reason itself. From God's standpoint, faith liberates reason from its blind spots and therefore helps it to be ever more fully itself. Faith enables reason to do its work more effectively and to see its proper object more clearly."[11] Archbishop J. Michael Miller, who was then secretary of the Vatican Congregation for Catholic Education, expanded on that point in a 2005 address at Notre Dame:

[In the words of John Paul II:] "In carrying out its research, a Catholic university can rely on a superior enlightenment which, without changing the nature of this research, purifies it, orients it, enriches it and uplifts it. . . . This light is not found 'outside' rational research, as a limitation or an impediment, but rather 'above' it, as its elevation and an expansion of its horizons."

From Justin Martyr in the second century down to the present day, the Catholic tradition has . . . held that the more we probe the mystery of God with the help of faith, the more we understand reality. . . . The gift of faith empowers the intellect to act according to its deepest nature.[12]

The Hiring Process

In other words, a Catholic university owes no apology for insisting that its faculty be predominantly Catholic. The roadblock to achieving that objective is the hiring process. "In Catholic universities, as in their secular peers, the academic department constitutes the key entity where hiring decisions are made. Today at Notre Dame, however, few departments conscientiously and enthusiastically support the mission statement's call for a predominant number of Catholic faculty."[13] One reason for that attitude is an insistence by present faculty and administrators that "any practices adopted to recruit Catholic faculty cannot be allowed to compromise the University's academic quality."[14] Or, as the Faculty Senate recommended in 2008, "The University should not compromise its academic aspirations in its effort to maintain its Catholic identity."[15] Fr. Wilson D. Miscamble, C.S.C., a Notre Dame professor of history, analyzed "the faculty problem" in 2007. "The matter of hiring Catholic faculty," he said, "has been of concern at Notre Dame for some time. The Rev. Robert Sullivan, of the history department and the Erasmus Institute, now heads an effort to identify able Catholic scholars. He also heads an ad hoc committee on recruiting outstanding Catholic faculty members, appointed by Provost Thomas G. Burish. One of the charges for this committee is to identify 'the best practices for hiring Catholic faculty members.' One can only hope and pray for the success of these endeavors. It must be understood, however, that this is not a matter that can be massaged by minor measures. . . . A major change in the hiring process is required . . . whatever faculty resistance it generates. If the . . . downward trend . . . is to be . . . reversed, a . . . decision calling for two-thirds of all future appointments to be committed Catholic scholars is essential. This would require very different ways of hiring from the department-based procedures of today. The university would need to engage in . . . strategic hiring or hiring for mission. A recognition that this approach is crucial to its identity could drive the endeavor. It would require Notre Dame (and other schools that want to preserve their Catholic mission and character) to be truly different from their secular 'preferred peer' schools. Failure to take such action, however, will lead schools like Notre Dame to merely replicate such secular institutions and to surrender what remains of their distinctiveness."[16]

Cardinal Dulles

Notre Dame administrators could draw inspiration for such an effort by reflecting on the address, "Catholic Colleges and Universities Today," by Cardinal Avery Dulles, S.J., at Assumption College in 2007. Perhaps the foremost American convert of the twentieth century and the son of John Foster Dulles, President Eisenhower's Secretary of State, the Cardinal rendered distinguished service to Catholic higher education. Using as his "primary guides" *Ex Corde Ecclesiae* and Cardinal John Henry Newman's *The Idea of a University*, Cardinal Dulles addressed bluntly the hiring of Catholic faculty. He did so in the context of culture and the relation of the university to the Church and its Magisterium. A "Catholic institution," he said, "must be founded on three principles: that there is a God, that he has made a full and final revelation of himself in Jesus Christ and that the Catholic Church is the authorized custodian and teacher of this body of revealed truth."

Cardinal Dulles questioned the pursuit of diversity as a goal in itself: "Postmodern students . . . imagine that change and diversity are desirable for their own sakes. . . . [S]tudents should be educated for the world of today [and] a variety of cultures may be a source of enrichment. But for nations to live together in peace and friendship, they must share common convictions regarding . . . the basic norms of morality."

"Religious diversity," he said, "is not desirable in itself. It appeals chiefly to those who believe there is no truth in religion anyway. If we believe that God is one, and that Jesus is his incarnate Son, we will hope that all peoples . . . may someday unite in praising him. To make this goal persuasive in the contemporary atmosphere of subjectivism and relativism is a serious challenge. Still another challenge comes from the academic establishment in America today. In secular circles there is a virtual consensus that no courses ought to be taught from a distinctive religious point of view. Faith is generally held to have no place in the classroom, at least on the level of higher education. If this only means that faith should not be imposed in the classroom we can agree. But if it means that professors should not manifest their religious beliefs or seek to defend them, the objection is unsound."

Cardinal Dulles went on to relate the hiring of all faculty to mission without limitation to percentages. "A Catholic institution," he said, "has to be clear about its mission. An essential step . . . is that faculty be hired for mission. If the teachers are hostile to the mission of the college or indifferent about it, the college will suffer. It does not suffice to hire faculty who are nominally Catholic. If teachers are angry with the Church or unsympathetic toward her doctrines, no changes in the curriculum will succeed in making the institution truly Catholic."[17]

Executive Veto

The proportion of Catholic faculty at Notre Dame is declining, not because suitable candidates cannot be found, but because of the obstacle course any seriously Catholic candidate faces in obtaining departmental approval. The University's mission is subordinated to the contrary will of component departments.[18] Under the University Bylaws, however, "The President. . . . shall make appointments to the academic and non-academic staffs of the University."[19] The President, through his authority to appoint faculty, could solve the "Catholic" problem by executive veto of appointments. It is a question of will.

10
Autonomy at Notre Dame
Academic Freedom?

> It is [the] Magisterium's task to preserve God's people from
> deviations and defections and to guarantee them the objec-
> tive possibility of professing the true faith without error. –
> *Catechism of the Catholic Church*, no. 890.

Academic Freedom

AT LAND O'Lakes, Notre Dame cut itself off from the Magisterium,
which it wrongly regarded as an "external" authority. The Magisterium, or
teaching authority of the Church, is exercised by the Pope and the bishops
in union with the Pope.[1] As we shall see in Chapter Twelve, the
Magisterium's role is not that of an external, peremptory authority. *Ex
Corde Ecclesiae* specifies that, "Even when they do not enter directly into
the internal governance of the University, Bishops 'should be seen not as
external agents but as participants in the life of the Catholic University.'"[2]
With its self-proclaimed "autonomy and academic freedom," Notre Dame
was on its own in deciding what a Catholic university should be and do. In
this and the following chapter we note three instances where Notre Dame
failed in that effort:

1. The sponsorship and public showing of *The Last Temptation of Christ*;

2. The sponsorship and public performance over eight years of *The
   Vagina Monologues*;

3. Notre Dame's conflicted handling, and ultimate politicization, of the
   abortion issue. This will be discussed in Chapter 11.

Notre Dame's presentations of *The Last Temptation of Christ* and *The*

Vagina Monologues reflected the University's acceptance of an academic freedom that cannot be reconciled with the Church's understanding of that term as expressed by Pope Benedict XVI in his address to Catholic educators in Washington, D.C. The Pope said:

> In regard to faculty members at Catholic colleges and universities, I wish to reaffirm the value of academic freedom. In virtue of this freedom you are called to search for the truth wherever careful analysis of evidence leads you. Yet it is also the case that any appeal to the principle of academic freedom in order to justify positions that contradict the faith and the teaching of the Church would obstruct or even betray the university's identity and mission; a mission at the heart of the Church's *munus docendi* and not somehow autonomous or independent of it.
>
> Teachers and administrators, whether in universities or schools, have the duty and privilege to ensure that students receive instruction in Catholic doctrine and practice. This requires that public witness to the way of Christ, as found in the Gospel and upheld by the Church's Magisterium, shapes all aspects of an institution's life, both inside and outside the classroom. Divergence from this vision weakens Catholic identity and, far from advancing freedom, inevitably leads to confusion, whether moral, intellectual or spiritual.[3]

The Last Temptation of Christ

In 1989, Notre Dame sponsored public showings of *The Last Temptation of Christ*. The University decided there that the Second Commandment's prohibition of blasphemy[4] was superseded by the authority of the secular establishment. As Professor Dean Porter, Director of the Snite Museum, said, "when [the museum] was built nine years ago, we decided if a film could be seen at the Museum of Modern Art, it could be seen here."[5] Notre Dame President Father Edward A. Malloy c.s.c., defended the sponsorship of the film in light of Notre Dame's "mission as a Catholic university to provide a nurturing and supportive learning environment for our students. People of good will, however, can disagree about particular dimensions of this educational task. I believe that a university is a good setting in which to address the great issues of the day. Often it is through the prism of creative expression that these questions are most engagingly faced. It is a proper prerogative of our faculty to determine in our fine arts offerings what combination of plays, movies, art displays and musical performances are best chosen in a given year."[6]

The Notre Dame Department of Communication and Theatre sponsored four showings of the film at the Snite Museum. The showings were advertised and open to the public. Such public exhibitions could not be justified on the ground of academic freedom. If the film were privately shown to a class for examination and discussion, no objection would have been made. The fact that attendance at the public showings was recommended for some classes (objecting students were excused) does not change the nature of the event as a public exhibition. Nor is that public character changed by the fact that the communication department sponsored a public discussion of the film at a later date.

I refused to see the film. However, I read the film script; I also read "The Facts on 'The Last Temptation of Christ,'" by John Ankerberg, which compares the script with the movie as released and with the book, by Nikos Kazantzakis, on which the film is based; and I discussed the film in detail with persons who did see it. The film begins with a disclaimer, "This film is not based on the Gospels but is a fictional exploration of the eternal spiritual conflict." The film then portrays Christ in a light that was accurately summarized by Notre Dame Law School Professor Edward J. Murphy in his essay in *The Observer* of September 25, 1989:

> My wife and I were among those who picketed in protest when this movie was shown in Mishawaka last fall. . . . Because of the taunts of some patrons that I had no right to protest without having first seen the movie, I did see it. Actually, the movie was much worse, much more insidious than I had expected it to be. From beginning to end, it is a veritable tissue of falsehood and distortion. To be sure, there is a disclaimer at the beginning that the events are fictitious and not based on the Gospels. But the movie is about an historical figure, Jesus Christ, not Joe Messiah. Does one have a "right" to lie about historical events, even if one admits to doing so?
>
> Let me illustrate:
> 1. Do you believe that Jesus Christ was unsure of who he was? Do you believe that he doubted his divinity? Do

you believe he was a wimpy character whose message was tentative and incoherent? (Movie: Jesus: "I'm a liar, a hypocrite, I'm afraid of everything. I don't ever tell the truth. I don't have the courage. . . . You want to know who my God is? Fair! You look inside me and that's all you'll find. . . . . Lucifer is inside me.")

2   Do you believe that Jesus, voyeur-like, watched Mary Magdalene have sex with a customer? Do you believe Jesus asked her to forgive him? (Movie: Jesus: "I want you to forgive me. I've done many bad things. I'm going to the desert. I need you to forgive me before I go. Please." Mary Magdalene: "Oh, I see. You said I'll have a day with you. And then you come in here with your head down saying, 'Forgive me. Forgive me.' It's not that easy. Just because you need forgiveness, don't ask me to do it. . . . You're not the man. You're the same as all the others, only you can't admit it. You're pitiful. I hate you!")

3.   Do you believe Jesus asked Judas to betray him? (Movie: Jesus: "You promised me. Remember you told me that if I moved one step from revolution you'd kill me. Remember?" Judas: "Yes." Jesus: "I've strayed, haven't I? Then you must keep your promise, you have to kill me.")

4.   Do you believe Jesus made crosses which he sold to the Romans for use in crucifying Jews? (Movie: Judas: "You're a disgrace. Romans can't find anybody to make crosses, except for you. You do it. You're worse than them! You're a Jew killing Jews. You're a coward. How will you ever pay for your sins?" Jesus: "With my life, Judas. I don't have anything else.")

This is a sample of the lies about Jesus in this blasphemous film. But it is not only about Jesus that vicious lies are told. His friends fare no better. For example, the apostle Paul is portrayed as a liar and a hypocrite who invents the story of Jesus' resurrection to make people feel better. Virtually everyone who is close to Jesus is smeared, including his mother. Our Lady is cast as a bitter and frustrated woman who neither understands nor accepts the mission of her son.[7]

Notre Dame, seeing the world "through the prism of creative expression," could not even draw a line short of a direct blasphemy of the person of Christ. Some viewers found it difficult to distinguish fiction from fact and indicated that the film had altered their perception of Christ. One sophomore said that, "before she saw the movie, she pictured Christ as above all others and someone who was not tempted. Now [she] said, she sees Christ on a more personal level."[8] Another student described the film as "an effort to break a stereotype about Christ."[9] Sr. Mary O'Neill of the Theology Department said the film was "not a narrative but more of a burning image that stays in one's mind and helps one feel what Jesus has gone through." Professor Mark Pilkinton, Chairman of the Communication Department, said that "he was pleased to see a real Christ who could be genuinely tempted and who overcame the temptation."[10]

Ed Murphy, like Ed Cronin, was one of the great Notre Dame teachers. He taught Contracts and Jurisprudence. But the most effective class I ever saw him give was not in a classroom. It was on that September night when he led a handful of others in reciting the Rosary outside the Snite Museum in protest of, and reparation for, Notre Dame's showing of *The Last Temptation of Christ*. His witness, though quiet and dignified, was politically incorrect. Very few joined him. Yet Ed would have gone out there all by himself, even if no one had followed his lead. That night he was a great teacher at his best, for those who were there and for those who would later reflect upon his witness. Notre Dame should be seeking more of his kind.

The Vagina Monologues

Perhaps as a result of the heat generated by the Obama invitation, in 2009, "[f]or the first time in eight years, Notre Dame students will not perform The Vagina Monologues at an on-or-off-campus location."[11]

On January 23 and 24, 2006, Fr. Jenkins addressed the Notre Dame community and opened a 10-week campus-wide discussion of academic freedom in the context of *The Vagina Monologues* and the Queer Film Festival .[12] Hopes were high that this portended a solution is accord with *Ex Corde Ecclesiae* and Catholic morality. On April 5, 2006, Fr. Jenkins concluded the discussion by deciding, in his "Closing Statement on Academic Freedom and Catholic Character," that he would permit continued performances of *The Vagina Monologues* (TVM) and of the Queer

Film Festival (QFF). Fr. Jenkins ignored the defects of the QFF and gave it a license as long as it goes by its new name, "Gay and Lesbian Film: Filmmakers, Narratives, Spectatorships."[13] That is like dealing with a soiled diaper by changing the pins.

In his Closing Statement, Fr. Jenkins fell for the lie that the *Monologues* opposes violence against women. Instead, the *Monologues* encourage such violence by objectifying women. The human person, as Pope John Paul II put it, is a "unified totality" of body and soul. *The Vagina Monologues* fragments that unity by personifying a body part and equating the woman to that part.[14]

The *Monologues* presents the vagina as an entity with which the woman should establish a "conscious relationship." It includes such gems as, "If your vagina got dressed, what would it wear?" and "If your vagina could talk, what would it say, in two words?" The *Monologues* recounts the lesbian seduction of a 16-year-old by a 24-year-old, which the victim describes as "my . . . salvation." Another monologue consists of the repetition of a four-letter expletive describing a body part. Other monologists recount conversations with their vaginas or vulvae. Others describe lesbian sexual acts. One monologue recounts a group masturbation, with the aid of hand mirrors, in a workshop run by "a woman who believes in vaginas." The decisive moment came when a participant thought, "I didn't have to find it. I had to be it. Be it. Be my clitoris. My vagina, my vagina, me." This submoronic equation of a woman with her body part facilitates the violence the *Monologues* claims to oppose.

Fr. Jenkins would "suppress speech" only if it were "overt and insistent in its contempt for the values and sensibilities of this University, or of any of the diverse groups that form part of our community." Those, including Bishop John M. D'Arcy, who rightly see *The Vagina Monologues* as a "contempt for [their] values and sensibilities," do not count, in the Jenkins world, as one of those "diverse groups." Bishops, incidentally, "should be seen not as external agents but as participants in the life of the Catholic university."[15]

In his address to the Notre Dame community on January 23, 2006, Fr. Jenkins had said, of an anti-Semitic play, "I do not believe that such a performance could be permitted at Notre Dame." He said: "Its anti-Semitic elements are clearly and outrageously opposed to the values of a Catholic university." But what about TVM and the QFF? The Jenkins Closing

Statement says that "[The *Monologues'*] portrayals of sexuality [are] in opposition to Catholic teaching." So they should be banned, right? Guess again:

"It is essential," said Fr. Jenkins, "that we hear a full range of views. . . . But we must . . . bring these . . . views into dialogue with the Catholic . . . tradition. This demands balance . . . and the inclusion of the Catholic perspective. . . . [T]his year's [*Monologues*] was brought into dialogue . . . through panels which . . . taught me . . . that the creative contextualization of a play like [*The Vagina Monologues*] can bring certain perspectives on important issues into a constructive and fruitful dialogue with the Catholic tradition." Fr. Jenkins took Fr. Malloy's "prism of creative expression" to the higher level of "creative contextualization."

So, Fr. Jenkins, correctly, would bar an anti-Semitic play, even with a panel discussion after it. If a play is anti-Semitic, it is a lie. But so are the *Monologues* and the Queer Film Festival lies. Fr. Jenkins would allow the *Monologues* if it were followed by a panel including the Catholic "perspective" as a debatable alternative. The Catholic university "guarantees academic freedom . . . within the confines of the truth and the common good."[16] That truth, a unity of faith and reason, includes the ennobling Catholic teaching on women and sexuality. It is objective and normative, not one of the "perspectives" that might be nonjudgmentally included in a panel at Michigan State, or at today's Notre Dame.

Bishop D'Arcy

On this issue, as he did on Fr. Jenkins's effort to justify his honoring of Obama, Bishop D'Arcy nailed it:

> Father Jenkins . . . made mention of . . . documentary films shown recently on campus concerning the early days of Nazism, which he believes would also have to be banned if "The Vagina Monologues" were banned. But there is an enormous difference between showing a Nazi propaganda film in 2008 and showing it in 1938. One is a matter of historic and scholarly interest in a long-past event, and the other constitutes active cooperation in promoting a current and threatening evil ideology. . . . "The Vagina Monologues" . . . is . . . a propaganda piece for the sexual revolution and secular feminism. While claiming to deplore violence

against women, the play at the same time violates the standards of decency and morality that safeguard a woman's dignity and protect her, body and soul, from sexual predators.
The human community has generally refrained from exposing and discussing the hidden parts of a woman's body, pre-
ferring to consider them private and even sacred. Most
importantly, the sexual sin, which the play depicts in several scenes, desecrates women just as much as, if not more
deeply than, sexual violence does. The play depicts, exalts,
and endorses female masturbation, which is a sin. It depicts,
exalts, and endorses a sexual relationship between an adult
woman and a child, a minor, which is a sin and also a crime.
It depicts and exalts the most base form of sexual relationship between a man and a woman. These illicit sexual
actions are portrayed as paths to healing, and the implication
is that the historic, positive understanding of heterosexual
marriage as the norm is what we must recover from . . . .
[W]hat makes a Catholic university distinctive is the conviction that in the search for truth, we do not start from scratch;
we start from the truth that has been revealed to us in the
Word of God, the person of Jesus Christ, and the teaching of
his church. The notion that truth will emerge from a discussion in which many points of view are represented both dis-
respects revealed truth and separates the search for truth
from the certainty of faith; instead, as Pope John Paul II stated in "Ex Corde Ecclesiae": "A Catholic university's privileged task is 'to unite existentially by intellectual effort two
orders of reality that too frequently tend to be placed in
opposition as though they were antithetical: the search for
truth, and the certainty of already knowing the fount of
truth.'"[17]

Father Shanley

President Brian J. Shanley, O.P., got it right in banning *The Vagina
Monologues* at Providence College. "A Catholic college," said Fr. Shanley,
"cannot sanction the performance of works of art that are inimical to the
teaching of the Church in an area as important as female sexuality and the
dignity of women." Fr. Jenkins should have borrowed the Shanley statement.

11

Autonomy at Notre Dame
The Politicization of Abortion

> The inalienable right to life of every innocent human individual is a constitutive element of a civil society and its legislation: "The inalienable rights of the person must be recognized and respected by civil society and the political authority. . . . Among such fundamental rights one should mention in this regard every human being's right to life and physical integrity from the moment of conception until death." . . . As a consequence of the respect and protection which must be ensured for the unborn child from the moment of conception, the law must provide appropriate penal sanctions for every deliberate violation of the child's rights. – *Catechism of the Catholic Church*[1]

An Alternative Magisterium

NOTRE DAME defended its presentation of "The Last Temptation of Christ" and "The Vagina Monologues" on grounds of the "academic freedom" employed by secular universities. The Catholic Church has a more restrictive concept of academic freedom, as expressed in *Ex Corde Ecclesiae* and Pope Benedict XVI's address to Catholic educators at Washington, D.C.[2]

On abortion Notre Dame does more than exempt itself from a duty to follow the Church's understanding of academic freedom. It defines, in effect, what the Church teaching on abortion really is. Notre Dame, rather than the Magisterium (including the Catechism quoted above), makes that definition. The process is the same used by Fr. Jenkins in telling the American Bishops what they really meant in their 2004 mandate not to honor pro-abortion politicians.[3] Cardinal John Henry Newman foresaw that when a Catholic university cut itself off from the authority of the Church, it could "become the rival of the Church with the community at large in those theological matters which to the Church are exclusively committed, – acting as the representative of the intellect, as the Church is the representative of the religious principle."[4]

Missed Opportunities

The record supports Professor Alfred Freddoso's observation that, "During my thirty years on the faculty at the University of Notre Dame, the university as an institution has never been unambiguously pro-life." Permit me to mention one initiative which, in 1973, seemed to be what some today would call a no-brainer. In *Roe v. Wade*, decided a few months before, an entire class of human beings, the unborn, had been deprived of not only their personhood but also their right to live.[5] After discussing it with colleagues on the faculty, I wrote an open letter requesting "the Trustees to take a corporate position committing . . . Notre Dame to the proposition that all human beings, including unborn children, are entitled to the right to live guaranteed by the United States Constitution. . . . It is appropriate for the University of Notre Dame, as an institution, to take a stand against abortion. There is . . . precedent . . . in the . . . commitments made by the University to the cause of equal justice for racial minorities. . . . [I]t is indefensible for a Catholic university, as for an individual, to proclaim its advocacy of civil rights if it is unwilling to speak forcefully in support of the civil right to live of the most poor and defenseless of all minorities. Notre Dame has an opportunity to render a great service to the nation by advancing the cause of equal justice under law for all human beings."[6]

The letter generated some faculty discussion of abortion and of the propriety of a university taking stands on any issues.[7] But nothing happened. Over the succeeding years, Fr. Hesburgh himself has urged that abortion, which he described as "an abomination," ought to be treated as a policy issue like racial segregation.[8] Abortion is a civil rights issue of supreme importance.[9] It is fair to ask: What if? What would the pro-life scene, and even the entire culture, be like now if Notre Dame, as an institution, had stood firmly for the right to life for the past three decades and more?

As William McGurn pointed out, the Democratic Party was not always uniformly pro-abortion: "We forget it now, but back in the day, Jesse

Jackson was calling abortion 'genocide,' Al Gore had a pro-life record in the House, and even Ted Kennedy could write letters saying, 'Wanted or unwanted, I believe that human life, even at its earliest stages, has certain rights which must be recognized.' In this party, Catholic leaders such as the Rev. Theodore Hesburgh, then president of Notre Dame, still enjoyed tremendous influence. Had they used that influence to try to arrest the Democrats' slide on life, things might have been very different today. Instead, they became classic enablers, treating abortion as an irritating issue that needed to be placed off to the side."[10]

In the 1970s, as now, Notre Dame encouraged and supported campus activities in support of the right to life of the unborn. Fr. Hesburgh, for example, in celebrating a Mass on Right to Life Day, January 22, 1975, said, "We were brought up to respect the law, but if we think decisions should be refuted, we must refute them. . . . I believe in women's liberation but I cannot believe in abortion being a fundamental right of it. I think women have no more right over life than anyone else."[11] Various student pro-life groups remained active into the 1980s and through today. In an informal way, Notre Dame was significantly a pro-life campus. Notre Dame, however, took a defining step in 1984.

The Invitation of Governor Cuomo

Notre Dame's presentation in 1984 of the address, "Religious Belief and Public Morality: A Catholic Governor's Perspective," by New York Governor Mario Cuomo, aligned the University with the political movement promoting the abortion culture.

"Cuomo did not just happen to use a lecture at Notre Dame to address abortion politics," said Fr. Raymond de Souza, "He was brought to Notre Dame in a flagrantly provocative manner to undermine the Church's pro-life witness in politics. Recall the timeline. In March 1984, John O'Connor became archbishop of New York. That summer, Walter Mondale nominated New Yorker Geraldine Ferraro for vice president. Ferraro attempted to justify her pro-abortion position as being compatible with her Catholic faith, and Archbishop O'Connor corrected her. It became a high-profile controversy. The Catholic Church, in the person of the archbishop of New York, was at odds with a Catholic candidate for national office on a matter of fundamental importance. The Church's pro-life public witness was clear – painfully clear for some."[12]

Governor Cuomo had already been invited, in June, 1984, by Father Hesburgh and Father Richard McBrien, chairman of the theology department, to speak at Notre Dame that fall.[13] His address, sponsored by the Theology Department, was given on Sept. 13, 1984.

On August 30, 1984, two weeks before the Cuomo address, Fr. Richard McBrien, a very cordial person, had written to me that "I hope to invite a Catholic politician with a different perspective to address himself or herself to the same topic" as Governor Cuomo. That Catholic politician proved to be Congressman Henry Hyde (R-IL), who spoke on Sept. 24th, eleven days after Governor Cuomo, which meant that Cuomo had undivided attention at the time of his address.

"After the archbishop of New York," continued Fr. deSouza, "had clarified that a faithful Catholic could not promote abortion rights, the nation's premier Catholic university, led by two of the most famous Catholic priests in America, provided a forum to the leading Catholic politician in the country to explain why the archbishop of New York was wrong, all this two months before a presidential election in which a vice-presidential candidate was a pro-abortion Catholic. It almost did not matter what Cuomo said; the message Notre Dame sent was clear. The archbishop of New York and his brother bishops did not speak authoritatively for the Church in the United States; Notre Dame had an authoritative voice, too, and she would be heard on the pro-choice side."[14]

Governor Cuomo's Address

In his address, Governor Cuomo described his opposition to abortion as "my religious value." He said, "Our public morality, then – the moral standards we maintain for everyone, not just the ones we insist on in our private lives – depends on a consensus view of right and wrong. The values derived from religious belief will not – and should not – be accepted as part of the public morality unless they are shared by the pluralistic community at large, by consensus." He agrees that "[e]ven a radically secular world must struggle with the questions of when life begins, under what circumstances it can be ended, when it must be protected, by what authority; it too must decide what protection to extend to the helpless and the dying, to the aged and the unborn, to life in all its phases. As a Catholic, I have accepted certain answers as the right ones for myself and my family."

Cuomo states, however, that "in our pluralistic society we are not required to insist that <u>all</u> our religious values be the law of the land. Abortion is treated differently. Of course there are differences both in degree and quality between abortion and some of the other religious positions the Church takes: abortion is a 'matter of life and death,' and degree counts. But the differences in approach reveal a truth, I think, that is not well enough perceived by Catholics and therefore still further complicates the process for us. That is, while we always owe our bishops' words respectful attention and careful consideration, the question whether to engage the political system in a struggle to have it adopt certain articles of our belief as part of public morality, is not a matter of doctrine: it is a matter of prudential, political judgment. . . .

"As a Catholic . . . I accept the church's teaching authority. . . . I accept the bishops' position that abortion is to be avoided. . . . For me life or fetal life in the womb should be protected, even if five of nine Justices of the Supreme Court and my neighbor disagree with me. . . . But . . . the breadth, intensity and sincerity of opposition to church teaching . . . can't help but determine our ability . . . to translate our Catholic morality into civil law. . . .

"I believe that legal interdicting of abortion by either the federal government or the individual states is not a plausible possibility and even if it could be obtained, it wouldn't work. . . . Nor would a denial of Medicaid funding for abortion achieve our objectives. Given *Roe v. Wade*, it would be nothing more than an attempt to do indirectly what the law says cannot be done directly; worse, it would do it in a way that would burden only the already disadvantaged. Removing funding from the Medicaid program would not prevent the rich and middle classes from having abortions. It would not even assure that the disadvantaged wouldn't have them; it would only impose financial burdens on poor women who want abortions.

"Apart from that unevenness, there is a more basic question. Medicaid is designed to deal with health and medical needs. But the arguments for the cutoff of Medicaid abortion funds are not related to those needs. They are moral arguments. If we assume health and medical needs exist, our personal view of morality ought not to be considered a relevant basis for discrimination. We must keep in mind always that we are a nation of laws – when we like those laws, and when we don't. . . .

"The hard truth is that abortion isn't a failure of government. No agency or department of government forces women to have abortions, but abortion goes on. Catholics, the statistics show, support the right to abortion in equal proportion to the rest of the population. . . . Are we asking government to make criminal what we believe to be sinful because we ourselves can't stop committing the sin?"

"We must work to find ways to avoid abortions without otherwise violating our faith."[15]

The Cuomo Doctrines

Governor Cuomo took major positions that are inconsistent with Catholic teaching:

1. He persistently defined opposition to abortion as merely "our Catholic morality," a "religious" value or position. As Benedict XVI said, certain "non-negotiable principles" include the "protection of life in all stages, from the first moment of conception to natural death. . . . These principles are not truths of faith, even though they receive further light and confirmation from faith; they are inscribed in human nature itself and therefore they are common to all humanity. The Church's action in promoting them is therefore not confessional in character, but is addressed to all people, prescinding from any religious affiliation they may have."[16]

2. Cuomo said such principles, which he described as "values derived from religious belief . . . should not . . . be accepted as part of the public morality unless they are shared by the pluralistic community at large, by consensus." Cardinal Joseph Ratzinger, who is now Benedict XVI, delivered an address in 1999 on "Crises of Law." He named two. One is derived from a "spirit of utopia" which would justify Marxism, terrorism, etc., to achieve "the ideal model of the future world." The other crisis involves "the theory of consensus: if reason is no longer able to find the way to metaphysics as the source of law, the State can only refer to the common convictions of its citizens' values, convictions that are reflected in the democratic consensus. Truth does not create consensus, and consensus does not create truth as much as it does a common ordering. The majority determines what must be regarded as true and just. In other words, law is exposed to the whim of the majority. . . . Even human life is something that can be disposed of: abortion and euthanasia are no longer excluded from juridical ordering."[17] Having defined opposition to abortion as merely a religious belief, Governor Cuomo denied that we are obliged to work to

have the political system adopt "our belief as part of public morality." Whether to do so, he said, "is a matter of prudential political judgment." He denies that we are obliged to try to change the consensus by advocating full legal protection of unborn life.

3. Cuomo describes "the bishops' position" as merely that "abortion is to be avoided." On the contrary, the duty of the Catholic citizen or politician is not merely to avoid abortion in his or her personal life and then to wet a finger and hold it up to see which way the political consensus is blowing. "The mission of the lay faithful," as Benedict XVI put it, in accord with the teachings of his predecessors, is "to configure social life correctly."[18] The civil law is under a moral duty, imposed by the natural law and not somebody's "religious values," to protect innocent life. At the Capitol Mall in Washington, in 1979, Pope John Paul II declared, "If a person's right to life is violated at the moment in which he is first conceived in his mother's womb, an indirect blow is struck also at the whole of the moral order, which serves to ensure the inviolable goods of man. Among those goods, life occupies the first place . . . And so, we will stand up every time that human life is threatened. When the sacredness of life before birth is attacked, we will stand up and proclaim that no one ever has the authority to destroy unborn life." [19]

4. Cuomo maintained that Catholics should not attempt to prevent, and by clear implication should support, Medicaid funding for abortions for poor women. Where the law allows such funding "our personal view of morality ought not to be considered a relevant basis for discrimination. We . . . are a nation of laws." The Declaration on Procured Abortion, issued in 1974 with the approval of Pope Paul VI, said, "[W]hatever may be laid down by civil law in this matter, man can never obey a law which is in itself immoral, and such is the case of a law which would admit in principle the liceity of abortion. . . . Moreover, he may not collaborate in its application."[20]

Sister Marita Calls It

The Nazareth Life Center, in Garrison, New York, a home for unwed mothers, rejected the gift by Governor Cuomo of his $1,500 honorarium from Notre Dame. "He believes abortion is not for his wife," said Sister Marita, "but there are instances where he thinks there should be free choice. I do not believe abortion involves a free choice. I just feel abortion is murder. It's not simply a Catholic issue. There are no ifs, ands or buts about it."[21] Sister Marita should have been running some things at Notre Dame.

Congressman Hyde's Address

Where Governor Cuomo spoke in the large venue of Washington Hall, Congressman Hyde, invited to provide balance, was consigned to the student lounge in the basement of the Notre Dame Law School eleven days after Governor Cuomo's nationally noted address. His friends, family and staffers cared that he was there, but not too many others. Congressman Hyde, however, delivered a superb analysis of the application of natural law and Church teaching to practical political life. Notre Dame dropped the Hyde address down the memory hole. But we should look at it.

Congressman Hyde noted that

> Millions of people now take for granted that opposition to abortion can only be grounded in religious dogma. . . . and many Catholics are timorously eager to placate potential hostility and bigotry by pleading that although they are "personally opposed" to abortion, they would never "impose their views" on anyone else. At the extreme we have the sort of Catholic politician of whom it's been said that "his religion is so private he won't even impose it on himself." . . . [T]he constitutional separation of church and state. . . . was never intended to rule religiously-based values out of order in the public arena. . . . The "wall of separation," according to these activists, sundered not only religious institutions and the institutions of the state; it stood fast between religiously-based values and the debate over the public business. Any appeal to a religiously-based value to buttress an argument for this or that public policy option was thus a violation of the separation of church and state. However, the application of this secular principle has been schizophrenic to say the least. The clergy were revered when they marched at Selma, joined anti-war sit-ins and helped boycott lettuce. They are reviled when they speak out against abortion. . . . Catholics experienced the hypocrisy of the abortion debate. They saw an issue of the utmost importance to constitutional

first principles (Who shall be within the boundaries of our community's sense of obligation and protection?) dismissed as a "Catholic issue," an unconstitutional "mixing of religion and politics." We were accused of trying to impose our religious values on others. . . .

Another way of expressing one's reluctance to impose one's values on a society is to require a consensus before supporting any changes in the law. . . . [T]his is a . . . selective requirement applying only to abortion legislation. No consensus was demanded before adopting the Civil Rights Act of 1964 or Fair Housing legislation – these were right and their proponents helped <u>create</u> a consensus by advocacy and example and by understanding that the law itself can be an excellent teacher. . . . Here the question of consistency becomes clear.

Had the Archbishop of New York quizzed a conservative Catholic President about his commitment to nuclear arms control, would there have been impassioned hand-wringing at the *New York Times* editorial board about 'mixing politics and religion?' Yet this is precisely what happened when the Archbishop of New York questioned a liberal Democratic candidate for Vice President about her approach to the public policy of abortion. Why is it that Archbishop O'Connor threatens the separation of church and state when he tries to clarify Catholic teaching about abortion, and the Rev. Jesse Jackson doesn't when he organizes a partisan political campaign through the agency of dozens of churches? These confusions are not merely a matter of anti-Catholic bias, although that is undoubtedly present; they reflect the chaotic condition of public understanding on the larger questions of religious values and the public policy debate. . . .

[W]e ought to . . . make clear that abortion is not, at bottom, a "Catholic issue," but rather a moral and civil rights issue, a humanitarian issue and a constitutional issue of the first importance. The abortion liberty, we should insist, is a profoundly narrow-minded, illiberal position; it constricts, rather than expands, the scope of liberty properly understood. It draws in, rather than expands, the community of the protected. These are, or ought to be, issues of concern far beyond the American Catholic community. . . .

The duty of one who regards abortion as wrong is not to bemoan the absence of a consensus against abortion, but to help lead the effort to achieve one. . . . Samuel Johnson once observed, "Mankind more frequently requires to be reminded than informed." That is all we are doing: At a time when the moral consensus of the West is under assault, we are reminding this nation of its traditional membership in that consensus. . . . I am not referring here to the teaching authority of the Church as such. I'm talking about the authority of moral law in the experience of all mankind, the moral law written in our hearts, the moral law without which it is nonsense to speak of "rights." Catholics neither have nor claim any monopoly of that law. We do have a duty to maintain it, and to be willing to stand up to speak for it when the state violates it. This is a duty wholly distinct from our duty to propagate our faith. The Gospel is the good news; the moral law is not news at all, it is what we know in our hearts already. . . .

Especially called are you, the students of Notre Dame. Father Theodore Hesburgh, in an address to the faculty in January 1982, said: . . . "Moral relativism gives us a society that is only relatively moral and we are sick of that, very sick indeed." Nearly two weeks ago on this campus the Governor proposed a hypothetical: "Put aside what God expects – assume if you like there is no God – then the greatest thing still left to us is life," he said. That remark misses a point of terrifying importance, a point that was made by Professor Paul Eidelberg: "Unless there is a Being superior to man, nothing in theory prevents some men from degrading other men to the level of subhuman." Do we need to be reminded that this is the age of Dachau and Auschwitz and the Gulag? . . . St. Ambrose said, "Not only for every idle word must man render an account, but for every idle silence."[22]

The Hesburgh Proposal

One week after Congressman Hyde's address, Father Hesburgh wrote that, "Many thoughts have been running through my mind since listening to Governor Mario Cuomo's brilliant talk on religion and politics at Notre Dame. . . . If given a *choice* between the present law of abortion-on-demand, up to and including viability, or a more restrictive law, such as limitation of abortion to cases of rape, incest, and serious threat to the mother's life, the majority of Americans polled consistently have supported the more limited option. . . . [A]s Governor Cuomo and others . . . have pointed out, there is not a consensus in America for the absolute prohibition of abortion. But there is and was a moral consensus, one ignored by the Supreme Court . . . for a stricter abortion law. A . . . well-kept secret is that a minority is currently imposing its belief on a demonstrable majority. . . . If such a total solution is not possible in our pluralistic society . . . will Catholics cooperate with other Americans of good will and ethical conviction to work for a more restrictive abortion law? One might hope so. This would not compromise our belief in the sanctity of all human life."[23]

The Incremental Approach Depersonalizes the Unborn

Fr. Hesburgh urged Catholics to "work for" a law in accord with the existing consensus; such as a law allowing abortion in "cases of rape, incest, and serious threat to the mother's life." Such an incremental law would have an unintended negative impact. It would confirm the depersonalization principle of *Roe v. Wade*. If your life is legally subject to extinction at the discretion of another on account of the identity of your father because he is a close relative or a rapist, or even to save someone else's life when you are not an aggressor, then you are a nonperson in the eyes of the United States Constitution. The Supreme Court, in *Roe v. Wade*, stated that if the unborn child is a person, the case for abortion "collapses" and the Court indicated that abortion would not be allowed even to save the life of the mother.[24] For abortion opponents to advocate a compromise allowance of abortion contributes to the culture of death by fostering the impression that abortion and other "life" issues are negotiable, like a highway appropriation. In a just and free society, the only legitimate issue is *whether* innocent human beings may be legally executed. The incremental approach frames the issue in terms, not of whether, but of *which* innocent human beings may be legally executed. After three decades of "pro-life" incrementalism, a measure of the futility of the compromise approach is the pro-life focus on partial-birth abortion. That tactic frames the issue not in

terms of whether, and not even in terms of which innocents may be legally executed, but in terms of *how* the killing is to be done.[25]

Evangelium Vitae, no. 73

The active proposal of incremental restrictions on abortion would not
appear to be justified by *Evangelium Vitae's* limited statement, in 1995, on
the responsibility of legislators "where a legislative vote would be decisive
for the passage of a more restrictive law, aimed at limiting the number of
authorized abortions, in place of a more permissive law already passed or
ready to be voted on. . . .[W]hen it is not possible to overturn or completely abrogate a pro-abortion law, an elected official, whose absolute personal opposition to procured abortion was well known, could licitly support
proposals aimed at *limiting the harm* done by such a law and at lessening
its negative consequences at the level of general opinion and public morality. This [is] not in fact an illicit cooperation with an unjust law, but rather
a legitimate and proper attempt to limit its evil aspects."[26]

Thus, Congressman Hyde, when he had exhausted all alternatives,
agreed to some exceptions to the Hyde Amendment's prohibition of federal funding for abortion. But he did not himself initiate such compromise at
the outset. Nor did he personally favor it. And, unlike Fr. Hesburgh, he did
not himself propose the allowance of abortion for rape, incest or the life of
the mother on the ground that it is in accord with the consensus. When a
legislator, pursuant to *Evangelium Vitae*, votes for a "more restrictive law"
that would still permit abortion, that vote can be "a legitimate and proper
attempt to limit [the] evil aspects" of the more permissive law. This can be
a worthy tactic to save lives. The Pope says that a legislator "could" licitly
support such a proposal. He does not say that he "should." This leaves open
the prudential question of whether pro-life support for such compromise
measures might increase the "negative consequences" of legalized abortion "at the level of general opinion and public morality," especially when
such compromises are promoted by "pro-life" advocates themselves. In
any event, *Evangelium Vitae* is not a license for Catholic legislators to
become proponents of what John Paul II called "the culture of death." And
it surely does not validate the positions taken by Governor Cuomo in his
Notre Dame address, and by Fr. Hesburgh in his incremental proposal
which relied on the Cuomo address.

Notre Dame's Counter-teaching

In its sponsorship of Governor Cuomo's address, Notre Dame used its national platform to tell Catholics, and especially Catholic politicians, 1. That their opposition to abortion is a merely sectarian religious view that they should not try to impose on their fellow citizens by urging the enactment of a law in accord with that opposition; 2. That they are not obliged to seek a full restoration to the unborn child of the constitutional right to live; and 3. That they are morally obliged to support public funding for abortions for poor women.

By implicitly endorsing these positions, Notre Dame, in this respect, declared its autonomy not only from "external" authority but from the truth dictated by reason, that no innocent human being should ever be intentionally killed by anyone.

The Laetare for Hyde

Regrettably, Fr. Hesburgh, in his compromise proposal endorsing the Cuomo approach, did not even mention Congressman Hyde's address which occurred a week before the Hesburgh proposal. Hyde denied that we ought "to require a consensus before supporting any changes in the law." Rather, he urged that we follow the course of the civil rights proponents in the 1960s who did not wring their hands over the absence of a consensus. They "helped create a consensus by advocacy" of laws. They understood that "the law itself can be an excellent teacher." Professor Mary Ann Glendon declined the 2009 Laetare Medal. It ought to be awarded for 2009, posthumously and retroactively, to Congressman Hyde.

The Cuomo address was a decisive commitment of Notre Dame to support of the political agenda of the culture of death. Two other Notre Dame events were important but comparatively small change.

The Maguire-Burtchaell Debate

On February 9, 1987, the Theology Department sponsored a debate on abortion between Dr. Daniel Maguire and Fr. James T. Burtchaell, c.s.c. Maguire, a leader of Catholics for Free Choice, presented his pro-abortion view as a legitimate Catholic position. He congratulated Notre Dame on "allowing the multiple Catholic views on abortion to be heard and debated." Daniel Maguire gains notoriety in the media because he falsely passes his position off as authentically "Catholic." The objection I raised was that: "Notre Dame, in providing him a forum to present his claim . . . concedes that his view is at least a debatably legitimate Catholic position. Whether or not Fr. Burtchaell . . . regards the Maguire position as authentically Catholic and no matter how eloquently he speaks against abortion, he will have lost the real debate the moment he steps on the platform. By the . . . fact that the 'debate' is held under these auspices, Dr. Maguire will have gained the sanction of Notre Dame for the false claim that the Catholic position is defined not by the Vicar of Christ, the Councils and the bishops in union with him, but by universities and individual theologians."[27]

Professors Alfred Freddoso and Janet Smith made an important point. "Notre Dame was one of the first universities to give George Wallace a hearing during the 1960's. . . . Maguire [and] . . . Wallace both have . . . narrow views about which human beings should be treated with respect. But . . . George Wallace was not a Catholic representing a group called 'Catholics for a Free Choice on Racial Discrimination.' Suppose he had been. Would Father McBrien have invited such a George Wallace to propound the "Catholic" argument for racism? Would the campus have welcomed this event, or even tolerated it? Would Washington Hall have been filled with dignitaries?"[28] The answers are obvious. Notre Dame implements a double standard on the abortion issue. That double standard weighs on the "pro-choice" side.

The Laetare Medal to Moynihan

In 1992, Notre Dame awarded the Laetare Medal to Senator Daniel Patrick Moynihan (D- N.Y.). Later in his career, when he supported the ban on partial-birth abortion, Moynihan picked up an unjustified reputation as a moderate on the abortion issue. But at the time Notre Dame awarded him the Laetare Medal, his record showed Senator Moynihan to be relentless and unyielding in voting for the legalization and funding of the killing of the unborn.[29] Why did Notre Dame award the medal to Senator Moynihan? "His passion for scholarship," said the President, Rev. Edward A. Malloy, C.S.C., "has made him sensible to the realities of state, sensitive to the cry of the poor and commendably supportive of higher education. "At Notre Dame, we share that passion, and with this year's Laetare Medal, we celebrate it as well."

One of the "realities of state" to which Senator Moynihan, and apparently the Notre Dame administrators, are "sensible" is that the American state, with Moynihan's active approval, legalizes the execution of more than 4,000 innocent human beings every single day. The sensitivity of Moynihan and our leaders "to the cry of the poor" is selective. The poorest and most helpless of the poor is the unborn child who is murdered before he can utter a cry. Mother Teresa reminded us that the poorest nations are those which murder their young by abortion. Finally, we are told, Moynihan is "commendably supportive of higher education," including research universities like Notre Dame. Senator Moynihan is in a position to expedite the allocation of taxpayers' money and other supports to "higher education." Maybe that explains it. "Sensible to the realities of state," the "national Catholic research university" is not deterred from honoring this important person by a little thing like his support for legalized baby killing.

The net effect of the Maguire-Burtchaell debate and the Moynihan award was to reinforce the message that Notre Dame had sent with its sponsorship of Governor Cuomo's address. In those events, Notre Dame presented as legitimately Catholic a position contrary to the teaching of the Catholic Church.

An Alternative Magisterium

Notre Dame, having declared its autonomy from the Magisterium, became, with the Cuomo address, an alternative magisterium, providing Catholic politicians with a rationale to present their "pro-choice" positions as authentically Catholic. Notre Dame, in effect, was telling Catholics what the Church really teaches. And it was not true. Archbishop Raymond Burke, at the 2009 National Catholic Prayer Breakfast, described the resulting confusion and scandal:

> In a nation set so firmly on a path of violation of the most fundamental moral norms, Catholics and others who adhere to the natural moral law are pressured to think that their religious commitment to the moral law as the way of seeking the good of all is a merely confessional matter which cannot have any application in public life. . . . How often do we hear Catholic legislators who vote in favor of anti-life and anti-family legislation claim that they are personally opposed to what the legislation protects and fosters,

but that they as public officials may not allow religious beliefs to affect their support of such legislation? How often do we hear . . . Catholics supporting candidates . . . who are anti-life and anti-family, because of political . . . loyalties or for reasons of other policies . . . supported by the candidate, which they deem to be good? How often is such thinking justified by the claim that religious faith is a purely private matter and has no place in the public forum? On the contrary, the common good depends upon the active engagement of religious faith in the public forum. . . . In addressing the critical issues of our nation, the Church and we, as her faithful sons and daughters, intervene on the basis of reason and natural law . . . in accord with the nature of every human being. . . . Our . . . commitment to protect . . . innocent human life and to safeguard the integrity of marriage and the family are not based on peculiar confessional beliefs or practices but on the natural moral law, written on every heart and, therefore, a fundamental part of the Church's moral teaching.[30]

So what do we make of the Notre Dame record on abortion? Notre Dame has taken autonomy to a new level. His predecessors set the stage for Fr. Jenkins by staking their claim that Notre Dame has an authority to decide what the Catholic Church teaches on abortion. The decision to confer Notre Dame's highest honors on President Obama cannot be blamed exclusively on Fr. Jenkins. It had its roots in the false autonomy claimed at Land O'Lakes and the politicized acts of the University in the succeeding decades.

12

The Magisterium
Why Notre Dame Needs It

The Mistake That Keeps On Giving

IN THE first eleven chapters we described some results of Notre Dame's assertion of "autonomy" from the Church. It was evident in 1967, and is abundantly clear today, that Land O'Lakes, in that respect, was a mistake that continues to distort the life of Notre Dame and other "Catholic" universities. It gets worse as we go along.

For an individual Catholic, or a Catholic university, to reject the teaching authority of the Church is a very big deal. "For it is indeed Christ who lives in the Church, and through her teaches, governs and sanctifies."[1] Notre Dame avows its respect for the Magisterium but rejects a duty to obey it. In this, Notre Dame disserves its students. It tells its students that, contrary to explicit statements of the Magisterium, including *Ex Corde*, the teachings of the Church (through which Christ teaches) are optional, not only for the University but impliedly for the students as well. Notre Dame's officials insist on both the Catholic identity of the University and their own Catholic belief. But the rhetoric is hollow, because on the big issue – private judgment or recognition of the authority of the Church – they act, at least in their University capacities, like Protestants. It is a type of consumer fraud to claim to be a "Catholic university" and refuse to abide by the requirements of that term as defined by the only entity with authority to define it.

For a professedly Catholic institution to falsify the role of the Magisterium is especially serious because the Church does not teach a particular subject. Rather, it incorporates a subject, whether economics, natural law, etc., into its teaching of Christ. As John Paul II and Benedict XVI have made clear, the object of studying Church teaching involves more than learning doctrines. Its object is to know Christ, who is Truth and who speaks through the Church. When Notre Dame, as an institution, gives the back of its hand to the teaching authority of the Church, it puts Church teaching on the same level as some professor's "scholarly" article. The message to students is: "Take it or leave it. It's just his point of view." Jesus Christ, however, is not your friendly campus theologian. And neither is the Pope.

The social and moral teachings of the Church are rich in wisdom and tradition, they are sound in principle, and they work. In this and the remaining chapters we discuss several aspects of them. The purpose is to suggest the good that Notre Dame could do, especially now, if it accepted and promoted those teachings and the authority of the Church to issue them. Notre Dame students would profit. And so would many others who are looking for a way out of "the dictatorship of relativism."

Two Questions

* Can a Catholic university survive if it accepts the Magisterium? Answer: Yes.
* Can it survive if it doesn't? Answer: No.

The people running major Catholic universities would probably reverse those answers. The Magisterium, from the Latin *magister*, or teacher, is the teaching authority of the Church. Religious authority is suspect today as an externally imposed restriction on conscience and freedom. On the contrary, the Magisterium, as discussed in the remaining chapters, is the guarantor of liberty of conscience and true freedom. In this chapter, our concern is the special role of the Magisterium with relation to the Catholic university and its students. The "dictatorship of relativism," described by Cardinal Ratzinger in his homily before his election as Pope, affects not only social and political life, but also and especially the thought processes of all students.

Openness

"There is one thing a professor can be absolutely certain of," said Allan Bloom: "almost every student entering the university believes, or says he believes, that truth is relative."[2] Although Professor Bloom died thirteen years before Cardinal Ratzinger became Pope, the two were of one mind on this. The two decades since the publication of *The Closing of the American Mind* confirm Bloom's diagnosis. With the students, said Bloom, "[t]he relativity of truth is . . . the condition of a free society. . . . [T]his framework . . . is the modern replacement for the inalienable natural rights that used to be the traditional American grounds for a free society. . . . Relativism is necessary to openness, and this is . . . the only virtue, which all primary education for more than fifty years has dedicated itself to inculcating. Openness – and the relativism that makes it the only plausible stance in the face of various claims to truth . . . is the great insight of our times. The true believer is the real danger. The study of history and of culture teaches that all the world was mad in the past; men always thought they were right, and that led to wars, persecutions, slavery, xenophobia, racism, and chauvinism. The point is not to correct the mistakes and really be right; rather it is not to think you are right at all.

"The students . . . cannot defend their opinion. [T]hey have been indoctrinated. The best they can do is point out all the opinions and cultures there are and have been. What right, they ask, do I or anyone else have to say one is better than the others? If I pose the routine questions designed to . . . make them think, such as, 'If you had been a British administrator in India, would you have let the natives under your governance burn the widow at the funeral of a man who died?,' they either remain silent or reply that the British should never have been there in the first place. It is not that they know very much about other nations, or about their own. The purpose of their education is not to make them scholars but to provide them with a moral virtue – openness."[3]

Intellectual consistency is not a hallmark of openness. In teaching the natural law course at Notre Dame, I usually ask, "Apart from sense impressions, can you be absolutely sure of anything?" The usual response is, "No." "Are you absolutely sure of that?" "Yes." Or, if the student is not sure, he is sure that he is not sure. For most students, exposure to Aristotle, Aquinas and the reality of moral truth knowable to reason comes as a news flash and, apparently, a welcome one.

How the Catholic University Is Different

The "openness" described by Professor Bloom presents a special challenge to the Catholic university. Cardinal Avery Dulles, as we saw in Chapter 9, said that a "Catholic institution must be founded on three principles: that there is a God, that he has made a full and final revelation of himself in Jesus Christ and that the Catholic Church is the authorized custodian and teacher of this body of revealed truth."[4] While *Ex Corde Ecclesiae* affirms that, "A Catholic University possesses the autonomy necessary to develop its distinctive identity and pursue its proper mission,"[5] that autonomy is subject to recognition of the teaching authority of the Church. *Ex Corde* affirms, therefore, that "the *institutional* fidelity of the University to the Christian message includes a recognition of and adherence to the teaching authority of the Church in matters of faith and morals." [6]

Why do Catholic universities, and many Catholics, fail to obey the teaching authority of the Church? One reason is that the Church itself is misunderstood and not accepted on its own terms. The Church is neither the Democratic nor Republican Party at prayer, nor a Kiwanis Club nor a transnational corporation, although at times it resembles all three. The Catholic Church is "the Mystical Body of Christ. . . . 'We must accustom ourselves to see Christ Himself in the Church. For it is indeed Christ who lives in the Church, and through her teaches, governs and sanctifies; and it is also Christ who manifests Himself in manifold guise in the various members of His society.'"[7] "As Lord," says the *Catechism*, "Christ is also head of the Church, which is his Body."[8]

That is serious business because Christ is not some CEO or community organizer. He is God. He founded one Church. It has three functions:

To teach on matters of faith and morals.

To rule, that is, to establish disciplinary and regulatory standards for the governance of the Church.

To sanctify, that is, to provide access to sanctifying and actual grace through the sacramental system and other means.[9]

The Magisterium is exercised by the Pope and the bishops in union with the Pope.[10] Teachings of the Church on faith and morals are binding on Catholics even if they do not include an "infallible definition" or a "definitive" pronouncement, when they "propose in the exercise of the ordinary Magisterium a teaching that leads to better understanding of Revelation in matters of faith and morals."[11] "[A]ll acts of the Magisterium derive . . . from Christ who desires that His People walk in the entire truth. For this same reason, magisterial decisions in matters of discipline, even if they are not guaranteed by . . . infallibility, are not without divine assistance and call for the adherence of the faithful." [12] In his September 16, 1987, address to the American bishops assembled in Los Angeles, Pope John Paul II said that "there is a tendency on the part of some Catholics to be selective in their adherence to the Church's moral teachings. It is sometimes claimed that dissent from the *Magisterium* is totally compatible with being a 'good Catholic' and poses no obstacle to the reception of the Sacraments. This is a grave error that challenges the teaching office of the Bishops of the United States and elsewhere."[13] As Bishop D'Arcy and other bishops affirmed, the 2004 mandate of the bishops of the United States that forbade the honor that Notre Dame conferred on Obama was a proper, and binding, exercise of the Magisterium.

The Church Rescues Reason

What the teaching Church is doing today is counter-cultural but inspiring. Notre Dame should be fully a part of it, because the Church rescues reason from its false limitation to the empirical and affirms that the only coherent foundation of any university is the integration of faith and reason. "Faith and reason," said John Paul II, "are like two wings on which the human spirit rises to the contemplation of truth."[14]

In his 2007 address to the European Meeting of University Professors, Pope Benedict XVI rejected "narrow and ultimately irrational attempts to limit the scope of reason. The concept of reason needs instead to be 'broadened' in order to be able to explore and embrace those aspects of reality which go beyond the merely empirical. . . . The rise of the European universities was fostered by the conviction that faith and reason are meant to cooperate in the search for truth."[15] In his address, "Faith, Reason and the University: Memories and Reflections," at the University of Regensburg on September 12, 2006, Benedict identified two false "principles" of "the modern self-limitation of reason":

> First, only the kind of certainty resulting from the interplay of mathematical and empirical elements can be considered scientific. . . . Hence the human sciences, such as history, psychology, sociology and philosophy, attempt to conform themselves to this canon of scientificity.
>
> A second point . . . is that by its very nature this method excludes the question of God, making it appear an unscientific or pre-scientific question. . . . [T]he . . . questions about

our origin and destiny, the questions raised by religion and ethics, then have no place within the purview of collective reason as defined by "science" and must thus be relegated to the realm of the subjective.

The subject then decides, on the basis of his experiences, what he considers tenable in matters of religion, and the subjective "conscience" becomes the sole arbiter of what is ethical. In this way, though, ethics and religion lose their power to create a community and become a completely personal matter.[16]

Benedict said we will succeed in "broadening our concept of reason and its application . . . only if reason and faith come together in a new way, if we overcome the self-limitation of reason to the empirically verifiable."[17] When the Pope's address in January, 2008, at Rome's public Sapienza University was cancelled due to protests, he published the prepared address. In it he said the "purpose of knowing the truth is to know the good. . . . The truth makes us good and goodness is true: this is the optimism that shapes the Christian faith, because this faith has been granted the vision of the *Logos*, of creative Reason which, in God's Incarnation, revealed itself as the Good, as Goodness itself." He emphasized that "faith can only be given in freedom." But he said the "danger for the western world . . . is that . . . man will fail to face up to the question of the truth. . . . [I]f reason . . . becomes deaf to the great message that comes to it from Christian faith and wisdom, then it withers like a tree whose roots can no longer reach the waters that give life to it."[18]

Notre Dame should enthusiastically enlist in the efforts of John Paul II and Benedict XVI to restore reason to its proper place in the intellectual life of all universities. Professor Ralph McInerny has rightly called for a recognition of "the historical fact that the university began as a Catholic institution, arising 'out of the heart of the Church.' The medieval university, a tumultuous place, reestablished the *modus vivendi* between faith and reason that had been disturbed by the influx of Aristotle, convoyed into the West by Arabic commentators. . . . If ever there has been a time to trumpet and boast of the ameliorative effect of Christian faith on the life of learning, it is now. Yet what we hear are mumbled hopes that with time and money our institutions can be made to look more and more like their fallen secular sisters."[19]

Why Notre Dame Needs the Magisterium

Notre Dame offers to its students abundant opportunities to put their faith into practice. More than three decades of teaching Notre Dame alumni in law school, however, lead me to conclude that Notre Dame undergrads are shortchanged in that they are not afforded a predictable opportunity to learn what the Catholic Church actually teaches about itself and about the binding character of its moral teachings. What they do learn in this area, unless they are lucky or prudent enough to study with certain professors, is likely to be filtered through the lens of a hostile professor.[20] They tend to be no more deprived than the graduates of other Catholic colleges. But they should be better. Adherence by the University to the Magisterium, and specifically to *Ex Corde*, would improve that situation.

The *Application of Ex Corde* to . the United States requires that, "With due regard for the principles of religious liberty and freedom of conscience, students should have the opportunity to be educated in the Church's moral and religious principles and social teachings and to participate in the life of faith: 1. Catholic students have a right to receive from a university instruction in authentic Catholic doctrine and practice, especially from those who teach the theological disciplines. They also have a right to be provided with opportunities to practice the faith through participation in Mass, the sacraments, religious devotions and other authentic forms of Catholic spirituality. (Parenthetically, on this last sentence, Notre Dame is a model of compliance.) 2. Courses in Catholic doctrine and practice should be made available to all students. 3. Catholic teaching should have a place, if appropriate to the subject matter, in the various disciplines taught in the university. Students should be provided with adequate instruction on professional ethics and moral issues related to their profession and the secular disciplines."[21] In these and other respects, *Ex Corde* is a Students' Bill of Rights. The response of an authentically Catholic university to *Ex Corde* should not be a distancing autonomy but enthusiastic and full implementation.

Newman and Ex Corde Ecclesiae

"If [Cardinal John Henry] Newman were alive today," said Cardinal Avery Dulles, "[h]e would enthusiastically embrace the principles set forth by John Paul II in *Ex corde Ecclesiae*." Newman, according to Dulles, saw rationalism as a threat to the Catholic university. In Newman's view, said Dulles, "[t]he university, as a place of intellectual cultivation, tends to treat the human mind as the measure of all things. Absolutizing its own standards and goals, the university aspires to complete autonomy and becomes a rival of the Church even in the Church's own sphere of competence. To prevent this encroachment, the Church must exercise what Newman calls 'a direct and active jurisdiction' over the university. This should not be seen as a hindrance but as a help to the university. Ecclesiastical supervision prevents the university from falling into the kinds of skepticism and unbelief that have plagued seats of learning since the time of Abelard. Because the university cannot fulfill its mission without revealed truth, and because the Church has full authority to teach the contents of revelation, the university must accept the Church's guidance. . . .

"In [*Ex Corde*]," continued Cardinal Dulles, "the Holy Father sets forth the same general principles that I have tried to highlight in Newman's treatise. He teaches that university education should not be content to produce an efficient work force for the factory or the market place; it should not exalt [the] technical over the spiritual. He strongly opposes the multiplication of separate departments and institutes, which he sees as harmful to a rich human formation. He calls for a universal humanism and an organic vision of reality. He likewise holds that Catholic universities have the incomparable advantage of being able to integrate all truth in relation to Christ, the incarnate Logos, whom Christians recognize as the way, the truth, and the life for the whole world. On these and many other points the nineteenth-century English cardinal and the present Polish pope may be said to share a common point of view."[22]

Pope Benedict has stressed the need for Catholic universities to affirm that true reason is open to the reality of God: As "a criterion of rationality, empirical proof by experimentation has become ever more exclusive. The fundamental human questions – how to live and how to die – [are] excluded from . . . rationality and are left to the sphere of subjectivity. Consequently, the issue that brought universities into being – the question of the true and the good – . . . disappears to be replaced by the question of feasibility. This, then is the great challenge to Catholic Universities: to impart knowledge in the perspective of true rationality . . . in accordance with a reason open to the question of the truth and to the great values inscribed in being itself, hence, open to the transcendent, to God."[23]

The Real "Reality"

Secular academics may tell you that talk about God is unreal, and that the world of economics, politics, etc., is the real world. The Catholic university ought to know better. In 2007, Benedict asked whether "the priority of faith in Christ and of life 'in him'" could "perhaps be a flight towards emotionalism, towards religious individualism, an abandonment of the . . . economic, social and political problems of Latin America and the world, and a flight from reality towards a spiritual world?" He answered:

> [W]e can respond to this question with another: what is this "reality"? What is real? Are only material goods, social, economic and political problems "reality"? This was . . . the great error . . . of the last century, a most destructive error, as we can see from the results of both Marxist and capitalist systems. They falsify the notion of reality by detaching it from the foundational and decisive reality which is God. Anyone who excludes God from his horizons falsifies the notion of "reality" and . . . can only end up in blind alleys or with recipes for destruction.
>
> [O]nly those who recognize God know reality and are able to respond to it adequately and in a truly human manner. The truth of this thesis becomes evident in the face of the collapse of all the systems that marginalize God.
>
> Yet here a further question . . . arises: who knows God? How can we know him? . . . For a Christian, the . . . reply is simple: only God knows God, only his Son who is God from God, true God, knows him. And he "who is nearest to the Father's heart has made him known" (John 1:18). Hence the unique and irreplaceable importance of Christ for us, for humanity.
>
> If we do not know God in and with Christ, all of reality is transformed into an indecipherable enigma; there is no way, and without a way, there is neither life nor truth.
>
> God is the foundational reality, not a God who is merely imagined and hypothetical, but God with a human face; he is God-with-us, the God who loves even to the Cross.[24]

An Inspiring Mission for Notre Dame

Benedict urges all believers to pass on to others the "great truth" of the faith. The Christian faith, of course, is not reducible to documents and doctrines. Benedict emphasized that "One can never know Christ only theoretically. With great teaching one can know everything about the Sacred Scriptures without ever having met him. Journeying with him is an integral part of knowing him. . . . Catechesis . . . must always . . . become a practice of communion of life with Christ. . . . The encounter with Jesus Christ requires listening . . . prayer and . . . putting into practice what he tells us. By getting to know Christ we come to know God, and it is only by starting from God that we understand man and the world, a world that would otherwise remain a nonsensical question. . . . Those who have recognized a great truth . . . have to pass it on. . . . These great gifts are never intended for only one person. In Jesus Christ a great light emerged for us, *the* great Light; we cannot put it under a bushel basket, we must set it on a lampstand so that it will give light to all who are in the house (cf. Mt 5:15)."[25]

Notre Dame ought to be explicitly and fully a part of this inspiring mission of the Church. Instead, Notre Dame opted out to the extent of substituting for obedience to the Magisterium a subordination to the standards of the secular academic and political establishments. Listen again to Cardinal Dulles: "In the United States," he said, "Catholic universities have been very apologetic, almost embarrassed, by their obligation to adhere to the faith of the Church. For Newman and for John Paul II, any university that lacks the guidance of Christian revelation and the oversight of the Catholic magisterium is by that very fact impeded in its mission to find and transmit truth. It fails to make use of an important resource that God in his Providence has provided. Surrounded by powerful institutions constructed on principles of metaphysical and religious agnosticism, the Catholic universities of this nation have too long been on the defensive. They have tried too hard to prove that they are not committed to any truth that cannot be established by objective scientific scholarship. While making certain necessary adaptations to the needs of our own day, they should proudly reaffirm the essentials of their own tradition, so brilliantly synthesized by Newman in his classic work."[26]

Notre Dame, in the pursuit of autonomy, misleads and potentially gives scandal to students and others through the implication that the unity of the Church is not that big a deal.[27] The implication is that Catholics can regard Church teaching as optional advisories and that Catholics can be all over the lot on moral questions because contradictory moral positions can both be good. St. Thomas Aquinas saw it differently. "If," he said, "we consider one action in the moral order, it is impossible for it to be morally both good and evil." From the aspect of its moral quality, "the same act cannot be both good and evil."[28] Notre Dame adds to the confusion by its claim to be Catholic while rejecting any obligation to be bound by the Church's teaching as to what being Catholic requires.

It is not too late for Notre Dame to resume its historical witness to the fullness of Catholic truth. The succeeding decades have confirmed the imprudence of the Land O'Lakes assertion of autonomy. It is time for Notre Dame to return to the Church. As Fr. Miscamble said to the ND Response students, "there is so much that is good at Notre Dame that you can never relent in your efforts to call this place to be its best and true self – proud of its Catholic identity and its loyal membership in the Church."[29] As part of the Church again, Notre Dame could fill a great need. "At this hour in our nation's life," said William McGurn, "America thirsts for an alternative to the relativism that leaves so many of our young people feeling empty and alone. This alternative is the Catholic witness that Notre Dame was *created* to provide . . . that Notre Dame is *called* to provide . . . and that in many ways, only Notre Dame *can* provide."[30]

13
The Magisterium and the Dictatorship of Relativism

> To have a clear faith, according to the creed of the Church, is . . . labeled as fundamentalism. . . . . [R]elativism, . . . allowing oneself to be carried along with every wind of "doctrine," seems to be the only attitude that is fashionable. A dictatorship of relativism is being constituted that recognizes nothing as absolute and which only leaves the "I" and its whims as the ultimate measure. – Cardinal Joseph Ratzinger, *Homily at Mass for the Election of the Roman Pontiff*, April 18, 2005.

The Enlightenment

THE POINT of this chapter is not to survey American relativism. It is to offer the Magisterium's answer to the question: Does a relativist culture, which has no standard of right and wrong, tend to produce freedom or tyranny?

Fr. Francis Canavan, S.J., aptly described modern American culture as "the fag end of the Enlightenment,"[1] the project of philosophers and politicians, over the past three centuries and more, to build a society as if God did not exist. Relativism is only one aspect of the Enlightenment culture. "The fundamental dogma of the Enlightenment," wrote Cardinal Ratzinger, now Pope Benedict XVI, "is that man must overcome the prejudices inherited from tradition; he must . . . free himself from every authority in order to think on his own, using nothing but his own reason. . . . Truth is no longer an objective datum, apparent to . . . everyone. . . . It . . . becomes something merely external, which each one grasps from his own point of view, without ever knowing to what extent his viewpoint corresponds to the object in itself or with what others perceive. The same truth about the good becomes unattainable. . . . The only reference point for each person is what he can conceive on his own as good. Consequently, freedom is no longer seen positively as a striving for the good which reason uncovers with help from the community and tradition, but is rather defined as an emancipation from all conditions which prevent each one from following his own reason."[2]

The premises of the Enlightenment may be described as:

* **Secularism.** There is no God, or if there is, he doesn't care about us;
* **Relativism.** Reason cannot know objective moral truth. (Relativism is absurd in its own terms. If the statement, "All things are relative," is true, then that statement must be relative.); and
* **Individualism.** The human person is an isolated individual who is his own moral arbiter and who has relation to others only if he so chooses.[3]

Legal Positivism

In fact, reason can know reality, including moral truth and objective good.[4] The jurisprudence of a relativist culture, however, will be some form of legal positivism, which recognizes a law enacted by the prescribed procedures as valid regardless of its content. Hans Kelsen, probably the leading legal positivist of the 20th century, provides a useful example. He rejected what he called "philosophical absolutism," the view that there is "an absolute reality, i.e., a reality that exists independently of human knowledge." He thought that philosophical absolutism leads to "political absolutism," or tyranny, because the rulers, who claim they can know reality, including what is right and wrong, will impose on the people what the rulers "know" to be for the people's good. Instead, Kelsen adopted "philosophical relativism," the "empirical doctrine that reality exists only within human knowledge, and that, as the object of knowledge, reality is relative to the knowing subject. The absolute, the thing in itself, is beyond human experience; it is inaccessible to human knowledge and therefore unknowable."

Kelsen thought "philosophical relativism" leads to democracy and tolerance, because "what is right today may be wrong tomorrow," and the minority "must have the full opportunity of becoming the majority. Only if it is not possible to decide in an absolute way what is right and what is wrong is it advisable to discuss the issue and, after discussion, to submit to

a compromise." For Kelsen, a law is valid and binding if "it has been con-
stituted in a particular fashion, born of a definite procedure and a definite
rule." There is no higher law of nature or of God, and the positive law cannot be criticized as unjust. According to Kelsen, justice "is not ascertaina-
ble by rational knowledge at all. Rather, from the standpoint of rational
knowledge there are only interests and conflicts of interests. . . . Justice is
an irrational ideal."[5]

Kelsen applied his theory consistently. He said, "The legal order of
totalitarian states authorizes their governments to confine in concentration
camps persons whose opinions, religion, or race they do not like; to force
them to perform any kind of labor, even to kill them. Such measures may
be morally or violently condemned; but they cannot be considered as taking place outside the legal order of those states."[6] St. Thomas Aquinas
taught, in contrast, that if a human law "deflects from the law of nature" it
is unjust and "is no longer a law but a perversion of law."[7] Kelsen, understandably, dismissed Aquinas as "one of the classical examples [of the]
coincidence of philosophical and political absolutism."[8]

"Hans Kelsen," wrote Cardinal Ratzinger, "was expressing the
spirit of our age when he represented the question of Pilate, 'What is
truth?' as . . . the sole appropriate attitude for determining the structure of
society within the state. . . . Truth is replaced by the decision of the majority, he says, precisely because there can be no truth, in the sense of a binding and generally accessible entity for man. Thus the multiplicity of cultures serves to demonstrate the relativism of all cultures. Culture is set
against truth. This relativism, which is . . . a basic attitude of enlightened
people . . . is the most profound difficulty of our age. This is also the reason why practice is now substituted for truth . . . we do not know what is
true, but we do know what we should do: raise up . . . a better society, the
'kingdom,' as people like to say, using a term from the Bible and applied
to the profane and utopian sphere."[9]

Crises of Law

That comment from Cardinal Ratzinger relates to his address on
"Crises of Law" which we noted in Chapter 11 with respect to Governor
Cuomo's reliance on "consensus." The "end of metaphysics," which
includes the denial that reason can know moral truth, has led, in Ratzinger's
words, to "juridical positivism which today . . . has taken on the form of

the theory of consensus. . . . The majority determines what [is] true and just. . . . [L]aw is exposed to the whim of the majority. . . . This is manifested . . . by the . . . disappearance . . . of law inspired in the Christian tradition. Matrimony and family are . . . substituted by . . . problematic forms of living together. The relation between man and woman becomes conflictive, as does the relation between generations. . . . The sense of the sacred no longer has any meaning for law; respect for God and for that which is sacred to others is . . . displaced by . . . a limitless liberty in speech and judgment. Even human life . . . can be disposed of: abortion and euthanasia are no longer excluded. . . . [M]anipulation of human life [is] manifested in . . . embryo experimentation and transplants, in which man arrogates to himself not only the ability to dispose of life and death, but also of his being and of his development. . . . going so far as . . . selection and breeding for . . . development of the human species, and the essential difference between man and animal is up for debate." The second crisis of law identified by Cardinal Ratzinger is the "spirit of utopia," seen in Marxism and terrorism, in which the standard is "not the consensus of contemporaries, but . . . the ideal model of the future world."[10]

Pope Benedict has noted also the damaging effect on international relations of "a relativistic logic which would consider as the sole guarantee of peaceful coexistence . . . a refusal to admit the truth about man and his dignity [and] the possibility of an ethics based on . . . the natural moral law. This has led . . . to . . . a notion . . . which . . . makes consensus between States – a consensus conditioned at times by short-term interests or manipulated by ideological pressure – the only real basis of international norms. The bitter fruits of this relativistic logic are sadly evident: . . . the attempt to consider as human rights . . . certain self-centered lifestyles: a lack of concern for the economic and social needs of the poorer nations; contempt for humanitarian law, and a selective defense of human rights."[11]

The Remedy

The Magisterium offers the remedy for the exaltation of either consensus or the spirit of utopia. Hans Kelsen claimed that relativism is the philosophy which supports democracy. If no one can know what is just, the tendency, he thought, will be to compromise in order to get along. Pope John Paul II denied that a relativist culture would lead to peaceful, democratic compromise. He saw relativism as the precursor of totalitarianism:

Only God, the Supreme Good, constitutes the unshakable foundation . . . of morality. . . . The Supreme Good and moral good meet in truth: the truth of God . . . and the truth of man, created and redeemed by him. Only upon this truth is it possible to construct a renewed society and to solve . . . the problem of overcoming the various forms of totalitarianism, so as to make way for the authentic freedom of the person. "Totalitarianism arises out of a denial of truth in the objective sense. If there is no transcendent truth, in obedience to which man achieves his full identity, then there is no sure principle for guaranteeing just relations between people. Their self-interest as a class, group or nation would inevitably set them in opposition to one another. If one does not acknowledge transcendent truth, then the force of power takes over, and each person tends to make full use of the means at his disposal in order to impose his own interests or his own opinion, with no regard for the rights of others. . . . Thus, the root of modern totalitarianism is to be found in the denial of the transcendent dignity of the human person who, as the visible image of the invisible God, is therefore by his very nature the subject of rights which no one may violate – no individual, group, class, nation or state. Not even the majority of a social body may violate these rights, by going against the minority, by isolating, oppressing, or exploiting it, or by attempting to annihilate it."[12]

John Paul's analysis is realistic. If no governing principles are acknowledged as true, political life is reduced to a conflict of competing interests with no commonly accepted truths on which reasoned compromise can be based. The solution will be found instead in force. Justice Oliver Wendell Holmes, the father of American Legal Realism, said law is not an ordinance of reason but merely "a statement of the circumstances in which the public force will be brought to bear upon men through the courts."[13] Holmes defined truth as "the majority vote of the nation that could lick all others."[14] For Holmes, "the sacredness of human life is a purely municipal ideal of no validity outside the jurisdiction. I believe that force, mitigated so far as may be by good manners, is the *ultima ratio*, and between two groups that want to make inconsistent kinds of world I see no remedy except force."[15] There are no moral limits to that conflict because no one can know objective truth and thus there is no common acknowl-edgement of what John Paul called the "dignity of the human person," who has "rights which no one may violate." "I see," said Holmes, "no reason for attributing to man a significant difference in kind from that which belongs to a baboon or a grain of sand."[16]

"[W]ithout the transcendent foundation which is God," Pope Benedict said, "society risks becoming a mere agglomeration of neighbors; it ceas-es to be a community of brothers and sisters, called to form one great fam-ily."[17] The conflict of interests in a relativist culture is all about power. It will be resolved, predictably, by the power of the state. "A community," said Benedict, "that is built without respect for the authentic dignity of the human being, without remembering that every person is created in the image of God, ends by doing no one any good."[18]

The Magisterium has something to offer the world, and Notre Dame, as we will discuss in the remaining chapters. According to the Notre Dame Mission Statement, "The University is dedicated to the pursuit and sharing of truth for its own sake." Unfortunately, Notre Dame's autonomy from the Magisterium opens the door to a relativist interpretation of that principle. How is the Mission Statement's "truth" to emerge and be shared? And by what standard do you recognize it? Who, in the University, decides what "truth" on a specific question is? The President? The Fellows? The Faculty Senate? We are talking about serious questions on which the Body of Christ, the Church, has enunciated the objective moral truth in definitive terms. When Notre Dame rejects obedience to the Magisterium, it sets a bad example to its own students: "If the University can be its own inter-preter of the moral law, so can I." The result is the encouragement of a miniature "dictatorship of relativism" on the campus and, more important, in the students' own future personal, family and professional lives. Notre Dame could benefit its students – and could positively influence American culture – by abandoning its false autonomy and accepting the role of the Magisterium in its interpretation of the moral law through the integration of faith and reason.

Only a jurisprudence founded on that integration and on the ultimate reality – God – can insist on the transcendent rights of the human person against the state. The human person has such rights because he is created in the image and likeness of God, with an immortal destiny that necessar-ily transcends the state. Every state, corporation, university, etc., that has ever existed, or ever will exist, has already gone out of existence or will go out of existence. Every human being who has ever been conceived will live forever. Where do you hear that kind of talk today? Principally, from the Magisterium of the Catholic Church.

Fr. James Schall, s.j., professor of political philosophy at Georgetown University, described "the Pope [as] the only universal voice in the world today. This is the uncanny genius of founding the Church on the Rock of Peter. What is most embarrassing to the world today is that the most intelligent voice it confronts, or deliberately refuses to confront, is that coming from the papacy. We can spend all sorts of time digging up scandals in the Church or things the papacy should have done but did not. What we cannot do is read the basic documents of the Church, particularly those of recent popes, and claim that they do not strike at the very roots of all that is disordered in all of the public order of the world, not just the West, but Islam, China, India and the rest."[19]

Here again: What if? What if Notre Dame, instead of abasing itself by promoting *The Last Temptation of Christ*, *The Vagina Monologues*, the Cuomo Address, etc., had stood firmly with the Church over the past four decades? Would not Notre Dame students and alumni, as well as the nation, benefit from that more than they do from a Notre Dame which merits the applause of the AAUP by its "creative contextualization" of moral issues?

14

The Magisterium
Protector of Conscience and Freedom

> Certainly, if I am obliged to bring religion into after-din-
> ner toasts (which indeed does not seem quite the thing) I
> shall drink – to the Pope, if you please, – still, to con-
> science first and to the Pope afterwards. – Cardinal John
> Henry Newman, *Letter to the Duke of Norfolk*

LET'S TAKE a pop quiz: Would Benedict XVI agree with Newman that conscience comes first and the Pope afterwards? The answer, perhaps to your surprise, is: Yes. "[T]he toast to conscience indeed must precede the toast to the Pope," said Cardinal Ratzinger to the United States bishops in 1991, "because without conscience there would not be a papacy." The Magisterium is a protector not only of conscience but also of freedom. Hard to believe?

M.Y.O.B.

Let's stop right there. For most products of American education today, "conscience" means their right to make whatever decision they want as to what they are going to do. It is a decision, a product of the will. And it cannot be wrong, except in pragmatic terms upon later evaluation of its consequences. If the Pope tries to tell them that some things – like killing unborn babies – are always wrong and should never be done, the response is "M.Y.O.B." – Mind Your Own Business. Conscience has no relation to objective truth because there is no such thing. It is my power to decide. Period. Paragraph. Next case.

This concept of conscience fits neatly with the "Mystery Passage" of *Planned Parenthood v. Casey*, where the Supreme Court reaffirmed the holding of *Roe v. Wade* and said: "At the heart of liberty is the right to define one's own concept of existence, of meaning, of the universe, and of the mystery of human life."[1] If that is your idea of liberty and conscience – an unlimited power of decision over everything, including existence, the universe and "the mystery of human life," you might want to stop reading here. A different concept of conscience, however, has been around for a few thousand years.

What Is Conscience?

"Conscience is a judgment of reason whereby the human person recognizes the moral quality of a concrete act that he is going to perform, is . . . performing . . . or has . . . completed."[2] Our judgment of conscience may be wrong. Whether we are culpable for that error will depend on whether we have fulfilled three duties to conscience:

1. Form that judgment, just as you would form any other judgment, such as what car to buy, etc. The first duty, in forming that judgment, is to consult the directions given to us by God through the natural law, the Ten Commandments (which are specifications of the natural law) and the teachings of the Church. The Magisterium is the authoritative interpreter of the law of God, including the natural law and the Commandments. Those standards require interpretation. Without such an acknowledged interpreter, each of us would be on his or her own, with no objective and certain criterion. The result, as John Paul II made clear, would be relativism and a conflict of interests resolved in favor of the most powerful.
2. Follow the judgment of your conscience if it is clear and certain. If your judgment is objectively wrong, you may be culpable for failing to form it properly.
3. If in doubt, try to resolve the doubt. If the doubt persists, for example, as to whether it is right to claim that item on your expense report, don't claim it. Take the safer course.[3]

Anamnesis

Cardinal Joseph Ratzinger addressed the bishops of the United States on "Conscience and Truth" in February 1991 in Dallas. He endorsed Newman's toast, which put conscience first and then the Pope, because

Newman saw the papacy as "not put in opposition to the primacy of conscience but based on it and guaranteeing it." To appreciate Ratzinger's analysis, let's go back a few years. By Adam's original sin, the human nature of his descendants "is wounded . . . subject to ignorance, suffering and . . . death; and inclined to sin – an inclination to evil that is called 'concupiscence.'"[4] The Ten Commandments were given by God so man could "attain a complete and certain understanding of the requirements of the natural law." "[S]inful humanity needed this revelation. . . . Because the light of reason was obscured and the will had gone astray."[5]

So how do we figure out whether our particular action is right or wrong? What Ratzinger calls "the first . . . ontological level" of conscience "consists in the fact that something like an original memory of the good and true (both are identical) has been implanted in us. . . . This anamnesis [recollection]. . . . is not a conceptually articulated knowing, a store of retrievable contents. It is . . . an inner sense, a capacity to recall, so that the one whom it addresses, if he is not turned in on himself, hears its echo from within. He sees: 'That's it! That is what my nature points to and seeks.'

"The . . . right to 'mission' rests on this anamnesis of the creator. . . . The Gospel . . . must be proclaimed to the pagans because they themselves are yearning for it in the hidden recesses of their souls. . . . Mission is vindicated then when those addressed recognize in the encounter with . . . the Gospel that this indeed is what they have been waiting for. . . . The love of God which is concrete in the commandments, is not imposed on us from without. . . . but has been implanted in us beforehand. The sense for the good has been stamped upon us."

Conscience and the Pope

"We can now appreciate," Ratzinger continued, "Newman's toast first to conscience and then to the Pope. The Pope cannot impose commandments on . . . Catholics because he . . . finds it expedient. Such a modern, voluntaristic concept of authority can only distort the true theological meaning of the papacy. The true nature of the Petrine office has become so incomprehensible . . . because we only think of authority in terms which do not allow for bridges between subject and object. . . . [E]verything which does not come from the subject is thought to be externally imposed. But the situation is . . . different [with] conscience. . . . The anamnesis instilled in our being needs . . . assistance from without so that it can become aware of itself. But this 'from without' . . . imposes nothing foreign, but brings to fruition what is proper to anamnesis . . . its interior openness to the truth. . . . [T]his teaching authority of the Pope consists in his being the advocate of the Christian memory. The Pope does not impose it from without. Rather, he elucidates the Christian memory and defends it. For this reason, the toast to conscience indeed must precede the toast to the Pope because without conscience there would not be a papacy. All power that the papacy has is power of conscience. It is service to the . . . memory upon which the faith is based . . . which . . . must be . . . defended against . . . a subjectivity forgetful of its own foundation as well as the pressures of social and cultural conformity."[6]

Everyone has a pope, a visible authority on moral questions. If it is not the real Pope, it will be a pope of the individual's own choosing – whether Rush Limbaugh, Bill Clinton, or the individual himself. It makes sense that we have one Pope instead of 7 billion, which would involve the natural law and its Lawgiver in a chaos of contradictions. "Christians have a great help for the formation of conscience *in the Church and her Magisterium*," said John Paul II. "In forming their consciences," John Paul continued, "the Christian faithful must give careful attention to the . . . teaching of the Church. For the Catholic Church is by the will of Christ the teacher of truth. Her charge is to . . . teach . . . that truth which is Christ, and at the same time with her authority to declare and confirm the principles of the moral order which derive from human nature itself."[7] Here again, Notre Dame becomes relevant. Instead of isolating itself by declaring its autonomy from this positive service of the Magisterium, Notre Dame would better serve its students by its own example of accepting that service on its own helpful terms as the teaching of "that truth which is Christ."

Judgment and Decision

The second level of conscience is the act of judgment and decision. Cardinal Ratzinger emphasized the duty to form the judgment of conscience. "It is never wrong to follow the convictions one has arrived at – in fact, one must do so. But it can . . . be wrong to have come to such askew convictions in the first place, by having stifled the protest of the anamnesis of being. The guilt lies then in a different place, much deeper – not in the present act, not in the present judgment of conscience but in the neglect of my being which made me deaf to the internal promptings of truth."[8]

Freedom

Pope John Paul II, in *Veritatis Splendor*, built upon this analysis. "In *the practical judgment of conscience,* which imposes on the person the obligation to perform a given act, *the link between freedom and truth is . . . manifest. . . .* [C]onscience expresses itself in acts of 'judgment' which reflect the truth about the good, and not in arbitrary 'decisions.'. . . [T]he authority of the Church . . . in no way undermines the freedom of conscience of Christians. This is so not only because freedom of conscience is never freedom 'from' the truth but always and only freedom 'in' the truth, but also because the Magisterium does not bring to the Christian conscience truths which are extraneous to it; rather it brings to light the truths which it ought to possess. . . . The Church puts herself . . . at the *service of conscience,* helping it to avoid being tossed to and fro by every wind of doctrine proposed by human deceit . . . and helping it not to swerve from the truth about the good of man, but rather . . . to attain the truth with certainty and to abide in it."[9]

As with conscience, freedom cannot be separated from objective truth. But what does that mean? The first, self-evident principle of the natural law is to seek good and avoid evil. The good is that which is in accord with the nature of the thing we are talking about. I am, in a strict sense, free to decide to put water instead of gasoline in the tank of my car. But if I put the water in, I will have violated the truth of the nature of my car. The nature of the car, built into it by its manufacturer, is that it runs on gasoline, not water, which is therefore not good for the car. When I put the water in, I am pro-choice. But I am also a pedestrian. I was "free" to put the water in, but now I am no longer free to drive my car.[10]

Similarly, I am "free" to decide to violate my own nature by violating my own maker's directions in the natural law and its specifications in the Commandments. For example, "the direct and voluntary killing of an innocent human being is always gravely immoral."[11] If I do that, I will have violated not only the truth and good of the victim, but my own as well. In short, when I violate my own good and the truth of my nature, I get all messed up.[12] "Pilate's question: 'What is truth' reflects the . . . perplexity of a man who . . . no longer knows *who* he is, *whence* he comes, and *where* he is going. Hence we not infrequently witness the . . . plunging of the human person into . . . gradual self-destruction. According to some . . . one no longer need acknowledge the . . . absoluteness of any moral value. All around us we encounter contempt for human life after conception and before birth; the ongoing violation of basic rights of the person; the unjust destruction of goods minimally necessary for a human life. Indeed, something more serious has happened: man is no longer convinced that only in the truth can he find salvation. The saving power of the truth is contested, and freedom alone . . . is left to decide by itself what is good and what is evil. This relativism becomes . . . a lack of trust in the wisdom of God, who guides man with the moral law."[13]

The deeper cause of such disorder relates to faith. "The attempt to set freedom in opposition to truth . . . is the consequence . . . of *another more serious and destructive dichotomy, that which separates faith from morality.* This separation represents one of the most acute pastoral concerns of the Church amid today's growing secularism, wherein many . . . people think and live as if God did not exist. . . . In a . . . dechristianized culture, the criteria employed by believers . . . in making judgments and decisions often appear . . . contrary to . . . the Gospel. . . . Christians should rediscover *the newness of the faith and its power to judge* a prevalent and all-intrusive culture. . . . It is urgent to rediscover . . . the . . . reality of the Christian faith, which is not simply a set of propositions to be accepted with intellectual assent. Rather, faith is a lived knowledge of Christ, a living remembrance of his commandments, and a *truth to be lived out.*"[14]

No Real Freedom Without God

Freedom is not merely an absence of restraint. Rather, "Jesus reveals by his whole life, and not only by his words, that freedom is acquired in *love,* that is, in the *gift of self.* . . . Contemplation of Jesus Crucified [shows] the full meaning of freedom: the gift of self in *service to God and one's brethren.*"[15] The bottom line, which the Magisterium offers for everyone whether Catholic or not, is that a society from which God is excluded is not a nice place to live. "[W]hen man eliminates God from his horizon, declares God really 'dead,' is he really happy? . . . When men proclaim themselves . . . the sole masters of creation, can they . . . build a society where freedom, justice and peace prevail? Does it not happen instead . . . that arbitrary power, selfish interests, injustice and exploitation and violence . . . are extended? In the end, man reaches the point of finding himself lonelier and society is more divided and bewildered."[16]

Why do we instinctively know that Benedict is right? In *Spe Salvi*, his second encyclical, which we discuss in Chapter 18, he tells us: "A world without God is a world without hope." The secular society can tell us nothing definite about what happens to us when we die. The "distinguishing mark" of Christians is "the fact that they have a future."[17] They don't know the details, but they know their life will not end in nothingness. Without that great hope, how can you really be free and happy here? If this life is all there is, you have to look out for yourself, for Number One. But so does everyone else. Life is a contest to see who ends up with the most power, money or toys. It tends to become a sort of Hobbesian state of nature where "there exist only lawless individuals, in whom is found no natural tendency to live in society; and man's life is 'solitary, poore, nasty, brutish and short.'"[18]

Our Creator, through his Church, offers not only the great hope but also, paradoxically, rules that guarantee freedom. Gilbert K. Chesterton gave us the classic illustration of why we should welcome the teachings of the Magisterium:

> Catholic doctrine and discipline may be walls; but they are the walls of a playground. Christianity is the only frame which has preserved the pleasure of Paganism. We might fancy some children playing on the flat grassy top of some tall island in the sea. So long as there was a wall round the cliff's edge they could fling themselves into every frantic game and make the place the noisiest of nurseries. But the walls were knocked down, leaving the naked peril of the precipice. They did not fall over; but when their friends returned to them they were all huddled in terror in the centre of the island; and their song had ceased.[19]

In his 1967 Advent Pastoral Letter, Archbishop John Murphy, of Cardiff, Wales, addressed "an unjustified fear" among some that if they follow the teaching of the Church they will have "lost their freedom, forgetting that by some glorious paradox, it is only in the bosom of the Church that they will find their freedom:

> It is the Church which fights for the unborn child, for the rights of parents to educate their children, for the dignity of the marriage contract, for the dignity of the individual being.

And in some secular humanistic future, when the only sin will be pain, the only evil ill health; when childbearing will be looked upon as a disease, and terminal illnesses will not be tolerated, when it is just possible that the free, human beings will be forbidden to have a child, or a smoke, or a drink, save by prescription of the National Health; in that cold, clinical future, you will search in vain for the rebels save in the ranks of the Catholic Church.[20]

15
God Is Love

> Being Christian is not the result of an ethical choice or a
> lofty idea, but the encounter with an event, a person, which
> gives life a new horizon and a decisive direction. – *Deus
> Caritas Est*, no. 1.

Four Encyclicals

IN CHAPTERS 12, 13 and 14 we discussed various ways in which the
Magisterium has upheld civil and personal freedom and the rights of conscience. In this and the following three chapters we examine four encyclicals, and related documents, that offer insights that could be of great benefit to Notre Dame and society in general. Those teachings are decisively
important because they emanate not from an academic committee or bull
session but, in the words of Fr. James Schall, s.J., from "the only universal
voice in the world today."[1] They deal with some pretty important topics,
including God, love, life, hope, justice and peace and economics, among
others. Notre Dame has impoverished itself and its students by distancing
itself from the Magisterium as an authoritative interpreter of the moral law.
The general community is similarly impoverished by its failure to recognize such an interpreter, a role which can be credibly undertaken only by
that "universal voice." Moreover, the insights offered by the Magisterium
make sense. They deserve acceptance on their merits and because of their
source. So let's look at four encyclicals in detail: *Deus Caritas Est*,
Humanae Vitae, *Caritas in Veritate* and *Spe Salvi*.

A Twofold Commandment

Deus Caritas Est (God Is Love) (DCE), signed in 2005 on the first
Christmas Day of his pontificate, packs a lot of instruction into 25 readable

pages. Part I analyzes human and divine love in terms of eros and agape. Addressed to "a world where the name of God is sometimes associated with vengeance or even a duty of hatred and violence," DCE tells that world of "the love which God lavishes upon us and which we in turn must share with others."[2] That love has many implications, including the fact that "Marriage based on exclusive and definitive love becomes the icon of the relationship between God and his people and vice versa."[3] DCE is also loaded with cultural, political and legal implications, arising from its assertion that "[l]ove of God and love of neighbor" are "inseparable."[4] We are commanded to love both God and neighbor. "Love can be 'commanded' because it has first been given."[5] "God loved us first . . . and this love of God has appeared in our midst" in Jesus.[6] Love of neighbor proceeds from "the love of God who has loved us first. "It is not a 'commandment' imposed from without and calling for the impossible, but rather . . . a freely-bestowed experience of love from within, a love which by its very nature must then be shared with others."[7] In the parable of the Good Samaritan,[8] we see that "[a]nyone who needs me, and whom I can help, is my neighbor."[9]

Caritas

Part II of DCE, on "Caritas," gets down to the practicalities of love of neighbor, which seeks the "integral good of man."[10] That good includes the material as well as the spiritual. While love of neighbor is a duty of the Church, it is "first and foremost a responsibility for each . . . member of the faithful."[11]

Caritas, or "Christian charity," is "first of all the . . . response to immediate needs . . . feeding the hungry, clothing the naked, caring for . . . the sick, visiting those in prison, etc."[12] But people "need . . . more than technically proper care. . . . They need heartfelt concern." [13] Charity therefore cannot be "just another form of social assistance."[14] Nor is it "proselytism," using aid to induce conversions. "Love is free; it is not practiced as a way of achieving other ends."[15] Charity, therefore, must not be at the service of "parties, ideologies" or "worldly strategems."[16]

Benedict responds to the Marxist claim that the poor "do not need charity but justice."[17] Charity, they claim, serves injustice by making an "unjust system . . . appear . . . tolerable" and thus blocking "the struggle for a better world." Benedict rejects that approach as "an inhuman philosophy," sacrificing people of the present to "the moloch of the future. . . . One does not make the world more human by refusing to act humanely here and now. We contribute to a better world only by personally doing good now."[18]

Justice and the State

But what about justice? Doesn't the Church care about it? Yes, it does. But the "just ordering" of society and the State is the role of "politics" and not of the Church.[19] The "direct duty" to work for a just society belongs to the "lay faithful" rather than to the Church itself.[20] "Fundamental to Christianity," says DCE, "is the distinction between Church and State."[21] The Church should not be in politics, but it does have an educative role:

> Justice is . . . the aim and . . . criterion of all politics. . . . But what is justice? The problem is one of practical reason; but . . . reason . . . must undergo constant purification, since it can never be completely free of the danger of . . . ethical blindness caused by the dazzling effect of power and special interests.
> Here politics and faith meet. Faith . . . is an encounter with the living God. . . . But it is also a purifying force for reason itself. . . . [F]aith liberates reason from its blind spots and therefore helps it to be . . . fully itself. . . . This is where Catholic social doctrine has its place: it has no intention of giving the Church power over the State. Even less is it an attempt to impose on those who do not share the faith ways of thinking and modes of conduct proper to faith. Its aim is simply to help purify reason and to contribute . . . to the acknowledgement and attainment of what is just.[22]

DCE traces Cathlic social teaching from Leo XIII's *Rerum Novarum* in 1891 through John Paul II.[23] That teaching offers guidelines that are valid for everyone and not just for Catholics. It argues "on the basis of reason and natural law" so as "to help form consciences in political life" and to "reawaken the spiritual energy" needed for justice to prevail. [24] *Caritas in Veritate,* the newest expression of that social teaching, is analyzed in Chapter 17.

Civil justice, however, is not enough. "Love – caritas – will always prove necessary even in the most just society."[25] The claim that "just social structures would make works of charity superfluous," says DCE, "masks a materialist conception . . . that man can live 'by bread alone.'"[26] No "ordering of the State" can be "so just that it can eliminate the need for a service of love."[27] "The State which would provide everything, absorbing everything into itself, would . . . become a mere bureaucracy, incapable of guaranteeing the very thing which . . . every person . . . needs . . . loving personal concern. We do not need a State which regulates and controls everything."[28] DCE urges the State to follow "the principle of subsidiarity" by supporting efforts of "social forces." The Church, as one of those "forces," "does not simply offer people material help, but . . . care for their souls, which often is . . . more necessary than material support."[29]

Religious Freedom

DCE encourages "cooperation" between State and Church agencies but insists that the State "must guarantee religious freedom."[30] Three days before he signed DCE, Benedict addressed the Curia on the teaching of Vatican II that religious freedom is required because "the human person is capable of knowing the truth about God" and because such truth "cannot be externally imposed" and "can only be claimed with God's grace in freedom of conscience."[31]

A recurrent theme of Benedict's papacy is his criticism of the "dictatorship of relativism." DCE continues this theme in its insistence on religious freedom to enable the Church to act as a moral educator, a role that rests on the reality that the truth about God and morality is objective and knowable.

Not Suggestions

DCE has a special relevance to Notre Dame and to the admirable service projects in which Notre Dame students engage. It articulates the context that can raise such projects far beyond the mere provision of material aid. "Practical activity," DCE tells us, "will always be insufficient unless it validly expresses a love for man." That love is "nourished by an encounter with Christ. My . . . sharing in the needs . . . of others becomes a sharing of my very self with them. . . . I must give to others not only something that is my own, but my very self; I must be personally present in my gift."[32] Those service efforts of Notre Dame students exemplify love of neighbor which is "inseparable" from love of God. Regrettably, Notre Dame is missing something when its autonomy from the authoritative role of the Magisterium implies to students that for them, too, Church teachings like DCE are optional. Love of God and love of neighbor become merely suggestions. Instead, they form in reality "a single commandment,"[33] the observance of which can lead an "encounter with . . . a person" that "gives life a new horizon and a decisive direction."[34]

16
Of Human Life

> In destroying the power of giving life through contraception
> a husband or wife is doing something to self. This turns the
> attention to self and so destroys the gift of love in him or her.
> . . . Once that living love is destroyed by contraception, abor-
> tion follows very easily. . . . We cannot solve all the prob-
> lems in the world, but let us never bring in the worst prob-
> lem of all, and that is to destroy love. And this is what hap-
> pens when we tell people to practice contraception and abor-
> tion. – Mother Teresa of Calcutta at the 1994 National Prayer
> Breakfast[1]

UNTIL 1930, no Christian denomination had ever said that contraception could ever be morally right. The Anglican Lambeth Conference of
1930 declared that "in those cases where there is . . . a clearly felt moral
obligation to limit or avoid parenthood, and where there is a morally sound
reason for avoiding complete abstinence, the Conference agrees that other
methods may be used, provided that this is done in the light of the same
Christian principles."[2]

Pope Pius XI responded in 1931 with his encyclical, *Casti Connubii*
(Of Chaste Marriage), reaffirming the traditional Christian position. That
position is not a privately Catholic thing, as seen in the *Washington Post*'s
editorial response to the Federal Council of Churches' endorsement of
Lambeth:

> It is impossible to reconcile the doctrine of the divine insti-
> tution of marriage with any modernistic plan for the
> mechanical regulation or suppression of human birth. The
> church must either reject the plain teachings of the Bible or

reject schemes for the "scientific" production of human
souls. Carried to its logical conclusion, the committee's
report . . . would sound the death-knell of marriage as a holy
institution, by establishing degrading practices which would
encourage indiscriminate immorality. The suggestion that
the use of legalized contraceptives would be "careful and
restrained" is preposterous.[3]

Why Is Contraception Wrong?

Francis Fukayama called the introduction of the contraceptive pill in
the 1960s "the Great Disruption in relations between men and women."[4]
Pope Paul VI initiated a study in the 1960s of the possible impact of the
new technology. As described in Chapter 6, Notre Dame, through its
President, Fr. Hesburgh, cooperated with the Rockefeller Foundation,
Planned Parenthood and other entities in lobbying for a change in the
Church teaching on contraception. Paul VI issued *Humanae Vitae*, reaffirming the traditional position, in 1968. Papal teachings reject contracep-
tion for three reasons:[5]

1. *Contraception deliberately separates the unitive and procreative
   aspects of sex. Humanae Vitae* stated that "each and every marriage act
   . . . must remain open to the transmission of life."[6] "That teaching," it
   continued, "is founded upon the inseparable connection, willed by
   God and unable to be broken by man on his own initiative, between the
   two meanings of the conjugal act: the unitive meaning and the procreative meaning."[7] The encyclical excluded, as a "licit means of regulat-
   ing birth. . . . Every action which, either in anticipation of the conjugal act, or in its accomplishment, or in the development of its natural
   consequences, proposes, whether as an end or as a means, to render
   procreation impossible."[8]

2. *Contraception asserts that man (of both sexes), rather than God, is the
   arbiter of whether and when human life shall begin.* "[T]hrough contraception, married couples . . . claim a power which belongs solely to
   God: the power to decide, in *a final analysis*, the coming into existence
   of a human person. They assume the qualification not of being coop-
   erators in God's creative power, but the ultimate depositaries of the

source of human life. . . .[C]ontraception is . . . so profoundly unlawful as never to be, for any reason, justified. To think or to say the contrary is equal to maintaining that in human life situations may arise – in which it is lawful not to recognize God as God."[9] Contraception also accepts the premise that there is such a thing as a human life not worth living, including specifically the child that might result from that act if contraception had not been used.

3. *Contraception prevents the total mutual self-donation which ought to characterize the conjugal act.* "Contraception," said Denver Archbishop Charles Chaput in his 1998 *Pastoral Letter on Humanae Vitae*, "not only . . . attacks procreation . . . it necessarily damages unity as well. It is the equivalent of spouses saying: 'I'll give you all I am – except my fertility; I'll accept all you are – except your fertility.' This withholding of self inevitably works to isolate and divide the spouses, and unravel the holy friendship between them . . . maybe not immediately and overtly, but deeply, and in the long run often fatally for the marriage."[10] On the difference between contraception and natural birth regulation, or NFP (natural family planning), which can be moral when used for "serious reasons," John Paul II said, "[Natural birth regulation and contraception involve] two irreconcilable concepts of the human person and of human sexuality. The choice of the natural rhythms involves accepting the cycle of . . . the woman, and thereby accepting dialogue, reciprocal respect, shared responsibility, and self-control. To accept the cycle and to enter into dialogue means to recognize both the spiritual and corporal character of conjugal communion and to live personal love with its requirement of fidelity."[11]

Consequences

The practically universal acceptance of contraception contributes to other evils:

Abortion, euthanasia, and suicide. If, through contraception, I make myself the arbiter of whether and when life begins, I will predictably make myself the arbiter of when life shall end, through abortion, euthanasia or suicide. Abortion is a fail-safe backup for contraception. Pope John Paul described abortion and contraception as "fruits of the same tree." "[T]he pro-abortion culture," he said, "is especially strong . . . where the Church's teaching on contraception is rejected. . . . The close connection . . . in mentality, between . . . contraception and . . . abortion is . . . demonstrated . . . by the development of . . . products . . . which, distributed with the same ease as contraceptives, really act as abortifacients in the very early stages of . . . the life of the new human being."[12] The "morning after pill," marketed as an "emergency contraceptive," operates as an abortifacient and is now available over-the-counter without a prescription.[13]

The declining ratio of working-age people to the elderly, which is a world-wide result of contraception and abortion, creates economic pressure for euthanasia of the elderly, the disabled and other nonproductive people whose lives might not be worth continuing in light of the rising cost of health care.[14] The apparent intention of the Obama administration to ration health care is discussed in Chapter 1.

"We are witnessing on a planetary level, and in the developed countries in particular," said Pope Benedict, "two . . . interconnected trends . . . an increase in life expectancy, and . . . a decrease in birth rates. As societies are growing older, many nations . . . lack a sufficient number of young people to renew their population. This situation is the result of multiple . . . causes. . . . But its ultimate roots [are] moral and spiritual; they are linked to a disturbing deficit of faith, hope, and, indeed, love. To bring children into the world calls for . . . generosity . . . trust and hope in the future. . . . Perhaps the lack of such creative and forward-looking love is the reason why many couples today choose not to marry, why so many marriages fail, and why birth rates have significantly diminished."[15]

Homosexual activity. The contraceptive society cannot consistently deny the legitimacy of homosexual activity. If it is entirely man's decision whether sex will have any relation to reproduction, the objections to allowing two men or two women to marry each other are reduced to the aesthetic and arbitrary. Pastor Donald Sensing, of Trinity United Methodist Church in Franklin, Tennessee, injected a note of realism, that the general acceptance of the Pill made same-sex marriage inevitable:

> Opponents of legalized same-sex marriage say they're trying
> to protect a beleaguered institution, but they're a little late.
> The walls of traditional marriage were breached 40 years

ago; what we are witnessing now is the storming of the last bastion. . . . Sex, childbearing and marriage now have no necessary connection to one another, because the biological connection between sex and childbearing is controllable. The fundamental basis for marriage has thus been technologically obviated. . . . There's little left to save.[16]

Pornography and the lowering of the dignity of women (and children). In pornography, the woman is treated, not as a person, but as a sex object. With child pornography, children are targeted victims. *Humanae Vitae* warned that the acceptance of contraception would mean that "man, growing used to employment of anti-conceptive practices, may finally lose respect for the woman and . . . may come to the point of considering her as a mere instrument of selfish enjoyment, and no longer as his respected and beloved companion."[17] The accuracy of that prediction can be verified even on prime-time TV. [18] When *Humanae Vitae* made that prediction, the theologians of The Church of Where It's At, perhaps even at Notre Dame, laughed at Pope Paul. But now that the objectification of women is obvious, nobody is laughing any more.

Extra-marital sex and divorce. In the natural order of things, one reason why sex is reserved for marriage, and why marriage is permanent, is that sex has something to do with babies. But if it is entirely up to me to decide whether or not sex will have anything to do with babies, why should I be obliged to reserve sex for marriage? And why should marriage be permanent? Why marry at all? Why not just cohabit? "Since the 1960s, the easy availability of reliable contraception has helped to spur a revolution in sexual mores. . . . As the sexual revolution gathered steam, the idea that a nuclear family was the only acceptable environment in which to raise a child crumbled."[19]

In Vitro Fertilization (IVF) and Cloning. IVF is the flip side of contraception, taking the procreative without the unitive. We discussed these techniques and embryonic stem cell research (ESCR) in Chapter 1. It is futile to try to put the brakes on IVF, human cloning, or ESCR, as on abortion or euthanasia, without restoring the conviction that God, and not man, is the arbiter of when and how life begins and ends. This requires a reassessment and rejection of contraception.

Not Just a Catholic Issue

The Catholic Church has stood virtually alone in defense of what, until 1930, was the universal Christian position. In recent years, however, significant Protestant and Evangelical criticism of contraception has emerged. "The effective separation of sex from procreation," said R. Albert Mohler, Jr., president of the Southern Baptist Theological Seminary, "may be one of the most important defining marks of our age – and one of the most ominous. This awareness is spreading among American evangelicals and it threatens to set loose a firestorm. . . . A growing number of evangelicals are rethinking the issue of birth control – and facing the hard questions posed by reproductive technologies."[20] "At first," noted Allan Carlson, "pro-life Evangelicalism avoided the issue of contraception. However, over time, it has become ever more difficult for many to draw an absolute line between contraception and abortion, because – whatever theological distinctions they made between the two – the 'contraceptive mentality' embraces both, and some forms of 'contraception' are in practice abortifacients."[21]

Contraception is still the unmentionable issue. If you are pro-life you can mention your opposition to abortion and euthanasia without totally ostracizing yourself. But if you avow your opposition to contraception you will have certified yourself as not only politically incorrect but, worse still, a traditionalist. Abortion has been described as the sacrament of the Culture of Death. Not quite. Contraception, to borrow the Catholic phrase, is the "sacrament of initiation" of the Culture of Death. Once you have signed on for contraception, your trajectory is set. You may disagree on details, but predictably you will support the entire anti-life agenda.

While the Magisterium, practically alone, has been upholding the positive, hopeful Catholic teaching on marriage and the transmission of life, Notre Dame has been, at best, on the sidelines. Teaching moments have come and gone, unused. On November 21, 1977, Fr. Hesburgh told an audience of over 300 biology students that various types of contraception present "'a very difficult problem of conflicting judgments.' While stressing his 'abhorrence' to sterilization and abortion, Hesburgh left the listeners free to decide what their position should be on other methods. 'It's a question in my mind of following your own conscience in this matter,' he said."[22] That was nine years after *Humanae Vitae*. The students were entitled to a better analysis. If a student concluded in his conscience that contraception was morally permissible, that judgment of his conscience was incorrectly formed and was wrong. As discussed in Chapter 14, you are obliged to act on a clear conscience but you may be culpable for failing to form it correctly. Students and others are entitled to be fully informed on that point, rather than to be told, in effect, that they have a free pass to go either way on contraception.

It is fair to ask again: What if???? What if Notre Dame had joined the fight on the side of the teaching Church on this decisive issue? In this area, the Magisterium has stood up for the dignity of the person, the integrity of marriage and the family and, most important, the absolute inviolability of innocent life. It is long past time for Notre Dame to join totally in that fight.

17
Love in Truth

POPE BENEDICT'S third encyclical, *Caritas in Veritate* (Love in Truth), signed on the feast of Saints Peter and Paul, June 29, 2009, complements the themes of his first two, *Deus Caritas Est* and *Spe Salvi*, that God is love and that only in God do we have real hope.

Catholic Social Teaching

Before looking at *Caritas in Veritate* (CIV) itself, it will be helpful to explain what Catholic social teaching is. First, we distinguish "evangelization, Catholic social teaching, and policy statements."[1] Evangelization is bearing witness to Christ and the Gospel.[2] Catholic social teaching, based on "scripture, tradition, and reason,"[3] offers principles to guide the formation of a sound political, economic, and social order.[4]

CIV describes "the missionary aspect of the Church's social doctrine [as] an essential element of evangelization. The Church's social doctrine . . . bears witness to faith. It is an instrument and an indispensable setting for formation in faith."[5]

Policy statements, such as an endorsement by the American bishops of a debatable housing or welfare bill, apply the social teachings to particular problems. But those policy statements are prudential judgments rather than binding moral teachings. Bishops "have no greater insight into policy matters than anyone else."[6]

CIV is a development of previous social teachings dating back to Leo XIII's *Rerum Novarum* in 1891. "The permanent principles of the Church's social doctrine [are] the dignity of the human person . . . the common good, subsidiarity; and solidarity."[7] "[T]he human person . . . is . . . the principle, the subject and the end of all social institutions."[8] "[T]he foundation on which all human rights rest is the dignity of the person."[9] That dignity flows from man's creation with an immortal destiny which transcends the state. Because man is created in the image of God, relation to others is intrinsic to his person as it is to the Persons of the Trinity. From this it follows that the civil order should foster solidarity among persons rather than isolated individualism. "Solidarity is thus the fruit of the communion which is grounded in the mystery of the triune God, and in the Son of God who took flesh and died for all."[10]

As a person with an eternal destiny, man cannot find his fulfillment in the state. The principle of subsidiarity denies the claim of the state to total competence:

> Just as it is wrong to withdraw from the individual and commit to the community at large what private enterprise and industry can accomplish, so too, it is an injustice, a grave evil, and a disturbance of right order for a larger and higher organization to arrogate to itself functions which can be performed efficiently by smaller and lower bodies. This is a fundamental principle of social philosophy, unshaken and unchangeable, and it retains its full truth today. . . . The true aim of all social activity should be to help individual members of the social body, but never to destroy or absorb them.[11]

"*The principle of subsidiarity,*" says CIV, "*must remain closely linked to the principle of solidarity and vice versa,* since the former without the latter gives way to social privatism, while the latter without the former gives way to a paternalist social assistance that is demeaning to those in need."[12] The purpose of civil society and of human law is to promote the common good, which is "the sum total of social conditions which allow people, either as groups or as individuals, to reach their fulfillment more fully and more easily."[13]

Scope of This Chapter

We will not attempt here to summarize CIV, which discusses many issues. We will note, instead, some elements of CIV which have an immediate and striking relation to the issues of life, bioethics, personal responsibility and truth raised by Notre Dame's honoring of President Obama.

Truth, Love and Life

CIV revisits and applies Pope Paul VI's teaching on "integral human development," which is spiritual as well as material, in his 1967 social encyclical, *Populorum Progressio*.[14] Integral human development requires "*fidelity to the truth, which alone is the guarantee of freedom.*"[15] CIV's opening words set the tone: "Charity in truth, to which Jesus Christ bore witness in his earthly life . . . is the . . . driving force behind the . . . development of every person and of all humanity. . . . [I]t is the principle not only of micro-relationships (with friends, with family members or within small groups) but also of macro-relationships (social, economic and political ones)."[16]

"Truth and the love which it reveals" are not human creations. They "can only be received as a gift [from] God, who is himself Truth and Love."[17] It is a two-way street. "Charity is love received and given. It is grace (*cháris*). . . . As the objects of God's love, men and women . . . are called to make themselves instruments of grace, so as to . . . weave networks of charity."[18]

CIV carries forward the emphasis by the Second Vatican Council and John Paul II that "man can fully discover his true self only in a sincere giving of himself."[19] "The full meaning of freedom," said John Paul, is "the gift of self in *service to God and one's brethren.*"[20] "*Charity in truth* places man before the astonishing experience of gift. Gratuitousness is present in our lives in many different forms, which often go unrecognized because of a . . . consumerist and utilitarian view of life. The human being is made for gift, which expresses and makes present his transcendent dimension."[21]

The Moral Law Applies to Everything

CIV stresses that all areas of life, including economics and politics, are subject to the moral law. "The conviction that man is self-sufficient and can . . . eliminate . . . evil . . . by his own action alone has led him to confuse happiness and salvation with . . . material prosperity and social action. . . . [T]he conviction that the economy must be autonomous, that it must be shielded from 'influences' of a moral character, has led man to abuse the economic process in a . . . destructive way."[22] Integral human development cannot be left up to the invisible hand of "automatic or impersonal forces, [derived] from the market or from international politics."[23] In other words, we need more than good theories. We need good people: "*Development is impossible without upright men and women, without financiers and politicians whose consciences are finely attuned to the requirements of the common good.*"[24] Achieving that uprightness is a matter of the spirit. "The human being develops when he grows in the spirit, when his soul comes to know itself and the truths that God has implanted deep within, when he enters into dialogue with himself and his Creator. When he is far away from God, man is unsettled and ill at ease."[25]

When Notre Dame rejects the authority of Church teaching, it conveys to students the impression that the moral principles in the social doctrine of the Church are optional. Those principles, instead, are mandatory. "*The economy needs ethics . . . to function correctly* – not any ethics whatsoever, but an ethics which is people-centered. . . .[T]he adjective 'ethical' can be abused. . . .[I]t can lend itself to . . . interpretations [including] choices contrary to justice and authentic human welfare. Much . . . depends on the underlying system of morality. . . . [T]he Church's social doctrine can make a . . . contribution since it is based on man's creation 'in the image of God' . . . which gives rise to the inviolable dignity of the human person and the transcendent value of natural moral norms. When business ethics prescinds from these two pillars . . . [i]t risks being used to justify the financing of projects that are . . . unethical."[26]

Notre Dame is a university that should be counted on to affirm, as an institution, that "life in Christ is the first and principal factor of development."[27] The principles of the natural law and the dignity of the person are not optional equipment for any graduate, no matter what field he enters. When managers ignore those principles, they tend to make a mess of things. "Economy and finance, as instruments, can be used badly when those at the helm are motivated by purely selfish ends. Instruments that are good . . . can thereby be transformed into harmful ones. But it is man's darkened reason that produces these consequences, not the instrument *per se*. [I]t is not the instrument that must be called to account, but individuals, their moral conscience and their personal and social responsibility. . . . [I]n *commercial relationships* the *principle of gratuitousness* and the logic of gift as an expression of fraternity can and must *find their place within normal economic activity.*"[28]

Inconsistency

A recurrent theme of CIV is the interconnection of moral issues, including a striking passage on the fallacy of promoting "environmental ecology" while neglecting "human ecology":

The Church. . . . must defend not only earth, water and air as gifts of creation that belong to everyone. She must above all protect mankind from self-destruction. There is need for . . . a human ecology, correctly understood. The deterioration of nature is . . . connected to the culture that shapes human coexistence: *when "human ecology" is respected . . . environmental ecology also benefits.* . . . [T]he *decisive issue is the . . . moral tenor of society.* If there is a lack of respect for the right to life and to a natural death, if human conception, gestation and birth are made artificial, if human embryos are sacrificed to research, the conscience of society ends up losing the concept of human ecology and, along with it, that of environmental ecology. It is contradictory to insist that future generations respect the natural environment when our educational systems and laws do not help them to respect themselves. The book of nature is one and indivisible: it takes in not only the environment but also life, sexuality, marriage, the family, social relations: in a word, integral human development. Our duties towards the environment are linked to our duties towards the human person. . . . It would be wrong to uphold one set of duties while trampling on the other. Herein lies *a grave contradiction* in our mentality and practice today: one which demeans the person, disrupts the environment and damages society."[29]

In his Commencement address, President Obama told the graduates, "Your generation must decide how to save God's creation from a changing climate that threatens to destroy it." He encouraged them "to seek new sources of energy that can save our planet."[30] The opposition to Notre Dame's honoring of President Obama was based on Obama's destructive positions on "human ecology." Obama's positions exemplify the "grave contradiction" identified by CIV in the passage quoted above.

Rights and Duties

A related problem is the overemphasis on rights and neglect of duties:

"[H]uman solidarity . . . imposes a duty." Many . . . claim that they owe nothing to anyone, except to themselves. They are concerned only with their rights, and [not] their own and other people's integral development. . . . *[R]ights presume duties, if they are not to become mere license. . . .* [W]e are witnessing a grave inconsistency. On the one hand, appeals . . . to alleged rights, arbitrary and non-essential . . . accompanied by the demand that they be . . . promoted by public structures, while, on the other hand . . . basic rights remain unacknowledged and are violated in much of the world. A link [exists] between claims to a "right to excess," and even to transgression and vice, within affluent societies, and the lack of food, drinkable water, basic instruction and elementary health care in . . . the underdeveloped world and on the outskirts of . . . metropolitan centers. The link consists in this: individual rights, when detached from a framework of duties . . . can run wild. . . . An overemphasis on rights leads to a disregard for duties.[31]

Population Growth?

CIV takes direct issue with the population-control movement that infringes on family and personal rights in procreation and sexuality. CIV is counter-cultural in its encouragement of large families "founded on marriage between a man and a woman." "[R]ights and duties in development," it says, " must . . . take account of the problems associated with *population growth*. This . . . concerns the inalienable values of life and the family. To consider population increase as the primary cause of underdevelopment is mistaken. . . . Due attention must . . . be given to responsible procreation. . . . The Church . . . urges . . . full respect for human values in . . . sexuality. It cannot be reduced merely to pleasure or entertainment, nor can sex education be reduced to technical instruction aimed solely at protecting . . . from . . . disease or the 'risk' of procreation. This would be to . . . disregard the deeper meaning of sexuality. . . . It is irresponsible to view sexuality merely as a source of pleasure, and . . . to regulate it through . . . mandatory birth control. . . . Against such policies there is a need to defend the primary competence of the family in the area of sexuality, as opposed to the State and its restrictive policies, and to ensure that parents are suitably prepared to undertake their responsibilities."[32]

CIV goes on to call attention to a population problem. It is not, however, the politically correct specter of overpopulation. It is, instead, the "planetary" trends[33] Benedict has noted before, especially in "developed countries," of both "an increase in life expectancy and . . . a decrease in birth rates." "Morally responsible openness to life," CIV states, *represents a rich social and economic resource*. Populous nations have [emerged] from poverty thanks not least to the size of their population and the talents of their people. . . . [F]ormerly prosperous nations are . . . passing through . . . uncertainty and in some cases decline, . . . because of their falling birth rates; this [is] a crucial problem for highly affluent societies. The decline in births . . . puts a strain on social welfare systems, increases their cost, eats into . . . financial resources needed for investment, reduces the availability of . . . labourers, and narrows the 'brain pool.' . . . [S]maller and at times minuscule families run the risk of impoverishing social relations, and failing to ensure effective . . . solidarity. These situations are symptomatic of scant confidence in the future and moral weariness. It is . . . a social and even economic necessity . . . to hold up to future generations the beauty of marriage and the family, and the fact that these institutions correspond to the deepest needs and dignity of the person. . . . States are called to *enact policies promoting the centrality and the integrity of the family* founded on marriage between a man and a woman, the primary vital cell of society, and to assume responsibility for its economic and fiscal needs, while respecting its essentially relational character."[34]

Suppression of Life

"One of the most striking aspects of development . . . is . . . *respect for life*,"[35] which promotes integral human development. A disturbing reality, as noted in CIV, is the imposition on developing nations of anti-life policies that impede development. "Not only does . . . poverty still provoke high rates of infant mortality in many regions, but some parts of the world . . . experience . . . demographic control, on the part of governments that . . . promote contraception and even . . . impose abortion. In economically developed countries, legislation contrary to life is very widespread, and it [contributes] to the spread of an anti-birth mentality . . . attempts are made to export this mentality to other States as if it were a form of cultural progress.

"Some non-governmental Organizations work actively to spread abortion, at times promoting . . . sterilization in poor countries, in some cases not even informing the women concerned. [D]evelopment aid is sometimes linked to . . . the imposition of strong birth control measures. Further grounds for concern are laws permitting euthanasia as well as pressure . . . nationally and internationally, in favor of its juridical recognition.

"*Openness to life is at the center of true development.* When a society moves towards the denial or suppression of life, it ends up no longer finding the . . . motivation and energy to strive for man's true good."[36]

An intriguing aspect of CIV is its analysis of "a self-centered use of technology," especially in the matter of bioethics. "The supremacy of technology tends to prevent people from recognizing anything that cannot be explained in terms of matter alone."[37] The integration of faith and reason is necessary to address that problem: "[In] bioethics . . . a self-centered use of technology . . . implies a . . . rejection of meaning and value. . . . [C]losing the door to transcendence brings . . . a difficulty: how could being emerge from nothing, how could intelligence be born from chance? Faced with these dramatic questions, reason and faith can come to each other's assistance. Only together will they save man. *Entranced by an exclusive reliance on technology, reason without faith is doomed to flounder in an illusion of its own omnipotence. Faith without reason risks being cut off from everyday life.*[38]

Technology is placing life under man's control. "*In vitro* fertilization, embryo research, the possibility of manufacturing clones and human hybrids: all this is . . . being promoted in today's . . . disillusioned culture, which believes it has mastered every mystery, because the origin of life is now within our grasp. Here we see the clearest expression of technology's supremacy. . . . To the . . . scourge of abortion we may well have to add . . . the systematic eugenic programming of births. [A] pro-euthanasia mindset is [asserting] control over life that . . . is deemed no longer worth living. . . . Who could measure the negative effects of this kind of mentality for development? How can we be surprised by the indifference shown towards . . . human degradation, when such indifference extends even to our attitude towards what is and is not human? What is astonishing is the arbitrary and selective determination of what to put forward today as worthy of respect. Insignificant matters are considered shocking, yet unprecedented injustices [are] widely tolerated. While the poor of the world continue knocking on the doors of the rich, the world of affluence runs the risk of no longer hearing those knocks, on account of a conscience that can no longer distinguish what is human. [T]he natural law, in which creative

Reason shines forth, reveals our greatness, but also our wretchedness inso-
far as we fail to recognize the call to moral truth."[39]

A Spiritual Resource

CIV is a spiritual resource for students and others. At the end of its
extensive treatment of many aspects of development it concludes that
"*[d]evelopment needs* . . . Christians moved by the knowledge that truth-
filled love, *caritas in veritate*, from which authentic development proceeds, is not produced by us, but given to us. . . . Development requires
attention to the spiritual life, a serious consideration of the experiences of
trust in God, spiritual fellowship in Christ, reliance upon God's providence
and mercy, love and forgiveness, self-denial, acceptance of others, justice
and peace."[40]

The bottom line, which makes all kinds of sense: "Without God man
neither knows which way to go, nor even understands who he is."[41] Not a
bad message.

18

In Hope We Were Saved

THE MESSAGE of Benedict XVI's second encyclical, *Spe Salvi* ("In Hope We Were Saved"), in 2007, is simple: "A world without God is a world without hope."[1] The message is for everyone and not just for Catholics.[2]

We all have "many greater or lesser hopes," including "the hope of creating a perfect world . . . thanks to scientific knowledge and to scientifically based politics."[3] Benedict admits that "we need the . . . hopes that keep us going day to day. But these are not enough without the great hope which . . . can only be . . . the God who has a human face and who has loved us to the end, each one of us and humanity in its entirety."[4] A secularist culture, he insists, can offer no hope for anything after death. No future. In contrast, their "encounter with Christ" gives Christians their "distinguishing mark" which is "the fact that they have a future: it is not that they know the details . . . but they know in general terms that their life will not end in emptiness. Only when the future is certain as a positive reality does it become possible to live in the present as well."[5]

Spe Salvi explores the relation between the lack of hope and what Benedict had described at Regensburg in 2006 as "the self-imposed limitation of reason to the empirically verifiable" so that "questions of religion and ethics no longer concern it."[6] When reason is so limited, affirmations of God and objective morality are dismissed as non-rational. Benedict describes as "presumptuous and . . . false," the idea that "[s]ince there is no God to create justice . . . man himself is now called to establish justice." "It is no accident," he said, "that this idea has led to the greatest forms of cruelty and violations of justice. . . . A world which has to create its own justice is a world without hope."[7] Justice will be whatever man decrees. Thus Hans Kelsen, whom we discussed in Chapter 13, said, in accord with his legal positivism, that the Nazi extermination camps were valid law. He could not reasonably criticize them as unjust because justice, for him, is "an irrational ideal."

Spe Salvi traces "the foundations of the modern age" to Francis Bacon and others who thought that "man would be redeemed through science."[8] "[U]p to that time, the recovery of what man had lost through the expulsion from Paradise was expected from faith in Jesus Christ. . . . Now, this 'redemption,' the restoration of the lost Paradise is no longer expected from faith, but from the newly discovered link between science and praxis [practice, action or conduct]. It is not that faith is simply denied; rather it is displaced onto another level – that of purely private and other-worldly affairs – and . . . it becomes . . . irrelevant for the world. . . . This . . . vision . . . shapes the present-day crisis of faith which is . . . a crisis of Christian hope. Thus hope too . . . acquires a new form. Now it is called: *faith in progress*. . . . [T]hrough the interplay of science and praxis . . . a totally new world will emerge, the kingdom of man."[9]

Benedict affirms the achievements and potential of science, but he cautions that "[i]f technical progress is not matched by . . . progress in man's ethical formation. . . . it is not progress at all, but a threat for man and for the world."[10] The problem is that ethical formation is impossible unless reason can offer answers on moral right and wrong. But reason cannot do that if it is limited to the empirical, without "integration through . . . openness . . . to the differentiation between good and evil. . . . [R]eason . . . becomes human only if it is capable of directing the will along the right path and it is capable of this only if it looks beyond itself . . . . Let us put it very simply: man needs God, otherwise he remains without hope . . . God truly enters into human affairs only when, rather than being present merely in our thinking, he himself comes towards us and speaks to us. . . . Reason . . . and faith need one another in order to fulfill their true nature and their missions."[11]

We conclude this chapter with a story Benedict tells in *Spe Salvi*. It reminds us again that the Christian faith is not essentially about doctrines, theories and rules. What the Magisterium offers is hope gained through the encounter with a person, Jesus Christ. Early in the encyclical, he had said, "To come to know . . . the true God . . . means to receive hope. We who have always lived with the Christian concept of God, and have grown accustomed to it, have almost ceased to notice that we possess the hope that ensues from a real encounter with this God."[12] Then he said that the life of "a saint of our time can . . . help us understand what it means to have a real encounter with this God for the first time."[13]

"Josephine Bakhita, canonized by Pope John Paul II . . . was born around 1869 . . . in Darfur in Sudan. At the age of nine, she was kidnapped by slave-traders, beaten till she bled, and sold five times in the slave-markets of Sudan. Eventually she found herself working as a slave for the mother and the wife of a general, and there she was flogged every day till she bled; as a result . . . she bore 144 scars throughout her life. Finally, in 1882, she was bought by an Italian merchant . . . who returned to Italy as the Mahdists advanced. Here . . . Bakhita came to know a totally different kind of 'master' – in Venetian dialect, which she was now learning, she used the name '*paron*' for the living God, the God of Jesus Christ. Up to that time she had known only masters who despised and maltreated her, or at best considered her a useful slave. Now . . . she heard that there is a '*paron*' above all masters, the Lord of all lords, and that this Lord is good, goodness in person. She came to know that this Lord even knew her, that he had created her – that he actually loved her. She too was loved, and by none other than the supreme '*Paron*,' before whom all other masters are themselves no more than lowly servants. She was known and loved and she was awaited. What is more, this master had himself accepted the destiny of being flogged and now he was waiting for her 'at the Father's right hand.' Now she had 'hope' – no longer simply the modest hope of finding masters who would be less cruel, but the great hope: 'I am definitively loved and whatever happens to me – I am awaited by this Love. And so my life is good.' Through the knowledge of this hope she was 'redeemed,' no longer a slave, but a free child of God. She understood what Paul meant when he reminded the Ephesians that previously they were . . . without hope *because* without God. Hence, when she was about to be taken back to Sudan, Bakhita refused; she did not wish to be separated again from her '*Paron*.' On 9 Jaunary 1890, she was baptized and confirmed and received her first Holy Communion. . . . On 8 December 1896 . . . she took her vows in the Congregation of the Canossian Sisters and from that time onwards, besides her work in the sacristy and in the porter's lodge at the convent, she made several journeys round Italy in order to promote the missions: the liberation that she had received through her encounter with the God of Jesus Christ, she felt she had to extend, it had to be handed on to others, to the greatest possible number of people. The hope born in her which had 'redeemed' her she could not keep to herself; this hope had to reach many, to reach everybody."[14]

Benedict uses the story of Saint Josephine Bakhita to answer the question: "[C]an our encounter with the God who in Christ has shown us his face and opened his heart be for us too not just 'informative' but 'performative' . . . can it change our lives, so that we know we are redeemed through the hope that it expresses?"[15] In other words, is Christian faith "performative . . . a message which shapes our life in a new way, or is it just 'information' which . . . we . . . set aside and which now seems . . . to have been superseded by more recent information?"[16] The answer, of course, is that Christian faith is "performative." "That means: the Gospel is not merely a communication of things that can be known – it is one that makes things happen and is life-changing."[17]

The Magisterium of the Catholic Church exists to offer that hope to everyone. What a mistake, and what a needless one, for Notre Dame, over the past four decades, to renounce obedience to that source of Truth and of Hope. And what a missed opportunity to introduce students, and so many others, to that inspiring truth not only as an obligation but also as a gift. That mistake should be reversed.

19

The Question of Truth
Can "Autonomy" Be Fixed?

> It is the honor and responsibility of a Catholic University to
> consecrate itself without reserve to the cause of truth. – Pope
> John Paul II, *Ex Corde Ecclesiae*, no. 4.

A Hopeless Case?

NOTRE DAME'S honoring of President Obama was a highly visible
exercise of the autonomy from the Church under which Notre Dame has
operated for four decades. In Chapters 7 through 11 we saw applications
of that autonomy over those years. Chapter 12 offered reasons why a return
to acceptance of the Magisterium would benefit Notre Dame and its students. Chapters 13 through 18 analyze examples of magisterial teaching
from which society in general, as well as Catholic universities, could benefit. This book has criticized the Land O'Lakes declaration of "autonomy"
from "external" authorities including the Church, as a mistake which Notre
Dame has compounded by its actions taken in the exercise of that autonomy. A further question is whether Land O'Lakes "autonomy" can be fixed
by minor or even major adjustments to bring it fully in line with the nature
of the Catholic university as spelled out in *Ex Corde Ecclesiae*. Or is that
"autonomy" a hopeless case meriting only a swift repudiation?

The theme of this book is that the Land O'Lakes declaration of autonomy from the Church was a mistake in its inception. Notre Dame's experience with that autonomy over the past four decades confirms that the only
effective remedy for Notre Dame would be a repudiation of Land O'Lakes
and an explicit "recognition and adherence to the teaching authority of the
Church in matters of faith and morals."[1] The soundness of this conclusion

is confirmed, interestingly, by a major address delivered by Fr. Hesburgh
shortly after the Land O'Lakes statement.

"The Vision of a Great Catholic University in the World of Today"

On December 9, 1967, five months after Land O'Lakes, Fr. Hesburgh
addressed a special convocation commemorating the 125th anniversary of
the founding of Notre Dame. The address, "The Vision of a Great Catholic
University in the World of Today," applies to Notre Dame the theory and
practice of the "autonomy and academic freedom" from "external" authority claimed at Land O'Lakes. The tone of the address is positive and uplift-
ing. "In many ways," Fr. Hesburgh wrote in a foreword, "it is the most
important talk I have ever written, since it deals with the heart of all the
efforts during these recent years and, hopefully, is a realistic blueprint of
what we hope to realize at Notre Dame, as a great Catholic university, in
the years ahead."[2]

If you want a serious, thoughtful analysis of how a Catholic university can operate in the autonomy environment of Land O'Lakes, the
Hesburgh address is as good as you are going to get. The address, however, confirms instead that the autonomy concept of Land O'Lakes is fatally
flawed. That autonomy project rejects the authority of the Magisterium, but
it leads predictably to an on-campus "dictatorship of relativism" and the
emergence of an alternative magisterium.

Parenthetically, this is a difficult chapter for me to write. It includes
explicit and strong disagreements with positions taken by Fr. Hesburgh. I
very highly respect Fr. Hesburgh. In the four decades I have been at Notre
Dame, I have seen numerous examples of his integrity, his kindness and his
practical concern for others as persons. I ask the reader, therefore, please
do not interpret criticisms in this book of actions or policies as personal
disparagements of Fr. Hesburgh or anyone else.

Cardinal Newman

In his 1967 address, Fr. Hesburgh said the university "has developed
in modern times into a much different reality than it was, even a little over
a century ago when Cardinal Newman wrote his 'Idea of a University.'
That classic book can no longer be a complete model for the Catholic university of today. . . . There are timeless principles in Newman's 'Idea,' but

he wrote about a completely different kind of university in a completely different kind of world."[3]

In many ways the university today differs from what it was in Newman's day. The central role of research in major universities today is one difference. The emphasis in Newman's day was on liberal and classical education, with a structured and sequential curriculum. Today, the curriculum tends to be elective, non-sequential and utilitarian in content. Another difference is the focus today on social and community service, including apostolic work at places like Notre Dame, as part of the formation available to an undergrad student. It would be an oversimplification, however, to dismiss Newman because of such differences and others which could be mentioned. Newman's insights went to essential elements which have not changed. Indeed, one decisive change in the modern university provides a compelling reason to pay close attention to Newman. That change is the modern university's rejection of the synthesis of faith and reason which characterized the university in its origin, the vestiges of which endured even into the nineteenth and twentieth centuries. *Ex Corde* insists on a restoration of that synthesis. Newman's insights are important in effecting that restoration.

Contrary to Fr. Hesburgh's view, Cardinal Avery Dulles, as we saw in Chapters 12, 13 and 14, affirmed the relevance of Newman to the problems of universities and culture today. "Newman," Cardinal Dulles said, "writing in England in the mid-nineteenth century, proposed a vision of Catholic higher education that takes account of major difficulties that were prevalent in his day and are no less prevalent in ours. . . . His proposals [are] in contrast to four tendencies that Newman found unacceptable. I shall call these tendencies utilitarianism, fragmentation, secularism, and rationalism."[4] Cardinal Dulles affirms that Cardinal Newman, if he were alive today, "would enthusiastically embrace the principles . . . in Ex Corde Ecclesiae," including the jurisdiction of the Magisterium as binding on Catholic universities.[5]

The Modern University World

A problem is raised by Fr. Hesburgh's observation that "the Church did not create this modern university world, as it helped create the Mediaeval university world. Moreover, the Church does not have to be present in this modern world of the university, but if it is to enter, the reality and the terms of this world are well established and must be observed."[6] The issue presented by Land O'Lakes is not the role of the Church if it chooses to participate somehow in the secular "modern world of the university" at Stanford, Northwestern or wherever. The issue is the relation of the Church to the *Catholic* university. Fr. Hesburgh's implication is that before a university can be "Catholic" it must first be a university according to the standards of the "modern university world." Being Catholic seems to be an add-on. Real universities, it seems, are not Catholic and if Catholics want to do their thing as a university, they first must qualify by meeting the standards of the real, secular "university world."

On the contrary, the Catholic university comes, as did *all* universities, "ex corde ecclesiae," out of the heart of the Church. The payoff question between the Catholic university and the "modern" university is the question of truth. As Cardinal Dulles describes the teaching of *Ex Corde*, "Catholic universities have the incomparable advantage of being able to integrate all truth in relation to Christ, the incarnate Logos, whom Christians recognize as the way, the truth, and the life for the whole world."[7] In his comment on *The Vagina Monologues*, Bishop D'Arcy put it very plainly: "[W]hat makes a Catholic university distinctive is the conviction that in the search for truth, we do not start from scratch; we start from the truth that has been revealed to us in the Word of God, the person of Jesus Christ, and the teaching of his church."[8] Land O'Lakes requires the Church, in its own Catholic universities, to surrender its freedom to teach on faith and morals with the authority it derives from Christ who teaches through the Church, to which authority the university itself, as an institution, is bound to adhere.[9] Instead, the teachings of the Church, as far as the professedly Catholic university is concerned, are merely advisory. The Land O'Lakes concept, including its application at Notre Dame, reduces the teaching Church to a state of triviality beyond irrelevance.

Perhaps Fr. Hesburgh, and others who support Land O'Lakes autonomy, see a tension between being a "great" university and being a "Catholic" university. Fr. Hesburgh described his vision as an "attempt to create what to many seems impossible, a great Catholic university in our times. . . . A great Catholic university must begin by being a great university that is also Catholic."[10] Prof. Ralph McInerny, as we saw in Chapter 12, stated the more pertinent question: "Is a Non-Catholic University Possible?"[11] "For Newman and for John Paul II," said Cardinal Dulles, "any university that lacks the guidance of Christian revelation and the oversight of the Catholic magisterium is by that very fact impeded in its mission to find and transmit truth."[12]

The Catholic University without the Magisterium

In his address, Fr. Hesburgh said correctly that "The University is not the Church. It might be said to be *of* the Church, as it serves both the Church and the people of God, but it certainly is not the magisterium."[13] The issue, however, is the relation of the Catholic university *to* the Magisterium. *Somebody* has to make the call as to what is authentic Catholic teaching. Notre Dame itself assumed that role in its promotion of the Cuomo doctrine on abortion, discussed in Chapter 11. Notre Dame made itself a "super-magisterium," telling the Catholic people, and especially Catholic politicians, that the teaching of the Church on abortion is not what those people in Rome say it is. The Hesburgh address continues: "The University . . . is not the Church teaching, but a place – the only place – in which Catholics and others, on the highest level of intellectual inquiry, seek out the relevance of the Christian message to all of the problems and opportunities that face modern man and his complex world."[14] Apart from the self-validation involved in the claim that the Catholic university is the "only place" where such seeking out is done, the question left open is whether the Catholic university can do anything more than "seek out"? Can it provide answers as to "the relevance of the Christian message"? If so, whose answers? And why should anyone accept them?

At this point we confront the questions of truth and of obedience to those vested with authority, derived from Christ, to declare that truth in matters of faith and morals.

"The University," Fr. Hesburgh asserts, "is not the kind of place that one can or should try to rule by authority external to the university."[15] That begs the question of whether the Magisterium should be regarded as simply "external" to the Catholic university. "A Catholic University . . . is linked with the Church . . . by an institutional commitment made by those responsible for it."[16] "The *institutional* fidelity of the University to the Christian message includes a recognition of and adherence to the teaching authority of the Church in matters of faith and morals."[17] And Bishops "should be seen not as external agents but as participants in the life of the Catholic University."[18] If the Catholic university, pursuant to Land O'Lakes, rejects the authority of the Church as "external," what, if any, authority is there in the University? The officers and others, of course, exercise the authority conferred in the statutes, bylaws, etc. But the question here is authority as to the truth in faith and morals. Who has authority, with respect to the University, to decide what is true in faith and morals? Fr. Hesburgh's answer, in the world of Land O'Lakes, is frustratingly vague. "The best and only traditional authority in the university," he says, "is intellectual competence: this is the coin of the realm. This includes, in the Catholic university, especially, philosophical and theological competence."[19]

Someone, of course, has to decide who has such competence. If a person in the university is judged to have competence, how does he or she exercise it as authority? And if others have similar competence, we have to answer, in case they disagree, how the University decides who is right and what is true? The answer appears to be consensus, with somebody, of course, deciding what is the consensus. Recall Cardinal Ratzinger's observation, quoted in Chapter 11, that "Truth does not create consensus, and consensus does not create truth as much as it does a common ordering."[20]

As quoted from *Ex Corde* at the beginning of this chapter, "It is the . . . responsibility of a Catholic University to consecrate *itself* without reserve to *the cause of truth*." That means an institutional commitment to truth. The Magisterium, for the Catholic university, is the teacher of that truth.

One of the most puzzling aspects of Fr. Hesburgh's analysis is his discussion of commitment: "At Notre Dame, as in all universities, commitment to be meaningful must be personal rather than institutional, a thing of personal free conviction rather than institutional rhetoric."[21] Does this leave room for any commitment of the University, as an institution, on the truth of an issue of faith or morals? Fr. Hesburgh continues, "Whatever the personal faith of our variegated faculty and student body, I have sensed that we are united in believing that intellectual virtues and moral values are important to life and to this institution. I take it that our total community commitment is to wisdom, which is something more than knowledge and much akin to goodness and beauty when it radiates throughout a human person."[22] If "our total university commitment is to wisdom," obvious questions occur: Whose wisdom? Who defines it? And who decides whether a specific position on faith or morals proceeds from wisdom?

The more basic problem arises from Fr. Hesburgh's statement that "commitment to be meaningful must be personal, rather than institutional." Does this mean that the University, as an institution, will make no commitment as to what is true on an issue of faith or morals? If so, that position is itself a commitment to a position – the position of non-commitment. In reality, Notre Dame does, rightly, make institutional commitments on racial equality and other moral issues. But it does so in exercise of its own magisterium. The promotion of the Cuomo doctrine on abortion, discussed in Chapter 11, is an example.

Truth

The difficulties in the theoretical framework advanced by Fr. Hesburgh are attributable to the incoherence of the Land O'Lakes concept which he tries to apply. Fr. Hesburgh's effort is as strong a defense of the Land O'Lakes concept as one could make. The difficulty is that the Land O'Lakes concept is indefensible. The first casualty of that concept is truth. Fr. Hesburgh discusses the place of truth at Notre Dame:

"We can, in summary, give living vital witness to the wholeness of truth from all sources, both human and divine, while recognizing the inner sacredness of all truth from whatever source, and the validity and autonomy of all paths to truth. Somehow, the Notre Dame community should reflect profoundly, and with unashamed commitment, its belief in the existence of God and in God's total revelation to man, especially the Christian message; the deep age-long mystery of Salvation in history; the inner, inalienable dignity and rights of every human person, recognizing at the same time both man's God-given freedom and his human fallibility, an uneasy balance without God's grace; buttressing man's every move towards a more profound perception and articulation of truth and a more humane achievement of justice in our times – and Notre Dame must try to do all of this in the most ecumenical and open spirit."[23]

If "the Notre Dame community should reflect . . . its belief in . . . God's total revelation to man, especially the Christian message," who decides what the "Christian message" is? What do we do if a theology teacher wants to teach his students that abortion is the eighth sacrament? Who is to say he is wrong if the University rejects the authority of the Magisterium? In his Washington, D.C. address to Catholic educators, Pope Benedict XVI said that "any appeal to the principle of academic freedom in order to justify positions that contradict the faith and teaching of the Church would obstruct or even betray the university's identity and mission."[24] Notre Dame cannot have it both ways. It cannot play the politically correct games of "openness" and also claim to be Catholic.

For the Land O'Lakes concept, and Notre Dame, to reject obedience to the voice of truth given to us by Christ, is beyond unreasonable. Consider Cardinal Dulles' clear exposition:

> Depending on one's point of view, this institutional bond [of the Catholic university to the Church] may be seen as a burden or a help. Some . . . hanker for the freedom to teach whatever comes to their minds, without having to conform to any doctrinal norms. But on deeper consideration is becomes apparent that the Church says no only . . . to guide her members to a deeper yes – yes to God who is the source of all truth and to Christ, who said of himself, 'I am the truth' (Jn. 14:6). Since the truth makes us free (Jn. 8:32), it does not confine us; it liberates us from the shackles of ignorance and error."[25]

Fr. Hesburgh ascribes to the university a competence that the Catholic university, as an institution, pursuant to Land O'Lakes, would deny to the Magisterium: "Faith is unchangeable in what it believes, but as good Pope John said, there are many ways of expressing what we believe – and today, the words must be directed to the inner complexity of our times. . . . The university is best prepared to understand this human confusion, and to speak to it with faithful words that say something, to avoid the meaningless formulae, the empty phrases, the words without weight."[26]

This affirmation of the university as "best prepared" is followed by an astonishing anointing of "the Catholic university community" as the place where "the ultimate answers . . . must be found":

> Schema Thirteen of Vatican II addressed many problems of the Church in the world today. This document is an invitation rather than an ultimate answer. If the ultimate answers are to be found, these must be found within the Catholic university community which is in living contact with the faith and the world, the problems and all the possible solutions, the possibilities and despairs of modern man.[27]

This explicit proclamation of super-authority and super-competence on the part of "the Catholic university community" would surprise and amuse any veteran of faculty meetings, faculty senates, etc., at a Catholic university. But that statement also amounts to an explicit displacement of the teaching authority of the Church by the super-magisterium of the "university community." Fr. Hesburgh here is simply making a logical application of the Land O'Lakes concept. His position is unworkable because that concept does not, and cannot, work.

All the good things Fr. Hesburgh seeks in the Catholic university can be achieved and maintained through adherence to *Ex Corde*, which mandates acceptance of the teaching authority of the Church, more effectively than through Land O'Lakes' autonomy from the Magisterium.

The Remedy

The title of this book is a question: "What Happened to Notre Dame?" The answer is that Notre Dame made a wrong turn four decades ago. "The essential formula of Land O'Lakes," said Fr. Richard John Neuhaus, "is a perfect invitation to follow in the footsteps"[28] of the originally Protestant universities which, in the words of Prof. George Marsden, have gone "From Protestant Establishment to Established Nonbelief."[29]

The President, Fellows and Trustees who perpetrated the honoring of Obama have forfeited their right to continue in positions of responsibility at Notre Dame. A mere change in personnel, however, would not be a sufficient remedy.

If Notre Dame is to survive as a Catholic university, it must repudiate the mistake it made at Land O'Lakes. That would require a full acceptance of *Ex Corde Ecclesiae*, which guarantees appropriate autonomy and academic freedom but insists on "adherence to the teaching authority of the Church in matters of faith and morals."[30] The situation requires, however, more. As John Paul II was quoted at the beginning of this chapter, "It is the honor and responsibility of a Catholic University to consecrate itself without reserve to *the cause of truth*." Jesus Christ is Truth and he speaks through his Church. As Fr. Miscamble said at the ND Response rally on Commencement Day, "there is so much that is good at Notre Dame that you can never relent in your efforts to call this place to be its best and true self – proud of its Catholic identity and its loyal membership in the Church. . . . Let us labor in the vineyard, so that Notre Dame might regain its true soul . . . be faithful in its mission as a Catholic University . . . and truly become the 'powerful means for good' that Fr. Sorin dreamed about."[31]

ND Response was a proper response to the Obama Commencement because ND Response was essentially an act of prayer. And that still is the proper response. The primary weapons are Eucharistic Adoration and the Rosary. The most effective, practical thing we can do for Notre Dame is to pray, especially through the intercession of Mary, the Mother of God. It is her University.

20
Postscript
Notre Dame as a Lesson for Everyone

NOTRE DAME rejected obedience to the Magisterium as the authoritative teacher, in the Catholic tradition, of faith and morals. Without such an authoritative interpreter of the moral law, Notre Dame, as an institution, invited the resolution of moral issues by a "dictatorship of relativism" in which the community consensus became authoritative. The University, filling a vacuum, eventually assumed for itself, in some respects, the role of a substitute magisterium. In the Catholic tradition, the Magisterium teaches by the authority of Christ who is God and who teaches through the Church, which is the Body of Christ. When Notre Dame rejected the authority of the Magisterium while still claiming to be a "Catholic university," it reduced itself to incoherence.

One lesson of the Notre Dame experience is that everyone needs an authoritative interpreter of the moral law, a source to which, or to whom, he (or she) looks for authoritative answers to moral questions. In fact, every person already has one. The default choice – and perhaps the nearly universal choice – is the person himself. Unlimited private judgment on moral issues, however, is the foundation of the relativist culture, which evolves legally into positivist totalitarianism and culturally into a nihilism where even the intentional killing of the innocent is a culturally accepted problem-solving technique. Without a common morality, which requires an accepted authoritative interpreter of the moral law, society goes into the pits. This is a conclusion not of faith but of reason and common sense.

In its historical acceptance of its full Catholic character, including the teaching authority of the Church, Notre Dame had it all. And then walked away from it, with the consequences we have detailed in this book. The Notre Dame story reminds one of more than just the necessity, in reason, of an authoritative interpreter of the moral law. That story invites the conclusion that the most appropriate figure to fill that role of interpreter is the Pope who truly is the one "universal voice" on moral issues. His suitability for that role is a conclusion of reason, reinforced by a study of the positive, hopeful pronouncements that emanate from that source. Beyond the rational basis for that conclusion, but supportive of it, is the reality of Christ who happens to be God and who teaches through his Church, the head of which on earth is his Vicar, the successor to Peter.

There is, however, another angle. For many people, Notre Dame symbolized more than just "the Catholic thing." It symbolized the need – in a culture of meaninglessness – for a champion, for *somebody* to stand for "the permanent things." The Fighting Irish are my team on Saturday, many would say, because Notre Dame *means* something. When you pulled for Notre Dame, you were pulling for a truth. You knew that, even as the world went crazy, there was one place that held fast. Notre Dame had earned its place as a symbol of integrity – and truth.

The Obama fiasco was shocking because it seemed like a sudden collapse of a dam. It resulted, of course, from four decades of erosion. That collapse is a microcosm of the erosion and collapse of American culture. And here is where Americans other than Catholics have a stake in what happened at Notre Dame and what can be done to fix it.

Most people in the United States, who have an opinion on the point, if asked to identify the leading "religious" university in the land, would be likely to say, regardless of faith, "Notre Dame." As we have seen, Notre Dame is following the path of the Protestant universities, which have gone, in George Marsden's phrase, "from Protestant establishment to established nonbelief." The abandonment of truth by universities of whatever type affects the culture. As relativism and agnosticism filter into that culture from the universities, religion is privatized as nonrational and squeezed out of public life. In private life, relativism takes over along with an "I'm aboard, pull up the gangplank" individualism. Those cultural effects can be catastrophic as well as scandalous if the university that repudiates its own source of truth is the national icon of religious integrity.

You do not have to be Catholic, or even interested in that faith, to appreciate that the public interest is served by universities and other institutions that bring religious influence to bear on education and society.

What happened to Notre Dame can happen, or has happened, to other institutions of other religions. The Notre Dame experience can therefore be a helpful wake-up call for concerned persons of all faiths. Beyond that, persons of other faiths have an interest in the restoration of Notre Dame itself to the fullness of its Catholic identity. If Notre Dame were to return to its roots, it could start a trend.

In summary, this book is not a polemic against Notre Dame or those who now control its administration. It is rather an effort to suggest not only how Notre Dame could return to its roots but also how the Notre Dame experience could prompt a reintegration of faith and reason through the Body of Christ.

Appendix
Talk for ND Response Rally –
Sunday, May 17, 2009

Wilson D. Miscamble, C.S.C.
Professor History University of Notre Dame

TRUE FRIENDS of Notre Dame – I thank you for your presence.

I want to thank especially our treasured students in ND Response for inviting me to be with you. It is a great privilege and honor. As I look out on the good and decent people gathered here, I know one thing: There is no place I would rather be.

I have been a teacher at Notre Dame for more than two decades. But today I come before you primarily as a Holy Cross priest – a member of the Religious Order that founded Notre Dame more than a century and half ago.

On November 26, 1842, an extraordinary French priest named Edward Sorin and a small band of Holy Cross brothers arrived at this site – a place where French missionaries had once ministered to the Potawatomi Indians. Fr. Sorin christened the place Notre Dame du Lac. He and his Holy Cross confreres began the work of building a college with a small log chapel as their point of departure. They aimed to serve Christ here. And they sought to evangelize in His name under the patronage of the Blessed Mother.

When the young priest wrote home to his superior – Blessed Basil Moreau, the founder of the Holy Cross Order – he put it this way: Here in northern Indiana, he said, he hoped to establish "one of the most powerful means for good in this country." Since then, the university has prospered.

But building this university was not an easy task. The tiny school faced horrendous tribulations during its initial years. Damaging fires, a terrible cholera outbreak, and a series of financial crises failed to halt the onward march of the school. Whatever the odds against them, Father Sorin and his collaborators never gave up or quit.

Those of you familiar with Notre Dame's history would know that this tenacity had perhaps its finest moment on April 23, 1879. That was the day that the so-called "big fire" swept over the campus. In just three hours much of the work of the previous three decades lay in ashes. A few days later, Father Sorin trudged through the still-smoldering ruins of the venture to which he had devoted his life. Then he called the whole community into the campus church – which had miraculously survived the fierce blaze. With absolute faith and confidence, Father Sorin looked forward and told his anxious band of followers this: "If it were ALL gone I should not give up." The effect was "electric." As one observer put it, after that "there was never a shadow of a doubt as to the future of Notre Dame."

Under God's providential care, our university did recover and grow. Father Sorin . . . his determined band . . . and the generations of Holy Cross religious and their lay collaborators who followed them built something special. Their blood and sweat and tears are in the bricks and mortar – and they are reflected in the lives that they touched.

They were "educators in the faith" who understood in the words of Fr. Moreau "that the mind could not be cultivated at the expense of the heart." These folk built Notre Dame into a distinctive place that nurtured its students' religious and moral development, as well as their intellectual lives. Notre Dame challenged them to serve God and neighbor. And, as it did so, it proudly proclaimed its Catholic identity and its loyal membership in a Church that was and is unafraid to speak of moral truths and foundational principles and beliefs. In the process, Notre Dame came to hold a special place in the hearts of Catholics all across America.

Now friends, jump ahead to today. The formal leadership of the University still proclaims its fidelity to this vision.

– University leaders assert that Notre Dame is and will be different, so that it can make a difference;

– University leaders assure the parents of incoming freshmen that Notre Dame won't be like those 'other' schools that merely associate themselves with a Catholic or Jesuit 'tradition'. NO! – to the contrary – here at Notre Dame, their children will find an institution unashamedly Catholic and willing to embrace all the tenets of our faith. Notre Dame will instruct its students in the Church's moral truths and in its foundational beliefs and principles.

Of late, that rhetoric seems to ring rather hollow. The words have not been matched by deeds. Instead of fostering the moral development of its students Notre Dame's leaders have planted the damaging seeds of moral confusion.

By honoring President Obama, the Notre Dame Administration has let the students and their parents down. And it has betrayed the loyal and faith-filled alumni who rely on Notre Dame to stand firm on matters of fundamental Catholic teaching – and so to affirm the sanctity of life. The honor extended to Barack Obama says very loudly that support for practically unlimited access to abortion – and approval for the destruction of embryonic life to harvest stem cells – are not major problems for those charged with leading Notre Dame. They seem easily trumped by other issues, and by the opportunity to welcome the president to our campus. Bishop John D'Arcy, the great bishop of this diocese who so loves Notre Dame, said it well – Notre Dame chose "prestige over truth." How embarrassing for an institution dedicated to the pursuit of truth to settle for temporary attention over eternal honor.

Friends, just ask yourselves whether anyone – regardless of their other accomplishments – would be honored here at ND if they held racist or anti-Semitic sentiments. They would not – and rightly so! Yet Notre Dame honors at this Commencement a politician who readily proclaims his support for the Freedom of Choice Act, and who is clearly the most radically pro-abortion president in this great nation's history.

As you know well, Notre Dame undertook this sad action in the face of the 2004 instruction of the U.S. Catholic Bishops that "Catholic institutions should not honor those who act in defiance of our fundamental moral principles." In so doing, the administration has distanced the University from the Church that is its lifeblood – the ultimate source of its identity.

A number of my fellow Holy Cross priests and I believe that such a "distancing puts at risk the true soul of Notre Dame." Regrettably, this distancing also puts Notre Dame in the service of those who seek to damage the teaching authority of our Bishops. What a sad circumstance for an institution that should stand at the very heart of the Church.

Now, we can be sure that today the president will offer a fine address

– crafted by a talented speechwriting team to appeal to a "Catholic audience." No doubt too, President Obama will deliver it eloquently. There will surely be a tribute to Notre Dame's former president, Father Hesburgh, for his important work on civil rights. The president will claim that he is influenced by Catholic social teaching and will appeal for folk to work together in the areas where common ground can be found. Most of the crowd will cheer . . . the photos will be taken . . . and soon the event will be over. The President will board Air Force One and fly away.

But what matters for us here is less what President Obama says, but rather what the day will mean for Notre Dame and its place in American Catholic life.

The truth is this: This painful episode has damaged the ethos and spirit of Notre Dame. But there is another truth that we must also remember: IT IS NOT THE END OF THE STORY!

Some among the administration of Notre Dame will want the issue to "go away" quickly. It may even be likely that there are some among them who genuinely understand the evil of abortion, and who are inwardly troubled by these recent events whatever their outward bravado. – They will have a chance to show through future deeds and in very practical ways Notre Dame's commitment to the prolife cause. Let us hope and pray that they take up that opportunity.

But we cannot rely on them. As we have seen, on their own, their commitment will never be more than tepid.

Instead, let us link ourselves with those Holy Cross religious over the generations who never gave up – whatever the set-backs . . . whatever the trials . . . whatever the personal cost. In some ways, the task before us today is tougher than theirs. In those early days, the problems were clear – but so too was the mission.

Now we are engaged in a more intellectual and spiritual struggle. Will we be true to the founding vision? Can we resist the subtle and not so subtle temptations to surrender our distinct religious identity – and conform to the reigning and rather barren secular paradigm of what a university should be?

The Obama visit suggests that the University's leadership has succumbed to this temptation. Yet when we look back on these days, I have a sense that what will stand out is how a group of dedicated prolife students, wonderful alumni, and ordinary Catholics who cherish this place refused to acquiesce in the Administration's willingness to wink at its most funda-mental values in exchange for the public relations coup that attends a pres-idential visit.

The people who refuse to give up – and I speak especially of you stu-dents – have taken on the role of teachers here. While the administration and many of the faculty sold out easily for the photo-ops, etc., you and some of your alumni sisters and brothers showed the benefits of your Notre Dame education. You held firm to the foundational principles of respect for life and for the dignity of every person. You are the ones who have under-stood what really matters. You refuse to just go along. You have made your voice heard and led the way to a better future.

You represent the very best of Notre Dame. You – along with your good professors and faithful alums – are the ones who can help Notre Dame recover from this painful and self-inflicted wound. You will not find it easy, and you will have moments where you will be discouraged. But you must remember there is so much that is good at Notre Dame that you can never relent in your efforts to call this place to be its best and true self – proud of its Catholic identity and its loyal membership in the Church.

When I think of our courageous ND Response students my mind goes quickly to a marvelous passage in J.R.R. Tolkien's The Two Towers. Lord of the Rings aficionados will know the passage well. It is delivered as Frodo and Sam eat what may be their last meal together before going down into the Nameless Land.

Sam says: 'And we shouldn't be here at all, if we had known more about it before we started. But I suppose it's often that way. The brave things in the old tales and songs, Mr. Frodo: adventures, I used to call them. I used to think that they were things the wonderful folk of the stories went out and looked for, because they wanted them, because they were exciting and life was a bit dull, a kind of sport, as you might say. But that's not the way of it with tales that really mattered, or the ones that stay in the mind. Folk seem to have been just landed in them, usually their paths were laid that way, as you put it. But I suspect that they had lots of chances, like us, of turning back, only they didn't."

Friends:

– Let us move forward together and let us never turn back.

– Let us take our instruction from the Lord, in the words that the great champion of life, John Paul II, used at the outset of his papacy: BE NOT AFRAID.

– Let us labor in this vineyard, so that Notre Dame might regain its true soul . . . be faithful in its mission as a Catholic University . . . and truly become the "powerful means for good" that Father Sorin dreamed about.

Thank you for having me. May Our Lady – Our Lady of the Lake – keep you close. And may she ever watch over the university that bears her name.

Endnotes

I. Invitation and Reaction

1 Steven Ertelt, "Catholic Bishops' Leader and More Bishops Oppose Barack Obama at Notre Dame," Life News, www.lifenews.com, April 2, 2009; John Gerardi, "Bishops' Response to Obama Invite," *Irish Rover* (Notre Dame), April 14, 2009, 9.

2 Most Rev. Raymond L. Burke, Address, National Catholic Prayer Breakfast, May 8, 2009.

3 *Today's Catholic*, March 29, 2009, p. 1.

4 *University of Notre Dame Newswire*, March 20, 2009; *South Bend Tribune*, March 21, 2009, p. A1.

5 *Ibid.*

6 Gary Bauer, "Saddleback: A Defining Moment in Outreach to Evangelicals," *Human Events*, www.humanevents.com, August 22, 2008.

7 For the text and legislative history of SB1082 (2003), see Illinois Senate Republican Staff Analysis in National Right to Life Committee, "Obama Cover-up Revealed on Born-Alive Survivor Bill," National Right to Life Committee website, www.nrlc.org/ obamaBAIPA/ObamaCoverup.html; see also Terence Jeffrey, "The Obama Debate Every American Should See," www.townhall.com, October 8, 2008, recounting the debate in the Illinois Senate between Senator Obama and Senator Patrick O'Malley on SB 1095; see also Joel Mowbray, "Obama's Falsehood," *Washington Times*, August 21, 2008, p. A27.

8 S.1173 and H.R. 1964 (110th Cong., 1st Sess.)

9 See President Barack Obama, *Memorandum to Secretary of State and Administration of USAID, on Mexico City Policy and Assistance for Voluntary Population Planning*, January 23, 2009.

10 See www.rhrealitycheck.org, May 8, 2009; see Steven Ertelt, "Obama Administration Announces $50 Million for Pro-Forced Abortion UNFPA," Life News, www.lifenews.com, March 26, 2009.

11 See Steven Ertelt, "President Obama's New Budget Calls for Tax-Funded Abortion in Nation's

Capital," Life News, www.life-news.com, May 8, 2009.

12 Steven Ertelt, "President Obama's Pro-Abortion Record: A Pro-Life Compilation," Life News, www.lifenews.com, May 11, 2009.

13 www.whitehouse.gov, *Executive Order 13505*, March 9, 2009.

14 See Steven Ertelt, "Kansas Archbishop Urges Pro-Abortion Gov. Sebelius to Skip Communion," Life News, www.lifenews.com, May 9, 2009.

15 See Bernadine Healy, "Why Embryonic Stem Cells are Obsolete," *U.S. News and World Report*, March 4, 2009.

16 *Evangelium Vitae*, no. 60.

17 *Guidelines*, II A (1) (2). See http://stemcells.nih.gov/policy/2009guidelines.htm.

18 See Bernardine Healy, "Obama Lifts Stem Cell Ban But Opens Debate on Embryo Creation," *U.S. News & World Report*, March 9, 2009.

19 *Guidelines*, V A.

20 Omnibus Appropriations Act, 2009, Sec. 509 (a) (1) and (2).

21 See National Right to Life Committee, *Letter*, March 31, 2009, by Douglas Johnson to all Members of Congress. www.nrlc.org.

22 See discussion in Pontifical Academy for Life, *Human Cloning is Immoral*, July 9, 1997.

23 See Congregation for the Doctrine of the Faith, *Dignitas Personae* (2008), nos. 28–30.

24 Transcript provided by White House of President Obama's remarks on stem cell research, March 9, 2009, *New York Times* online edition, www.nytimes.com, Politics, March 9, 2009.

25 See National Right to Life Committee, *Letter*, March 31, 2009, by Douglas Johnson to all Members of Congress. www.nrlc.org

26 Cardinal Joseph Ratzinger, *God and the World* (2002), 133–35; see Charles E. Rice, "Christmas Messages," *The Observer*, December 9, 2008.

27 American Recovery and Reinvestment Act of 2009, Division A, Title XIII, and Division B, Title IV. Accessible online at www.thomas.gov.

28 "Rationing Health Care," *Washington Times*, editorial, April 21, 2009, p. A18.

29 Jim Mayers, "GOP's Coburn: Obama's Healthcare Will Devastate Seniors," www.newsmax.com, April 30, 2009.

30 Rob Stein, "Rule Shields Health Workers Who Withhold Care Based on Beliefs," *Washington Post*, December 19, 2008, p. A-10.

31 For example, the Church Amendments (42 USC 300a-7), the Coats-Snowe Amendment (42 USC § 238n, the Public Health Service Act), and the Weldon Amendment (PL 110–161). See E. Christian Brugger, "Obama and the Bush Conscience Regulations," (2009), Culture of Life Foundation, www.culture-of-life.org.

32 Statement of William J. Cox, president of the Alliance of Catholic Health Care, *Business Wire*, April 1, 2009.

33 See Steven Ertelt, "Obama Takes Next Step to Scrap Protections for Pro-Life Doctors on Abortion," LifeNews.com, May 11, 2009; Secretary, HHS, Proposed Rule Rescinding, 45 CFR Part 88, March 5, 2009; Matt Bowman, "Obama's Conscience Claws," *American Spectator*, July 7, 2009; http://spectator.org/archives2009/0 7/07/obamas-conscience-claws/ print.

34 *Today's Catholic*, March 29, 2009, 5.

35 "Obama Promises Conscience Protection," Zenit, July 2, 2009; www.zenit.org/article-26353?1= english.

36 See, for example, *Philip J. Berg v. Barack Obama*, 129 S. Ct. 1030 (Mem.), Jan. 21, 2009 No. 08A5050; see also Andrew C. McCarthy, "Suborned in the U.S.A., *National Review Online*, July 20, 2009 (http:// article.nationalreview.com/?q=Zm JhMzlmZWFhOTQ3YjUxMDE2 YWY4ZDMzZjZlYTVmZmU=).

2. The Justification: Abortion as Just Another Issue

1 Most Rev. John M. D'Arcy, "State ment to the Faithful," *Today's Catholic*, April 26, 2009, 3.

2 William McGurn, Address, "A Notre Dame Witness for Life," Notre Dame Center for Ethics and Culture, April 23, 2009.

3 Viewpoint, "Jenkins Responds,"

Statement of Rev. John I. Jenkins, C.S.C., March 23, 2009; *The Observer*, In Focus Edition, April 29, 2009, 7.

4 E-mail from Dennis K. Brown to Linda Bunda, April 4, 2009.

5 United States Conference of Catholic Bishops, Forming Consciences for Faithful Citizenship, No. 40.

6 *Evangelium Vitae*, no. 57

7 *Ibid.,* no. 62.

8 *Ibid.*, no. 65. The *Catechism of the Catholic Church* defines euthanasia as "an act or omission which, of itself or by intention, causes death in order to eliminate suffering." No. 2277.

9 *Evangelium Vitae*, no. 60.

10 *Instruction on Bioethics* (1987).

11 410 U.S. 113 (1973).

12 410 U.S. at 156–57.

13 410 U.S. at 158.

14 See Charles E. Rice, *The Winning Side* (South Bend, Ind.: St. Augustine's Press, 2009), 15.

15 *Planned Parenthood v. Casey*, 505 U.S. 833, 846, 846–53 (1992).

16 Tom Kuntz, "Legal Foreshadowing of Nazi Horror," *New York Times*, July 4, 1999, Section 4, 7, containing the texts of the Nuremberg Laws of 1935.

17 Dred Scott v. Sandford, 60 U.S. (19 How.) 393, 451–52, 15 L. Ed. 691 (1857).

18 See Cardinal Joseph Ratzinger, Worthiness to Receive Holy Communion, General Principles. See text of the letter in Catholic World Report, August-September 2004, 28, 30.

19 Archbishop John J. Myers, "Houses of Worship: A Voter's Guide," *Wall Street Journal, Weekend Journal*, September 17, 2004, W13.

20 E-mail from Dennis K. Brown to Linda Bunda, April 4, 2009.

21 Col. Daniel Smith, "World at War," The Defense Monitor (Center for Defense Information, Special Issue, May/June 2006), 4. http://www.rationalrevolution.net/articles/casualties_of_war.htm

22 Department of the Navy, "Law and Armed Conflict (Law of War) Program to Ensure Compliance by the Naval Establishment," Secnav Instruction, 3000.1B, December 27, 2005.

23 For a timeline of the key events in the Schiavo case, see Kathy Goodman, "Key Events in the Case of Theresa Marie Schiavo," http://www.miami.edu/ethics/schiavo/timeline.htm/; see, among the many rulings in the case, In re Guardianship of Schiavo, 780 So. 2d 176 (FL app.), cert. denied, 789 So. 2d 348 (FL, 2001); Bush v. Schiavo, 885 So. 2d 32 (FL, 2004).

24 Schiavo v. Schindler (Pinellas County Circuit Court, File no. 90-2908-GD-003), Order, Feb. 25, 2005, 3; see Charles E. Rice, "Schiavo Not to Be Overlooked," *The Observer* (Notre Dame, Ind.; April 7, 2005), 12.

25 See Matter of Conroy, 486 A.2d 1209 (N.J., 1985); Charles E. Rice, *50 Questions on the Natural Law* (San Francisco: Ignatius Press, 1999), 363.

26 See Charles E. Rice and Theresa Farnan, Where Did I Come From? Where Am I Going? How Do I Get There? (South Bend, Ind.: St. Augustine's Press, 2009. 2nd edition), 170–72.

27 See Robert Preidt, "FDA OKs Single-Dose Plan B Emergency Contraceptive," HONnews, July13, 2009; www.hon.ch/News/HSN/628986.html; see Charles E. Rice, "Implications of Plan B availability," *The Observer*, October 31, 2006, 8.

28 William McGurn, Address, April 23, 2009; available at Notre Dame Center for Ethics and Culture http://ethicscenter.nd.edu; The Notre Dame Fund to Protect Human Life; http://ethicscenter.nd.edu/lifefund.shtml (Emphasis in original).

29 Viewpoint, "Jenkins Responds," Statement of Rev. John I. Jenkins, C.S.C., March 23, 2009; *The Observer*, In Focus Edition, April 29, 2009, 7.

30 Evangelium Vitae, no. 73.

31 J. Bottum, "At the Gates of Notre Dame," *First Things*, May 13, 2009.

3. The Justification: The Bishops' Non-Mandate

1 http://usccb.org/bishops/catholicsinpoliticallife.shtml. Numbers added.

2 Kathleen Gilbert, "Leaked: ND Prez Comment on USCCB Document Prohibiting Honoring Pro-Abortion Politicians,"

www.lifesitenews.com, April 8, 2009.

3 Most Rev. John M. D'Arcy, "Statement to the Faithful," *Today's Catholic*, April 26, 2009, 3.

4 Congregation for the Doctrine of the Faith, Doctrinal Note, "The Participation of Catholics in Political Life," November 24, 2002.

5 Pope Benedict XVI, *Address*, March 30, 2006; *L'Osservatore Romano* (English edition), April 12, 2006, 4.

6 Statement by Ten Holy Cross Priests, The Observer, April 8, 2009.

7 Mary Ann Glendon, "Notre Dame's Laetare Medal Declined," 38 Origins 741 (May 7, 2009).

8 AAUP Statement, by General Secretary Gary Rhoades, April 23, 2009, www.aaup.org/AAUP/newsroom, *South Bend Tribune*, April 26, 2009, C2.

4. The Obama Commencement

1 The White House, Office of the Press Secretary, *Remarks by the President in Commencement Address at the University of Notre Dame,* May 17, 2009.

2 *New York Times*, May 18, 2009, A1.

3 Dawn Teo, "Arizona Politics," *Huffington Post,* April 11, 2009, http://www.huffingtonpost.com/dawn-teo/asu-stiffs-obama-claim-to_b_185296.html; *Los Angeles Times Blogs*, May 13, 2009,

http://latimesblogs.latimes.com/washington/2009/05/barack-obama-arizona-state-grad-speech.html.

4 For text of Fr. Jenkins' address, see www.southbendtribune.com , May 17, 2009. See also *South Bend Tribune*, May 18, 2009, A1; Michael Paulson, "Notre Dame's Jenkins on Obama, Abortion," Articles of Faith, www.boston.com, May 17, 2009; See also Gail Hinchion Mancini, President Obama and Jenkins stress importance of dialogue at 164th Commencement, *ND Newswire*, May 17, 2009, newsinfo.nd.edu/news.

5 Pope John Paul II, Address to Representatives from the World of Culture, Art and Science, Astana, Kazakhstan, Sept. 24, 2001; 47 *The Pope Speaks* (Mar.-Apr. 2002), 90, 92; see also www.vatican.va.

6 Cardinal Joseph Ratzinger, Homily at the Mass for the Election of the Roman Pontiff, April 18, 2005; see Vatican Radio www.oecumene.radiovaticana.org, April 18, 2005; www.vatican.va/gpII/documents/homily-pro-eligendo-pontifice_20050418_ en.html.

7 "Bishop Finn Interviewed on Notre Dame Commencement," *The Catholic Key* Blog, Diocese of Kansas City, Monday, May 18, 2009, http://catholickey.blogspot.com/2009_05_01_archive.html. See also "Bishop Says Obama's Address Halted Dialogue," Zenit, May 22, 2009, http://www.zenit.org/article-25968?l=english

8   Pope John Paul II, *Discourse,* September 17, 1983; see discussion in Chapter 16.

9   "Obama Promises Conscience Protection," *Zenit,* www.zenit.org, July 2, 2009.

10   *Today's Catholic,* May 31, 2009.

11   *Employment Division v. Smith,* 494 U.S. 872, 887 (1990).

12   *U.S. v. Ballard,* 322 U.S. 78 (1944).

13   George Weigel, "Obama and the 'Real' Catholics," *National Review Online,* May 18, 2009.

14   *South Bend Tribune,* May 16, 2009, A6.

5. ND Response

1   See J. Bowyer Bell, *The Secret Army: The IRA 1916-1979* (1979), 3–15; Peter de Rosa, *Rebels: The Irish Rising of 1916* (1990); Margery Forester, *Michael Collins: The Lost Leader* (1972); 34–49.

2   Rev. Wilson Miscamble, C.S.C.; ND '77 (M.A.), '80 (Ph.D.), '87 (M.Div.); *Professor of History at the University of Notre Dame*; Chris Godfrey, ND Law '93; *Life Athletes (Founder and President), starting offensive guard for Super Bowl XXI Champion New York Giants*; Lacy Dodd, ND '99; *Room at the Inn, Board of Directors, Charlotte, NC*; Jon Buttaci, ND '09; *graduating senior, president of Notre Dame's Orestes Brownson Council* (Jon presented to Professor Mary Ann Glendon, in absentia, the Council's Orestes Brownson Award); Elizabeth Naquin Borger; ND '78; *Former Chairman of the Board of the Women's Care Center*; Dr. David Solomon; *Associate Professor of Philosophy at University of Notre Dame; W.P. and H.B. White Director of the Notre Dame Center for Ethics & Culture; Chair of the steering committee for the Notre Dame Fund to Protect Human Life*; Rev. John J. Raphael, SSJ; ND '89, *Principal of St. Augustine High School in New Orleans, LA.* The talks are available in print and video from www.NDResponse. com.

3   *Today's Catholic,* May 24, 2009.

4   Lacy Dodd, "Notre Dame, My Mother," *First Things,* May 1, 2009.

5   Genevieve Pollock, "Notre Dame's Watershed Moment," *Zenit,* May 28, 2009, www.zenit.org.

6   Flannery O'Connor, *Wise Blood* (1952), 157.

7   Available in print and video from www.NDResponse.com.

6. Land O'Lakes

1   David J. O'Brien, "The Land O'Lakes Statement," *Boston College Magazine,* Winter 1988, 38.

2   Neil G. McCluskey, S.J., "The Catholic University of Today," *America,* August 12, 1967, 154.

3   George W. Rutler, "Newman and Land O'Lakes," *Homiletic & Pastoral Review,* March, 1990, 9, 14.

4 Leo McLauglin, S.J., Address to the Fordham University Alumni Federation, Jan. 24, 1967; see Charles E. Rice, *Authority and Rebellion* (1971), 189.

5 The *Maryland* case, *Horace Mann League v. Board of Public Works of Maryland*, disqualified many religious colleges as too sectarian to receive state grants, 242 Md 645, 220 A2d 51 (1966). That was the first case which so alarmed the Catholic educators. A later case which took the issue up through the federal courts led to a more agreeable conclusion, *Roemer v. Board of Public Works of Maryland*, 426 US 736 (1976). Similar judgment had meanwhile been given in the *Connecticut* case, *Tilton v. Richardson*, 403 US 672 (1971). In the interval between 1966 and 1976 there was considerable unresolved fear among Catholic and other religious educators about the degree to which governmental assistance would be available only on condition of forfeiture of all meaningful religious commitment by their colleges and universities.

6 James T. Burtchaell, *The Dying of the Light* (Grand Rapids, Mich.: Eerdmans, 1998), 589–90.

7 Donald T. Critchlow, *Intended Consequences* (New York: Oxford University Press, 1999); review by Prof. J. Philip Gleason quoted by Oxford University Press at http://www.oup.com/us/catalog/general/subject/HistoryAmerican/Since1945/~~/dmlldz11c2EmY2k9OTc4MDE5NTE0NTkzOQ==

8 Donald Critchlow, *Intended Consequences*, 62–64.

9 University of Notre Dame, *Faculty Handbook, 2006–07*, 4

10 http://nd.edu/leadership/fellows, accessed 4/28/2009.

11 Edward A. Malloy, C.S.C., Reflections on University Governance, *The Observer*, February 24, 1992, 17.

12 Mr. Hernandez and Judge Lewis were elected as Fellows, as announced in *ND Newswire* on May 28, 2009, to replace Shirley Ryan and Arthur Velasquez, who had attained retirement age and were elected Emeritus Trustees.

13 David J. O'Brien, "The Land O'Lakes Statement," *Boston College Magazine*, Winter, 1998, 38, 42

14 ECE, General Norms, Art. 2, Sec. 5.

15 U.S. Conference of Catholic Bishops, *Ex Corde Ecclesiae: An Application to the United States*, Part I, Sec. V, quoting ECE, Part I, no. 12.

16 See George Marsden, "The Soul of the American University," *First Things*, January, 1991; see also George Marsden, *The Soul of the American University* (Oxford University Press, 1994).

17 Editorial, The Death of Religious Higher Education, *First Things*, January 1991.

18 ECE, Part I, no. 13(3).

19 *Application*, Part I, Sec. V.

20 *Ex Corde Ecclesiae*, no. 27.

21 George M. Marsden, *The Soul of*

the American University, Oxford University Press, 1994.

22 James T. Burtchaell, C.S.C., *The Dying of the Light* (Eerdmans, 1998).

23 *Ibid*, 595.

24 James T. Burtchaell, "The Decline and Fall of the Christian College," *First Things*, April 1991, 16; May 1991, 30.

25 *First Things*, April 1991 at 25.

26 *First Things*, May 1991 at 37–38. (Emphasis in original)

27 Statement by AAUP General Secretary Gary Rhoades, April 23, 2009.

28 See Charles E. Rice, "Academic Freedom Safe with Ex Corde," *The Observer*, October 29, 1999, 14.

29 Charles E. Rice, "Bring Notre Dame Back," *The Observer*, April 28, 2009, 13.

The University of Notre Dame Anscombe Society, The Identity Project of Notre Dame, Notre Dame Knights of the Immaculata, Notre Dame Children of Mary, the Orestes Brownson Council, and the Law School St. Thomas More Society. See www.NDResponse.com.

3 To obtain the 2009 film produced in Bangladesh by the boxers themselves, contact www.strongbodiesfight.org.

4 Contact Project Sycamore (e-mail: news@sycamoretrust.org; website: http://www.sycamoretrust.org).

5 Alasdair MacIntyre, Address, "Catholic Universities: Dangers, hopes, choices," Conference on Higher Learning and Catholic Traditions, University of Notre Dame, October 13–14, 1999.

7. Autonomy at Notre Dame: "A Small Purdue with a Golden Dome"

1 "A Death in the Family," *Notre Dame Magazine*, Spring 2005.

2 ND Response, the ad hoc coalition of Notre Dame-sponsored student groups that organized the protests includes Notre Dame Right to Life, *Jus Vitae* (Notre Dame Law School Right to Life), Notre Dame Knights of Columbus Council 1477, the Irish Rover (independent student newspaper), Notre Dame College Republicans,

8. Autonomy at Notre Dame: The "Research University"

1 *The Observer*, February 12, 1992, 7.

2 David Lipsky, "Young, Eager, and Deep in Debt," *New York Times,* December 29, 1994.

3 Gary Wolfram, "Making College More Expensive," *Policy Analysis* (Cato Institute, January 25, 2005), 1; see Daniel J. Flynn, "Blame Federal Subsidies for Spiraling Tuition," *Washington Times*, September 15, 1997, 28.

4 *South Bend Tribune*, February 15, 1993, B1.

5 See Allan Carlson, "'Anti-Dowry'? The Effects of Student Loan Debt on Marriage and Childbearing," *The Family in America*, Dec. 2005, 1.

6 Kimberly Blackwell, "Best of Both Worlds," *Scholastic*, February 28, 2002, 14, 18.

7 See Charles E. Rice, "2010: An Education Odyssey," *Observer*, January 14, 2004.

8 Ralph McInerny, "The Dangers of Research," *Fellowship of Catholic Scholars Newsletter*, March 1992, 1, 2.

9 David W. Lutz, "Can Notre Dame Be Saved?" *First Things*, January 1992, 35.

10 David W. Lutz, "What Does It Mean for a University to Be Catholic?" *The Observer*, February 17, 1993, 10.

9. Autonomy at Notre Dame: A Catholic Faculty?

1 Part II, General Norms, Art 4, Sec. 4.

2 United States Conference of Catholic Bishops, *Ex Corde Ecclesiae: An Application to the United States*, Particular Norms, Art. 4, Sec. 4a.

3 See discussion in Robert Sullivan, C.S.C. The University of Notre Dame's catholic and Catholic future: professors, teaching and scholarship. A white paper, 2008. www.nd.edu.

4 *Application of Ex Corde Ecclesiae to the United States.*

5 See Chapter 7.

6 James T. Burtchaell, "The Decline and Fall of the Christian College (II), *First Things*, May, 1991, 30, 38.

7 *Fides et Ratio*, no. 16.

8 *Fides et Ratio*, no. 42.

9 *Fides et Ratio*, no. 43.

10 *Fides et Ratio*, No. 8.

11 Pope Benedict XVI, *Deus Caritas Est*, no. 28.

12 Archbishop J. Michael Miller, Address, October 31, 2005; Originsonline.com, December 15, 2005, quoting Pope John Paul II, Address to International Meeting of Catholic Universities, April 25, 1989.

13 Wilson D. Miscamble, C.S.C., "The Faculty Problem," America, Sept. 10, 2007.

14 Report, Ad Hoc Committee on Recruiting Outstanding Catholic Faculty, Sept. 18, 2007, 13.

15 Faculty Senate, Response to Universities Initiative on Hiring Catholic Faculty, April 16, 2008.

16 Wilson D. Miscamble, C.S.C.., "The Faculty Problem, America, Sept. 10, 2007.

17 Cardinal Avery Dulles, S.J., "Catholic Colleges and Universities Today," Assumption College, Worcester, Mass., October 11, 2007.

18 See Charles E. Rice, Catholic Faculty and the ND Mission, Observer, November 14, 2007, 10.

19 Bylaws, Section II(3).

10. Autonomy at Notre Dame: Academic Freedom?

1 Vatican II, *Lumen Gentium* (Dogmatic Constitution on the Church), no. 25.

2 *Ex Corde Ecclesiae*, no. 28, quoting Pope John Paul II, *Address to Leaders of Catholic Higher Education*, September 12, 1987.

3 Pope Benedict XVI, *Address to Catholic Educators of the United States*, April 17, 2008.

4 The Ten Commandments of God, given to Moses and reaffirmed in the New Covenant, are: 1. I am the LORD your God; you shall not have strange Gods before me. 2. You shall not take the name of the LORD your God in vain. 3. Remember to keep holy the LORD's Day. 4. Honor your father and your mother. 5. You shall not kill. 6. You shall not commit adultery. 7. You shall not steal. 8. You shall not bear false witness against your neighbor. 9. You shall not covet your neighbor's wife. 10. You shall not covet your neighbor's goods. See *Catechism*, no. 2052.

5 *South Bend Tribune*, September 29, 1989, C1, col. 1.

6 Letter, December 1, 1989, from Fr. Malloy to Andrew Duff.

7 Edward J. Murphy, "The Temptation of Notre Dame," *Observer*, September 25, 1989; *The Wanderer*, October 5, 1989.

8 *South Bend Tribune*, September 30, 1989, 1.

9 *Ibid.*

10 *The Observer*, October 5, 1989, 1.

11 *The Observer*, April 7, 2009.

12 Rev. John I. Jenkins, C.S.C., Address, "Academic Freedom and Catholic Character: An Invitation to Reflection and Response," January 23 and 24, 2006. http://president.nd.edu/academic-freedom/address_text.shtml.

13 *South Bend Tribune*, April 6, 2006, p. A1; http://president.nd.edu/closingstatement.

14 See Charles E. Rice, "Jenkins' Closing Statement a Serious Misstep," *Observer*, April 25, 2006.

15 *Ex Corde Ecclesiae*, Application, III.

16 *Ex Corde Ecclesiae*, no. 12.

17 *Today's Catholic*, March 16, 2008, 3.

11. Autonomy at Notre Dame: The Politicization of Abortion

1 CCC, no. 2273, quoting *Donum Vitae*, III.

2 See Chapter 10.

3 See Chapter 3.

4 John Henry Newman, *The Idea of a University Defined and Illustrated* (London: 1929), 218; see George W. Rutler, "Newman and Land O'Lakes," *Homelitic & Pastoral Review*, March 1990, 9, 14.

5 *Roe v. Wade*, 410 U.S. 113 (1973).

6 Charles E. Rice, "A Call to Condemn Abortion," *The Observer*, October 31, 1973, 7.

7 See *The Observer*, November 2, 1973.

8 *The Harmonizer* (Diocese of Fort Wayne-South Bend), August 17, 1986.

9 See Richard John Neuhaus, "The Pro-Life Movement as the Politics of the 1960s," *First Things*, January 2009.

10 William McGurn, "Obama Gets Their Irish Up," *Wall Street Journal*, Opinion Main Street, March 24, 2009.

11 *The Observer*, January 23, 1975.

12 www.fatherdesouza.ca, April 27, 2009.

13 *The Observer*, September 13, 1984.

14 www.fatherdesouza.ca, April 27, 2009.

15 Mario Cuomo Address; "Religious Belief and Public Morality: A Catholic Governor's Response," September 13, 1984. *A Report on Religion*, Notre Dame Department of Public Relations and Information, Vol. IV, no. 1 (Fall 1984).

16 Pope Benedict XVI, *Address*, March 30, 2006.

17 Cardinal Joseph Ratzinger, *Address to LUMSA Faculty of Jurisprudence*, November 10, 1999.

18 *Deus Caritas Est*, no. 29.

19 Pope John Paul II, *Homily*, Washington, D.C., Capitol Mall, October 7, 1979.

20 Congregation for the Doctrine of the Faith, *Declaration on Procured Abortion* (1974), no. 22.

21 *New York Times*, September 15, 1984, 9.

22 Henry J. Hyde, Address, "Keeping God in the Closet: Some Thoughts on the Exorcism of Religious Values from Public Life," September 24, 1984. *A Report on Religion*, Notre Dame Department of Public Relations and Information, Vol. IV, no. 2 (Fall 1984).

23 Rev. Theodore M. Hesburgh, C.S.C., "Reflections on Cuomo: The Secret Consensus," *The Observer*, October 1, 1984, 6.

24 *Roe v. Wade* 410 U.S. 113, 156–57, 157, n. 54 (1973).

25 See *Gonzales v. Carhart*, 550 U.S. 124 (2007), upholding the federal prohibition of partial-birth abortion.

26 *Evangelium Vitae*, no. 73.

27 Charles E. Rice, "Sponsorship of Debate Misrepresents Labels," Letter, *The Observer*, February 5, 1987, 9.

28 Prof. Alfred Freddoso and Prof. Janet Smith, Guest Column, *The Observer*, February 20, 1987.

29 See Charles E. Rice, "Moynihan's Voting Record Is Clearly Pro-Abortion," *Observer*, April 13, 1992, detailing eighteen pro-abortion Moynihan votes.

30 Most Rev. Raymond L. Burke, *Address*, National Catholic Prayer Breakfast, Washington, D.C., May 8, 2009.

12. The Magisterium: Why Notre Dames Needs It

1 Pope Paul VI, *Ecclesiam Suam* (1964), no. 35.

2 Allan Bloom, *The Closing of the American Mind* (1987), 25–26.

3 *Ibid.*

4 Cardinal Avery Dulles, S.J., "Catholic Colleges and Universities Today," Assumption College, Worcester, Mass., October 11, 2007.

5 *ECE*, General Norms, Art. 2, Sec. 5.

6 *ECE*, no. 27.

7 Pope Paul VI, *Ecclesiam Suam* (1964), nos. 30, 35, quoting Pope Pius XII, *Mystici Corporis* (1943).

8 *Catechism*, no. 669.

9 See *Catechism of the Catholic Church* , nos. 888–96.

10 Vatican II, *Lumen Gentium* (Dogmatic Constitution on the Church), no. 25.

11 *Catechism*, no. 892.

12 Congregation for the Doctrine of the Faith, *Instruction on the Ecclesial Vocation of the Theologian* (1990), no. 17.

13 32 *The Pope Speaks*, 378, 381 (1987); see also *VS*, nos. 113, 116.

14 Pope John Paul II, *Faith and Reason* (1998), Preamble.

15 Pope Benedict XVI, *Address to European Meeting of University Professors*, June 24, 2007.

16 Pope Benedict XVI, *Address*, September 12, 2006; *L'Osservahtore Romano*, September 20, 2006.

17 *Ibid.*

18 *L'Osservatore Romano* (English), January 23, 2008.

19 Ralph McInerny, "Is a Non-Catholic University Possible?" *Crisis*, February 2000.

20 Charles E. Rice, "Adherence to Church Teaching Is Not Option," *The Observer*, January 18, 1993.

21 *Ex Corde Ecclesiae, An Application to the United States*, Particular Norms, Art. 4, Sec. 5.

22 Cardinal Avery Dulles, *Address*, Washington, D.C., November 10, 2001.

23 Pope Benedict XVI, Address, "The Key Service of Today's Catholic University," November 25, 2005.

24 Pope Benedict XVI, Address to Aparecida Conference of CELAM (Episcopate of Latin America and the Caribbean), May 13, 2007; *L'Osservatore Romano* (English), May 16, 2007.

25 Pope Benedict XVI, *Address to the Roman Curia*, December 21, 2007.

26 Cardinal Avery Dulles, *Address*, November 10, 2001, Washington, D.C.

27 See *Catechism*, nos. 813–22, on unity as one of the four marks of the Church.

28 *Summa Theologica*, I, II, Q. 20, art. 6.

29 Wilson D. Miscamble, C.S.C., *Address to ND Response*, May 17, 2009.

30 William McGurn, Address, April 23, 2009.

13. The Magisterium and the Dictatorship of Relativism

1 Francis Canavan, S.J., "Commentary," *Catholic Eye*, December 10, 1987, 2.

2 Cardinal Joseph Ratzinger, *Address to Consistory of College of Cardinals*, April 4, 1991.

3 See Heinrich A. Rommen, *The Natural Law* (1998), chapters 4, 5 and 6; Charles E. Rice, *50 Questions on the Natural Law* (1999), 266–70.

4 See Charles E. Rice, *50 Questions on the Natural Law* (1999), 125–39.

5 Hans Kelsen, "Absolutism and Relativism in Philosophy and Politics," 42 *American Political Science Review* 906 (1948). *Ibid.*, at 908, 913; *Ibid.*, at 906; *Ibid.* at 913. Hans Kelsen, "The Pure Theory of Law, Part II," 51 *Law Quarterly Review* 517, 518–19 (1935); Hans Kelsen, "The Pure Theory of Law, Part I," 50 *Law Quarterly Review* 474, 482 (1934). See Charles E. Rice, *The Winning Side* (2000), 98–99; see Charles E. Rice, *50 Questions on the Natural Law* (1999), 90–92.

6 Hans Kelsen, *Pure Theory of Law* (1967), 40; see R.S. Clark, "Hans Kelsen's Pure Theory of Law," 22 *Journal of Legal Education*, 170, 182 (1969); see Charles E. Rice, *50 Questions on the Natural Law* (1994), 94.

7 Thomas Aquinas, *Summa Theologica*, I, II, Q. 95, Art. 2.

8 42 *American Political Science Review* at 912.

9 Cardinal Joseph Ratzinger, *Truth and Tolerance* (2004), 72.

10 Joseph Cardinal Ratzinger, *Crises of Law*, Address to LUMSA Faculty of Jurisprudence, November 10, 1999.

11 Pope Benedict XVI, *Address to Non-Governmental Organizations*, December 1, 2007; *L'Osservatore Romano* (English), December 12, 2007, 5.

12 Pope John Paul II, *Veritatis Splendor*, no. 99, quoting from *Centisimus Annus* (1991), no. 44.

13 2 *Holmes-Pollock Letters* (1941), 212.

14 2 *Holmes-Pollock Letters* (1942), 36; See Oliver Wendell Holmes, "The Natural Law," 32 *Harvard Law Review* 40 (1918).

15 Oliver Wendell Holmes, *The Natural Law: Collected Legal Papers* (1920), 310.

16 2 *Holmes Pollock Letters* (1942), 252; see discussion in William Kenealy, s.j., "The Majesty of the Law," 5 *Loyola Law Review* 101, 107-8 (1950); Charles E. Rice, *Beyond Abortion: The Theory and Practice of the Secular State* (1979), chs. 2 and 6; Francis E. Lucey, s.j., "Natural Law and American Legal Realism: Their Respective Contributions to a Theory of Law in a Democratic Society," 30 *Georgetown Law Journal*, 493 (1942).

17 Pope Benedict XVI, *Angelus Reflection*, January 20, 2008.

18 Pope Benedict XVI, *Address to Congress* on "Values and Perspectives for the Europe of the Future," March 24, 2007.

19 Carrie Gress, "Father James Schall on 'Spe Salvi,'" ZZenit, February 1, 2008, ZE080201.

14. The Magisterium: Protector of Conscience and Freedom

1 *Planned Parenthood v. Casey*, 505 U.S. 833, 851 (1992) (joint opinion of Justices O'Connor, Kennedy and Souter, which in this respect was the opinion of the Court.)

2 *Catechism*, no. 1778.

3 *Catechism*, nos. 1776–1802.

4 *Catechism*, no. 405.

5 *Catechism*, no. 2071.

6 Joseph Cardinal Ratzinger, *Conscience and Truth,* 10th Workshop for Bishops, February 1991, Dallas, Texas.

7 Pope John Paul II, *Veritatis Splendor(VS)* (1993), no. 64, quoting Vatican II, *Dignitatis Humanae*, no. 14.

8 Cardinal Joseph Ratzinger, *Address*, "Conscience and Truth," Dallas, Texas, 1991.

9 *VS*, nos. 61, 62.

10 See Charles E. Rice, *50 Questions on the Natural Law* (San Francisco: Ignatius, 1999), 30–33, 50–53.

11 *Evangelium Vitae*, no. 57.

12 See Charles E. Rice and Theresa Farnan, *Where Did I Come From? Where Am I Going? How Do I Get There?* (South Bend, Ind.: St. Augustine's Press, 2009), 89–101.

13 *VS*, no. 84.

14 *VS*, no. 88.

15 *VS*, no. 87.

16 Pope Benedict XVI, *Cappella Papale for the Opening of the 12th Ordinary General Assembly of the Synod of Bishops*, October 5, 2008.

17 Benedict XVI, *Spe Salvi* (2007), no. 2.

18 Heinrich A. Rommen, *The Natural Law* (Liberty Fund, 1998), 73–74, quoting Thomas Hobbes, *Leviathan, or the Matter, Forme & Power of a Commonwealth, Ecclesiaticall and Civill*, ed. by A.R. Waller (Cambridge: The University Press, 1904. Part I, chap. 13).

19 Gilbert K. Chesterton, *Orthodoxy* (Dodd, Mead, 1940), 260.

20 Archbishop John Murphy, *Advent Pastoral Letter*, November 1, 1967; see *The Wanderer*, December 14, 1967.

15. God Is Love

1 See Chapter 13.

2 *Deus Caritas Est (DCE),* no. 1

3 DCE, no. 11.

4 DCE, no. 18.

5 DCE, no. 14.

6 DCE, no. 17.

7 DCE, no. 18.

8 Lk 10:25–37.

9 DCE, no. 15.

10 DCE, no. 19.

11 DCE, no. 20.

12 DCE, no. 31 (a).

13 *Ibid.*

14 DCE, no. 31.

15 DCE, no. 31 (c).

16 DCE, no. 31 (b).

17 DCE, no. 26.

18 DCE, no. 31 (b).

19 DCE, no. 28 (a).

20 DCE, no. 29.

21 DCE, no. 28 (a).

22 *Ibid.*
23 DCE, no. 27.
24 DCE, no. 28 (a).
25 DCE, no. 28 (b).
26 *Ibid.*
27 *Ibid.*
28 *Ibid.*
29 *Ibid.*
30 DCE, no. 28 (a).
31 Pope Benedict XVI, Address, December 22, 2005; *L'Osservatore Romano*, January 4, 2006.
32 DCE, No. 34.
33 DCE, no. 18.
34 DCE, no. 1.

16. Of Human Life

1 *Family Resources Center News*, May 1994, 13.
2 E. Christian Bruegger, "A Defense of Marital Conjugal Chastity," *Fellowship of Catholic Scholars Quarterly*, Winter, 2004, 10, 16.
3 "Forgetting Religion," *Washington Post,* editorial, March 22, 1931.
4 Francis Fukayama, *The Great Disruption: Human Nature and the Reconsitution of the Social Order* (London: Profile Books, 1999), 101–3, 120–22.
5 See Charles E. Rice and Theresa Farnan, *Where Did I Come From? Where am I Going? How Do I Get There?* (South Bend, Ind.: St. Augustine's Press, 2009), 141–52.
6 *Humanae Vitae*, no. 11 (Latin translation omitted).
7 *Ibid.*, no. 12.
8 *Ibid.*, no. 14.

9 Pope John Paul II, Discourse, September 12, 1983; 28 *The Pope Speaks* (1983), 356, 356–57.
10 Charles J. Chaput, "Of Human Life," *Catholic World Report* (October 1998): 56, 58–60 (Emphasis added.)
11 Pope John Paul II, *Familiaris Consortio*, No. 32.
12 *Evangelium Vitae*, no. 13.
13 Charles E. Rice, "Implications of Plan B availability," *The Observer*, October 31, 2006, 8. See Chapter 2, note 27.
14 *Population Research Institute Review*, September-October 2006, 10.
15 Pope Benedict XVI, Message to Prof. Mary Ann Glendon, President of the Pontifical Academy of Social Sciences, April 27, 2006; *L'Osservatore Romano*, May 10, 2006, 5.
16 Donald Sensing, "Save Marriage? It's Too Late." *Wall Street Journal*, Opinion Journal, March 15, 2004.
17 *Humanae Vitae*, no. 17.
18 Jennifer Harper, "Family hour goes down the tubes," *Washingeon Times*, September 6, 2007, A10.
19 "The Frayed Knot – Marriage in America," *The Economist* – U.S. Edition, May 26, 2007.
20 Russell Shorto, "Contra-Contraception," *New York Times Magazine*, May 7, 2006, 48, 50.
21 Allan Carlson, "Children of the Reformation," *Touchstone*, Feature, May, 2007, 1, 8.
22 Mark Rust, "Hesburgh speaks on birth control," *The Observer*, November 22, 1977, 1.

17. Love in Truth

1   J. Brian Benestad, "Catholic Social Teaching, Political Philosophy and Pope John Paul II's *Laborem Exercens*," *Proceedings of the Fifth Convention of the Fellowship of Catholic Scholars* (1982), 53, 58.

2   See the call for a "new evangelization" in *Veritatis Splendor*, no. 106; see also William E. May, ed., *The Church's Mission of Evangelization* (1996).

3   J. Brian Benestad, 58, 59.

4   On the human community generally, see *Catechism of the Catholic Church*, nos. 1877–1948; on the social teaching of the Church in the context of the Seventh Commandment, see nos. 2419–63.

5   *Caritas in Veritate*, no. 15.

6   Benestad, 59.

7   Pontifical Council for Justice and Peace, *Compendium of the Social Doctrine of the Church* (2005), no. 160.

8   CCC, no. 1881, quoting *Gaudium et Spes*, no. 25.

9   *Ecclesia in America*, no. 57.

10 *Ibid.*, no. 52.

11 Pope Pius XI, *Quadregisimo Anno* (1931), no. 79; see also *Letter to Families*, no. 16.

12 CIV, no. 58.

13 CCC, no. 1906, quoting *Gaudium et Spes*, no. 26.

14 CIV, no. 8.

15 CIV, no. 9.

16 CIV, nos. 1 and 2.

17 CIV, no. 52.

18 CIV, no. 5.

19 Vatican II, *Gaudium et Spes*, no. 24.

20 *Veritatis Splendor*, no. 87.

21 CIV, no. 34.

22 *Ibid.*

23 CIV, no. 71.

24 *Ibid.*

25 CIV, no. 76.

26 CIV, no. 45.

27 CIV, no. 8.

28 CIV, no. 36.

29 CIV, no. 51. Emphasis added.

30 Remarks by the President in Commencement Address at University of Notre Dame, May 17, 2009 (The White House, Office of the Press Secretary).

31 CIV, no. 43.

32 CIV, no. 44.

33 Pope Benedict XVI, *Message to Prof. Mary Ann Glendon*, April 27, 2006; *L'Osservatore Romano* (English), May 10, 2006, 4.

34 CIV, no. 44.

35 CIV, no. 28.

36 *Ibid.*

37 CIV, no. 77.

38 CIV, no. 74.

39 CIV, no. 75.

40 CIV, no. 79.

41 CIV, no. 78.

.

18. In Hope We Were Saved

1   *Spe Salvi* (SS), no. 44.

2   See Charles E. Rice, "Reason Depends of Faith," *The Observer*, February 20, 2008.

3   SS, no. 30.

4   SS, no. 31.

5   SS, no. 2.

6   See Chapter 12.

7   SS, no. 42.

8   SS, nos. 16, 25.

9 SS, no. 17.

10 SS, no. 22.

11 SS, no. 23.

12 SS, no. 3.

13 *Ibid.*

14 *Ibid.*

15 SS., no. 4.

16 SS, no. 10.

17 SS, no. 2.

19. The Question of Truth: Can "Autonomy" Be Fixed?

1 *Ex Corde Ecclesiae*, no. 27.

2 Theodore M. Hesburgh, C.S.C., "The Vision of a Great Catholic University in the World of Today," in *Thoughts IV* (University of Notre Dame, 1968), 1.

3 Hesburgh, "The Vision of a Great Catholic University," 3.

4 Cardinal Avery Dulles, Address, "Newman's Idea of a University and its Relevance to Catholic Higher Education," Washington, D.C., November 10, 2001.

5 *Ibid.*; See also, George William Rutler, "Newman and Land O'Lakes," *Homiletic & Pastoral Review*, March 1990, 9; see Chapter 12.

6 "The Vision of a Great Catholic University," 4.

7 Cardinal Avery Dulles, Address, Washington, D.C. November 10, 2001.

8 *Today's Catholic*, March 16, 2008; see Chapter 10.

9 *Ex Corde Ecclesiae*, no. 27.

10 Hesburgh, *op. cit.*, 8-9.

11 Ralph McInerny, "Is a Non-Catholic University Possible?" *Crisis*, February 2000, 60.

12 Cardinal Avery Dulles, *Address*, November 10, 2001, Washington, D.C.; see Chapter 12.

13 Hesburgh, 7.

14 Hesburgh, 7.

15 Hesburgh, 8.

16 ECE, General Norms, Art. 2, Sec. 2.

17 ECE, no. 27.

18 ECE, no. 28, quoting Pope John Paul II, *Address to Leaders of Catholic Higher Education*, September 12, 1987.

19 Hesburgh, 8.

20 Cardinal Joseph Ratzinger, Address to LUMSF. Faculty for Jurisprudence, November 10, 1999.

21 Hesburgh, 11.

22 Hesburgh, 11.

23 Hesburgh, 11–12.

24 Pope Benedict XVI, *Address to Catholic Educators of the United States,* April 17, 2008.

25 Cardinal Avery Dulles, Address, October 11, 2007.

26 Hesburgh, 14.

27 Hesburgh, 15.

28 Editorial, "The Death of Religious Higher Education," *First Things*, January 1991; see Chapter 6.

29 George Marsden, *The Soul of the American University: From Protestant Establishment to Established Nonbelief* (Oxford University Press, 1994).

30 ECE, no. 27.

31 Wilson D. Miscamble, C.S.C., Address, May 17, 2009; Chapter 5.

INDEX